REBECCA
JACQUELINE MARTIN

UNLOCKING
THE ENGLISH
LEGAL SYSTEM

SERIES EDITORS:
JACQUELINE MARTIN & CHRIS TURNER

Hodder Arnold

A MEMBER OF THE HODDER HEADLINE GROUP

Orders, please contact Bookpoint Ltd, 130 Milton Park, Abingdon, Oxon OX14 4SB. Telephone: (44) 01235 827720.
Fax: (44) 01235 400454. Lines are open from 9.00–5.00, Monday to Saturday, with a 24-hour message answering service. You can also order through our website www.hoddereducation.co.uk

If you have any comments to make about this, or any of our
other titles, please send them to educationenquiries@hodder.co.uk

British Library Cataloguing in Publication Data
A catalogue record for this title is available from the British Library

ISBN: 978 0 340 88693 9

First published 2005
Impression number   10 9 8 7 6 5 4 3
Year   2009 2008 2007

Cover photo of Old Bailey Law Courts © Rupert Horrox/Corbis.
Typeset by Phoenix Photosetting, Chatham, Kent
Printed in Malta for Hodder Arnold, an imprint of Hodder Education, and a member of the Hodder Headline Group,
an Hachette Livre UK company, 338 Euston Road, London NW1 3BH by Gutenberg Press.

CONTENTS ■

PREFACE

The *Unlocking the Law* series is an entirely new style of undergraduate law textbook. Many student texts are very prose dense and have little in the way of interactive materials to help a student feel his or her way through the course of study on a given module.

The purpose of this series, then, is to try to make learning each subject area more accessible by focusing on actual learning needs, and by providing a range of different supporting materials and features.

All topic areas are broken up into 'bite-size' sections, with a logical progression and extensive use of headings and numerous sub-headings. Each book in the series will also contain a variety of charts, diagrams and key facts summaries to reinforce the information in the body of the text. Diagrams and flow charts are particularly useful because they can provide a quick and easy understanding of the key points, especially when revising for examinations. Key facts charts not only provide a quick visual guide through the subject but are useful for revision purposes also.

The books have a number of common features in the style of text layout. Important cases are separated out for easy access and have full citation in the text as well as in the table of cases, for ease of reference. The emphasis of the series is on depth of understanding much more than breadth. For this reason, each text also includes key extracts from judgments, where appropriate. Extracts from academic comment from journal articles and leading texts are also included to give some insight into the academic debate on complex or controversial areas. In both cases these are indented to make them clear from the body of the text.

Finally, the books also include much formative 'self-testing', with a variety of activities ranging through subject-specific comprehension, application of the law, and a range of other activities to help the student gain a good idea of his or her progress in the course.

Symbols used in this series:

J	This is a small extract from a judgment in a case. It may follow a case example or the case may be identified immediately above.

 This is a section from an Act.

(A) This is an Article of the EC Treaty or of the European Convention on Human Rights.

This is a clause from a Draft Bill or Code.

Q	This is a quote from a government paper, Royal commission report or similar.

Where a paragraph is indented, this is an extract from an academic source such as an article or a leading textbook.

Note also that for all incidental references to 'he', 'him', 'his', we invoke the Interpretation Act 1978 and its provisions that 'he' includes 'she' etc.

English Legal Method and the English Legal System are important as they underpin understanding of the development and practice of all substantive areas of law. This book starts with an outline of the sources of law, followed by detailed consideration of the operation of judicial precedent and statutory interpretation. There are also additional exercises on these topics in Appendix 1. The court structure in England and Wales is then explained, together with how cases are funded. Chapters 8–11 concentrate on the personnel, both professional and lay, in the legal system. Finally, there is a chapter on sentencing. The book should provide students with a clear understanding of our legal system.

The book is designed to cover all of the main topic areas on undergraduate and professional syllabuses and help provide a full understanding of each.

The law is stated as we believe it to be on 1st March 2005.

Rebecca Huxley-Binns
Jacqueline Martin

First, a note on the terminology. When we refer to the '*English* Legal System', we are usually deliberately not referring to Scotland, Northern Ireland, the Isle of Man and the Channel Islands, which have separate legal systems; but to England and, on the whole, Wales. According to context, however, we might use the terms 'Great Britain' or the 'United Kingdom' where relevant, especially when considering the broader sources of law, such as the European Union and the European Convention on Human Rights, each of which has affected the UK as a whole.

1.2 The sources of law

Where does the law come from? The obvious answer is the law-makers. The key law-makers in the ELS are:

Parliament	Parliament is the principal law-maker in the ELS because of the doctrine of **parliamentary sovereignty**.
The courts	Historically vital as law-makers because we had judges before we had a Parliament. The courts continue to be integral to the constitutional framework of the ELS under the **Rule of Law** and the **Separation of Powers doctrine**.

Note the following key terms:

Parliamentary sovereignty	Parliament is able pass laws on any subject; these laws can regulate the activities of anyone, anywhere; Parliament cannot bind its successors as to the content of subsequent legislation; and laws passed by Parliament cannot be declared void by the courts.
The Rule of Law	Individuals' liberties can be ensured only by regulating behaviour **by** the law (not arbitrarily), punishing only **according** to law and making all citizens **subject** to the law.
The Separation of Powers doctrine	Abuse of State power can be prevented only by sharing the power of the State among the Executive (the Government), the Legislature (Parliament) and the judiciary (the courts). In this way, checks and balances are in place to reduce the risk of abuse.

The key law-makers from outside the ELS but which affect the citizens governed by English law are:

The European Union	The UK's membership of the EU dictates an obligation to incorporate into UK law the laws of the institutions established by the Treaty of Rome (see section 1.7 below).
The Council of Europe	As you will see at section 1.8 below, the European Convention on Human Rights is the work of the Council of Europe (not the EU) and is fundamental to the operation of UK law – whether made by Parliaments or the courts – because of the Human Rights Act 1998.

There are some other sources of law which are considered later in this chapter (for example, law reform agencies and academics).

1.3 The courts

There is no legislative or express democratic authority for the courts to be law-makers but, nevertheless, it is clear that judges do make the law (see section 2.5 for more information). How do the judges make the law? In two key ways:

- developing the common law
- interpreting Acts of Parliament.

We will consider each of these roles below. First, you need to understand that there is a court hierarchy. The structure you will see in Figure 1.1 below does not merely indicate which courts hear which cases (the basic jurisdiction of each court is shown, but note that this is not detailed and you must refer to Chapters 4, 5 and 6 for more detail), but also that because there is a clear hierarchy, courts at the top of the diagram have more seniority and authority than the courts below. This is one of the reasons the courts at the top of the hierarchy hear appeals. Appeals are almost always on points of **law**, so this is where the law made by the judges stems from.

PRIVY COUNCIL	HOUSE OF LORDS	EUROPEAN COURT OF JUSTICE
Devolution issues (esp. Wales and Scotland). Appeals from the Commonwealth on civil and criminal law.	Appeals on civil and criminal law from English courts and Northern Ireland. Appeals on civil law from Scotland.	References from any court on a question of EU law and disputes between member states and institutions of the EU.

COURT OF APPEAL	
CRIMINAL DIVISION Appeals in criminal cases from the Crown Court.	CIVIL DIVISION Appeals in civil cases from the High Court and County Courts.

THE HIGH COURT		
QUEEN'S BENCH DIVISIONAL COURT	FAMILY DIVISIONAL COURT	CHANCERY DIVISIONAL COURT
Judicial review and appeals in some criminal cases.	Appeals in family matters from the County Courts.	Appeals in land and tax cases from the County Courts.
QUEEN'S BENCH DIVISION	FAMILY DIVISION	CHANCERY DIVISION
Hearings in civil cases according to value of claim.	Hearings in family and child law cases.	Hearings in land, trusts and tax cases.

CROWN COURT	MAGISTRATES' COURT	COUNTY COURT
Criminal trials on indictment and appeals in criminal cases from the Magistrates' Courts.	Criminal trials Family cases Non-payments of bills.	Hearings in civil cases according to value of claim, and family matters.

Figure 1.1 The court hierarchy

1.4 The common law

As stated above, one of the ways in which the judges make the law is by developing the common law. However, the phrase 'common law' is not a particularly easy one to get to grips with because it can have up to five different meanings, according to the context in which it is used:

	Meaning	Example
1.	The term 'common law' can be taken to refer to the system of law which is common to the whole country.	*Murder is an offence under the common law of England; however, walking on the grass in a local park may be an offence under a local byelaw, but is not part of the common law of England.*
2.	The term may also be used to distinguish that law which is not equity (see further below).	*Damages (a monetary award; compensation) are common law remedies, whereas the injunction is an equitable remedy.*
3.	It might be used to mean case law; that is law developed by judges through cases. This is the context in which the term was used at section 1.3 above.	*The common law principle that a manufacturer is liable in negligence to the ultimate consumer of its products derives from the case of* Donoghue v Stevenson *[1932] AC 562.*
4.	It could be used to indicate law which has not been made by Parliament (the law made by Parliament is called a statute or legislation).	*Murder is a common law offence, but the defences of diminished responsibility and provocation are statutory under ss 2 and 3 Homicide Act 1957.*
5.	The term may also be used to describe those legal systems that developed from the English system. In this final sense, a common law system is distinguished from a civil law system. Civil law developed from the Romano–Germanic legal system and is the dominant legal system in continental Europe including the European Union itself.	*France does not have a common law system because it developed from the Roman tradition with a civil law system. On the other hand, England, Australia and New Zealand are common law jurisdictions.*

An understanding of the historical development of the common law of England will assist you in using the term correctly; but to understand this, you also need to have a grasp of the development of equity.

1.4.1 Problems of the common law

The story starts before William the Conqueror conquered England in 1066. Before this date, there was no national legal system. Local laws were enforced by local lords or sheriffs. When William took the throne in 1066, he was a shrewd leader and he recognised that he would have to establish a system of central or national government and, with that, a centralised system of justice over which he would have control. Only in this way would he attain real power and control over his new subjects.

William travelled throughout the land, listening to people's grievances. He and his most powerful advisers would judge the merits of the complaints and deliver judgments. This travelling court system became known as the *Curia Regis* (King's Court) and it is from this court that we see the development of the common law. Subsequent kings appointed judges to the *Curia Regis* and over time a national but uniform system of laws was put in place. In this way many local customary laws were replaced by new national laws. As these national laws would apply to everyone, they would be common to all. These laws therefore became known as the common law. However, there were a number of problems with the operation of the common law.

- First, the common law operated on the basis of *stare decisis*; that means binding precedent. One of the main criticisms of this doctrine is that a court is bound to follow a previous decision even if the judge disagrees with that previous decision. Mechanisms do exist in the modern ELS for a judge to avoid this process today, but such mechanisms did not exist, or were rarely used, in the more antiquated system. This meant that the common law did not develop and parties could not persuade a judge to change the law, even when it was obviously in need of change.

- Second, cases in the common law courts were started by means of a writ. A writ is a document used by a party to commence a legal action. Documents are still used today, but in a different form (for example, in order to start a civil action, the claimant must issue a 'claim form'). Under the old common law system, the bureaucracy of the rules dictated that if the wrong writ had been chosen or a mistake had been made on the writ, that writ was void and could not be amended as happens today. Instead the plaintiff (the old term for 'claimant') had to go to the expense and trouble of starting all over again. Additionally, the common law rules required that certain civil actions (this was in the days before a formal legal system for the resolution of criminal cases existed) had to involve certain types of conduct. For example, an action for trespass had to involve an allegation that violence had been used against the plaintiff. Therefore, in theory, if no violence had been used, the action could not succeed. In practice, some common law judges were prepared to imply that violence had occurred when they knew very well that none had.

- Third, the only remedy available at common law was damages. This is a monetary award (compensation). In many cases, for example a breach of contract, this remedy was perfectly adequate, but if we continue with the trespass example above, the successful plaintiff would not have found money to be an adequate remedy – he wanted the trespasser to stop (but the order we now call an injunction did not exist).

1.4.2 Development of equity

Many people felt let down by the common law system because it was unable to remedy these defects for itself so, as had been the practice before the *Curia Regis*, they petitioned the king directly for a remedy. Initially, kings would consider these petitions themselves but at some time during the fifteenth century this work was handed over to the Lord High Chancellor, known subsequently just as the Lord Chancellor. The number of petitions rose dramatically, so the Lord Chancellor established a court to hear the petitions. This court was called the Court of Chancery. The rules which the Lord Chancellor adopted in this court were not the rules from the common law courts. Actions were started by a petition rather than a writ, and the Lord Chancellor was not bound by precedent. Instead, rules were established to ensure that justice was obtained in those cases where the parties were able to show that the common law courts were not able or prepared to provide a suitable remedy. These rules became known as the **rules of equity**, 'equity' meaning even-handedness and fairness. It was never intended that the principles of equity would replace the common law rules simply that they would fill the gaps in it and make up for its defects.

Maxims of equity

One of the ways in which equity was able to plug the gaps of the common law was by using guidelines called **maxims of equity**. One of the better-known maxims is 'He who comes to equity must come with clean hands'. This means that equity will not assist a party who has acted in bad conscience.

CASE EXAMPLE

D & C Builders v Rees [1966] 2 QB 617, CA

The plaintiff company sued Mr and Mrs Rees for failure to pay a bill in full for building work done to their home. The plaintiffs had sent three bills and the defendants had paid only one-third 'on account'. The defendants then made complaints about the quality of the work and, knowing that the plaintiff company was in severe financial difficulty, offered to pay a further third, but 'in full settlement'. The plaintiff company agreed, only because without the money the company would have gone bankrupt. The company later sued the defendants for the outstanding amount.

Lord Denning MR (denoting that he was, at the time of the judgment, the Master of the Rolls) held at the Court of Appeal:

> 'The creditor [the plaintiff] is only barred from his legal rights when it would be *inequitable* for him to insist upon them. Where there has been a *true accord*, under which the creditor voluntarily agrees to accept a lesser sum in satisfaction, and the debtor *acts upon* that accord by paying the lesser sum and the creditor accepts it, then it is inequitable for the creditor afterwards to insist on the balance. But he is not bound unless there has been truly an accord between them.

CONTINUED ▶

There are two Standing (ie permanent) Committees on Statutory Instruments. These committees allow for parliamentary discussion to take place and thus help to relieve the pressure on the House of Commons which often does not have enough time to consider all statutory instruments, but the committees do not have the power to change the wording of the SIs.

There is a Commons Select Committee on European Secondary Legislation and a Lords Select Committee on the European Communities. These two committees bring to the attention of Parliament the more important pieces of European legislation.

The Delegated Powers Select Committee scrutinises those Bills that are intended to become parent Acts for inappropriate grant of power or legislation with inappropriate delegation (a Lords-only committee).

1.6.5 Judicial control of secondary legislation

The Judiciary cannot generally review primary legislation, but can review delegated legislation. The process is called **judicial review**. This review can take place only after the delegated legislation has come into force. The court may declare it void for being *ultra vires* (beyond the powers of the person or body who made it). There are two types of *ultra vires*:

- **procedural *ultra vires*:** this is where the parent Act lays down procedural rules which must be followed by the subordinate authority. If these rules are not followed, the court can find the delegated legislation *ultra vires* and void

- **substantive *ultra vires*:** where the delegated legislation goes beyond what Parliament intended then the court can declare it void on substantive grounds.

ASE EXAMPLE

*R v Secretary of State for Education and Employment, ex p National Union of Teachers,
The Times*, 8th August 2000

The National Union of Teachers sought judicial review of the Education (School Teachers' Pay and Conditions) (No 2) Order 2000 which proposed changes to the contracts of employment of school teachers and teachers' eligibility for higher rates of pay by introducing a system of performance-related pay. The NUT argued that the Secretary of State had failed to use the necessary statutory procedure for altering teachers' pay and conditions as detailed in s 2 of the School Teachers' Pay and Conditions Act 1991 and also that he had used a consultation process that was unfair.

The High Court allowed the application and quashed the statutory instrument. The court held that the Secretary of State had bypassed the independent review that was required when a significant and controversial change was to be made to teachers' pay and conditions of service. The court also held that the four-day consultation period was wholly inadequate because the Order introduced a change that was outside the scope of any previous consultations.

Advantages and disadvantages of secondary legislation

Advantages	Disadvantages
Expertise – MPs have expertise in party politics. They may also have interests in broader areas of social policy, but are unlikely, as a body, to have the requisite expertise to enact legislation in very specialised or technical areas of the law or more local requirements (byelaws). Through a consultation process, those with the necessary expertise can be relied on to contribute to the effective regulation of the law in the form of delegated legislation.	*Democratic accountability* – The real source of law in this regard is civil servants and experts, with a Government Minister providing supervision only. The law-makers are thus not democratically elected and it is difficult to hold them to account.
Time – It is far quicker to introduce, amend and repeal laws that are in urgent need of change by way of delegated legislation than by following the full enactment procedure required by an Act of Parliament outlined above. The use of delegated legislation also saves parliamentary time so that Parliament can focus its resources on the general principles of the law rather than the minutiae.	*Sub-delegation* – The parent Act delegates the law-making power onto a Government Minister or a local authority or the Privy Council; but in the case of the former, it is not the named individual who will make the law but he will be able to pass the authority to someone else. They may in turn sub-delegate the task to another (an expert, for example). The question arises of how far from the authority and sovereignty of Parliament the law-making stretches.
Flexible – Linked to the point above, the speed allows changes to the law to be made quickly, as and when the need arises.	*Publishing* – The process for bringing delegated legislation into force is subject to cursory glance only by Parliament, to save parliamentary time. If MPs are unlikely to keep abreast of changes in the law by delegated legislation, how are normal individuals supposed to discover and abide by secondary laws? As you might imagine, from the sheer bulk of delegated legislation, few publications contain reference to all of them introduced in any year. (NB The *New Law Journal* contains a regular list of statutory instruments but by title only.)

ACTIVITY

Practice essay title

'Delegated legislation is not a democratic method of law-making, but it is a necessary one.'

Discuss.

1.7 The European Union

1.7.1 A brief history of the European Community

Following the effective destruction of the European economy caused by the Second World War, many of the Allied countries made legal moves towards increased co-operation in the fields of trade and energy. In 1951, the Treaty of Paris established the European Coal and Steel Community and, in 1957, two Treaties of Rome established Euratom (the European Atomic Agency) and, most importantly for the student of law, the European Economic Community. It is this latter body which has affected English law so much in the last three decades. In 1986, the Single European Act established a single market across the member states and in 1993 the European Economic Community became the European Community (EC) by means of the Maastricht Treaty (the Treaty on European Union). This Treaty also created a new body – the European Union (EU). The EU is a far larger body than the EC. The EU includes the EC and it deals with common foreign and security policies as well as co-operation between states on criminal matters. For our purposes, all of the law emanating from the EC and the EU shall be referred to as 'EC law'.

Another change made by the Maastricht Treaty was to renumber the articles of the Treaty of Rome, so you will often see an article referred to by two numbers. The one in brackets after the first is the original number; the first is the new number under the Treaty of Maastricht. For example, Article 234 (ex 177) means that 234 is the Maastricht number and 177 is the original number under the Treaty of Rome.

Country	Year joined the EU
Austria	1995
Belgium	1958
Cyprus	1st May 2004
Czech Republic	1st May 2004
Denmark	1973
Estonia	1st May 2004
Finland	1995
France	1958
Germany	1958
Greece	1981
Hungary	1st May 2004
Ireland	1973
Italy	1958
Latvia	1st May 2004
Lithuania	1st May 2004
Luxembourg	1958
Malta	1st May 2004
Netherlands	1958
Poland	1st May 2004
Portugal	1986
Slovak Republic	1st May 2004
Slovenia	1st May 2004
Spain	1986
Sweden	1995
UK	1st January 1973

Figure 1.4 The member states of the European Union

Summary

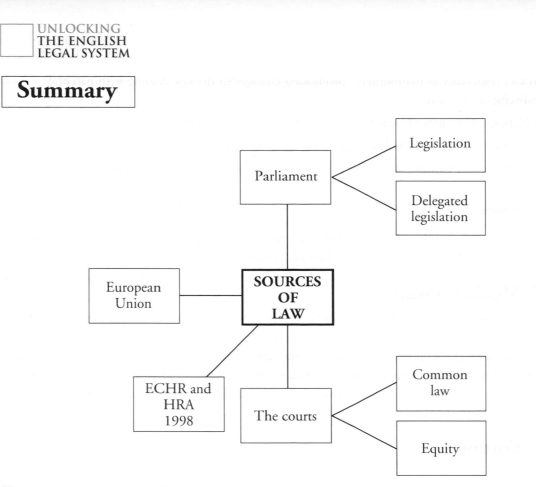

Figure 1.7 The sources of law

Further reading

Bailey, S H, Gunn, M, Ormerod, D and Ching, J (eds), *Smith, Bailey and Gunn on the Modern English Legal System* (4th edn, Sweet & Maxwell, 2002), Chapters 1 and 5.

Rivlin, G, *Understanding the Law* (3rd edn, Oxford University Press, 2004), Chapters 1, 3, 5 and 7.

Slapper, G and Kelly, D, *The English Legal System* (7th edn, Cavendish, 2004), Chapter 2.

chapter 2 THE DOCTRINE OF JUDICIAL PRECEDENT

Imagine that you have developed a mysterious illness and that you visit your doctor. He has never encountered this illness before, but remembers that a partner in the practice described something similar a while ago. Your doctor consults the other partner to find out what was prescribed.

Next, imagine that you are a solicitor in private practice. A wealthy client has asked you to draw up his will which is to contain an extremely complex trust. You have not drafted such a clause before, but you know that one of your partners has previously prepared this sort of will. You go in search of the file containing the clauses you need.

What is happening in both of the above cases is that the professional who is faced with an unfamiliar problem seeks a **precedent** to help him in arriving at the best solution to that problem. Using previous decisions to help resolve a current problem is a technique employed in all walks of life, but particularly in the courts of most legal systems.

In the English legal system this is referred to as the principle of *stare decisis* (which means 'stand by cases already decided') or the doctrine of **precedent** and these two terms are interchangeable. It is a concept which has a vital part to play in the day-to-day decision-making which takes place in our courts. Note at the outset that there is a difference between *stare decisis*, which describes the doctrine of precedent, and *res judicata*. This latter term means that a court's decision binds the **parties** to the case. The term is Latin for 'the matter has been settled' and is a principle that when a court has decided a case between the parties, after all the appeals if any are brought, the case is not to be re-opened by those parties or their successors. *Stare decisis*, which is the focus of this chapter, is the doctrine of following the legal reasoning from one case in a later case when the same points of law arise again.

In this chapter, the operation of the doctrine of precedent *(stare decisis)* in the courts of the English legal system will be examined. This chapter will develop your understanding of the way in which the courts and the judges work, and enable you to make some evaluation of the importance of decisions made in different courts.

2.1 What is the doctrine of precedent?

The doctrine simply means that a judge who is hearing a particular type of court case does not have to make a decision using simply his own knowledge of the relevant legal rules, but that similar previous decisions can be consulted to guide and justify the conclusion reached in the instant case. In fact, where a judge in a lower court is aware of a legal principle set by a higher court in a similar case, then this previous decision **must** be followed. It is this element of **binding** precedent which is distinctive within the English system.

So, for example, imagine that Parliament has created a new statute which regulates the activities of accountants. A dispute arises concerning the interpretation of one of the sections of the Act, and a court case ensues. The case reaches the Court of Appeal, which makes a decision about the definition of an 'accountant'. In all future cases in which the definition of an 'accountant' is in issue, lower courts must follow this binding precedent, and apply the decision from the previous case in these situations.

Clearly, if this system is to operate effectively, then it is essential that there is an efficient and reliable system of reporting court cases. This is achieved in three ways. First, all superior courts publish decided cases on the Internet. The second way is through the work of the Incorporated Council of Law Reporting for England and Wales, which produces the authoritative version of case reports (known as the Law Reports) and, third, through the publication of alternative series of reports by private publishers such as Butterworths. For example, see;

- www.publications.parliament.uk/pa/ld199697/ldjudgmt/ldjudgmt.htm
- www.lawreports.co.uk
- www.bailii.org
- www.butterworths.com

(For more information on law reporting, the different types of law reports, how to cite cases and how to use reported and unreported cases, refer to another text in this series: *Unlocking Legal Learning*, by R Huxley-Binns, L Riley and C Turner (Hodder Arnold, 2005), Chapters 4 and 5.)

Because of the vast number of cases decided every year, not every case from every court is published in this way, but the system does provide access to nearly all decisions of the superior courts which concern appeals on points of law. By consulting both the official and the privately published law reports, lawyers and judges are able to obtain valuable information about the way in which cases involving particular facts and legal principles have been decided on previous occasions. Because these precedents are regarded as binding, solicitors and barristers are thus able to give more accurate advice to their clients, and the judges are able to follow the reasoning of previous courts.

2.2 How does the doctrine of precedent operate?

2.2.1 The court hierarchy

The hierarchy of the courts is an important factor in the operation of the doctrine in practice. In Figure 2.1 you will find a basic outline of the court hierarchy, with a summary of the types of cases heard in each court. You should refer to Chapters 4, 5 and 6 for more information on the jurisdiction of each court.

HOUSE OF LORDS Appeals in civil and criminal cases		

COURT OF APPEAL	
Civil Division (appeals)	Criminal Division (appeals)

HIGH COURT		
Queen's Bench Divisional Courts (appeals)	Family Divisional Court (appeals)	Chancery Divisional Court (appeals)
Queen's Bench Division (first instance)	Family Division (first instance)	Chancery Division (first instance)

CROWN COURT (first instance criminal cases)	COUNTY COURT (first instance civil cases)

MAGISTRATES' COURT (first instance civil and criminal cases)	

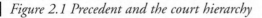

Figure 2.1 Precedent and the court hierarchy

A summary of how the doctrine of precedent operates within the hierarchy was made by the authors Twining and Miers in their book *How to Do Things with Rules* (Weidenfeld & Nicolson, 1991) and it is worth learning these few simple principles which apply whenever a court wishes to know whether or not to follow the decision of a previous case:

(a) If the precedent is a decision of a court **superior** to it in the hierarchy then it **must** follow that precedent in the present case (ie it is bound by the precedent).

(b) If the precedent is one of the court's **own** previous decisions, then, subject to certain exceptions, it **must** follow the precedent.

(c) If the precedent is a decision of a court **inferior** to it in the hierarchy, then it is **not bound** to follow the precedent, but **may** do so if it chooses.

These statements provide a useful outline of the rules and are therefore worth memorising, but, like all summaries, they do not tell the whole story, and in practice the situation is rather more complicated. In order to obtain the full picture, it is necessary to examine the position of each individual court in turn, and so details about the way in which precedent is applied in the different courts can be found below. Before that, however, it is important to appreciate a few of the technical aspects of the doctrine.

2.2.2 *Ratio decidendi* and *obiter dicta*

It is important to be aware of which part of the decision of a previous case is to be regarded as binding. The decision itself, ie who wins and who loses, is only really of interest to the parties in the case. What really matters, from the point of view of lawyers who wish to apply the doctrine of precedent, is the principle which can be drawn from the case by combining the relevant legal principles with the material facts on which the decision is based. This principle is known as the *ratio decidendi* (literally, the reason for deciding) and it is this part of the case which is absorbed into the general law, and which forms the basis of future legal reasoning. In discussion, lawyers generally abbreviate the term '*ratio decidendi*' to 'the *ratio*'.

The *ratio decidendi* is often contrasted with other parts of the judgment which are said to be *obiter dicta* (that is, sayings by the way). These are remarks made by a judge which are less central to the decision, for example hypothetical examples, statements of law which support dissenting judgments, and remarks concerned with broader principles of law which may not be directly in issue in the instant case.

The *ratio decidendi* is therefore that part of a previously decided case which later judges regard as binding on them, because it embodies the legal rule which justifies a particular decision. But how is it identified in any particular case? Discerning the *ratio* of a case requires a close analysis of the judgment or judgments in the case, and is made more difficult by the fact that the judges do not identify it for the benefit of later readers.

ACTIVITY

> In Appendix 1 to this book, you will find an extract from the famous case of *Carlill v Carbolic Smoke Ball Co* [1892] All ER Rep 127. Read it, and try to find the key (or most important or material) facts, the *ratio decidendi* and an example of an *obiter dictum.*

The *ratio decidendi* of *Carlill v Carbolic Smoke Ball Co* (1892) is that a contract cannot be made with the whole world, but an offer can be made to the world at large. This advert was such an offer. It was accepted by any person who (like Mrs Carlill) bought the product and used it in the prescribed manner. The offer was accepted by conduct. The plaintiff had not been asked to inform the company of her acceptance. It is worth noting at this stage that this 'rule of law' did not in fact exist until Mrs Carlill brought the case – precedents can be made too. This is called an 'original precedent' or a case of 'first impression'.

There are plenty of examples of *obiter dicta*, but one of the better known is where Bowen LJ said:

> J
>
> 'If I advertise to the world that my dog is lost and that anybody who brings him to a particular place will be paid some money, are all the police or other persons whose business is to find lost dogs to be expected to sit down and write me a note saying that they have accepted my proposal? Of course they look for the dog, and as soon as they find the dog, they have performed the condition.'

It is later judges who decide the *ratio* of an earlier case. In *Scruttons v Midlands Silicones* [1962] AC 446, the House of Lords endeavoured to clarify the reasoning used in its own previous decision of *Elder Dempster v Paterson Zochonis* [1924] AC 522. Lord Reid, in *Scruttons v Midlands Silicones* (1962), stated that a later court is entitled to question or limit a previous *ratio decidendi* of an earlier court:

(1) where it is obscure; and

(2) where it is out of line with other authorities (as in that case); and also

(3) where it is much wider than was necessary for the decision.

Academic writers such as Professor A Goodhart have attempted to formulate methods of finding the *ratio*. Goodhart's theory is that the *ratio* can be found by taking account of the facts treated by the judge as material, and the judge's decision as based on them. But it should be noted that this is only a theory and finding the *ratio* tends to be an intuitive process. It is more of an art than a science. Some help may be derived from the headnote in some of the reported cases. The headnote is the summary of the facts and the decision in each case, inserted by the editor of the reports, but it is unwise to rely on these as a method of finding the *ratio*. There is, unfortunately, no substitute for reading carefully through all the judgments of the case under discussion. In fact, this can reveal that a case may have more than one *ratio*, either because a judge has identified several reasons for a decision, providing several *rationes decidendi*, or because several members of the Divisional Court, the Court of Appeal or the House of Lords have given separate judgments with slightly different *rationes*.

2.2.3 Persuasive precedent

It is easy to focus on the binding nature and the binding element (*ratio decidendi*) of the system of precedent to the exclusion of all other factors. However, the final element to be examined before we look at how each court operates in the system is that of persuasive precedent. If something is persuasive it is 'influencing', 'inducing' or 'urging' you to go along with it or agree with it. A persuasive precedent is exactly that. Examples of persuasive precedent include:

- all *obiter dicta*
- a dissenting judgment (that is, where there is more than one judge, where one disagrees with the majority decision)
- a minority judgment (that is, where there is more than one judge, where one agrees with the majority decision but does so for a different reason)
- the *ratio* of a decision of a lower court in the hierarchy
- the *ratio* of a decision of a court abroad or the Privy Council (see below)
- writings of authors of repute, also known as books of authority
- reports of law reform bodies, such as the Law Commission
- custom.

You should now have a reasonable grasp of the following technical expressions:

- *stare decisis*
- *ratio decidendi*
- *obiter dicta*
- persuasive precedent.

ACTIVITY

Self-assessment questions

1. What is the doctrine of binding precedent?
2. What does the term '*ratio decidendi*' mean?
3. Suggest how the *ratio decidendi* of a case can be found.
4. What does the term '*obiter dicta*' mean?
5. How does a persuasive precedent differ from a binding precedent?

2.3 The doctrine as applied in individual courts

2.3.1 The House of Lords

The *ratio* of a decision of the House of Lords binds all inferior courts in this country.

From the end of the nineteenth century until 1966, the House regarded itself as bound by its own previous decisions, according to the law as stated in *London Tramways Co Ltd v London County Council* [1898] AC 375. This was because it was felt that there had be an end to litigation, ie it had to be possible for people to see that once a case had been to the House of Lords, then there would be no further debate on that legal point. The question of law would be conclusive and, if wrong, could be set right only by an Act of Parliament.

However, this approach proved to be unduly restrictive, in that it effectively prohibited any development in the law. Therefore in 1966, Lord Gardiner LC, on behalf of himself and the other Law Lords, issued a Practice Statement:

> **J**
>
> *Practice Statement* [1966] 3 All ER 77
>
> 'Their Lordships regard the use of precedent as an indispensable foundation upon which to decide what is the law and its application to individual cases. It provides at least some degree of certainty upon which individuals can rely in the conduct of their affairs, as well as a basis for orderly development of legal rules.
>
> Their Lordships nevertheless recognise that too rigid adherence to precedent may lead to injustice in a particular case and also unduly restrict the proper development of the law. They propose therefore to modify their present practice and, while treating former decisions of this House as normally binding, to depart from a previous decision when it appears right to do so.
>
> In this connexion they will bear in mind the danger of disturbing retrospectively the basis on which contracts, settlements of property and fiscal arrangements have been entered into and also the especial need for certainty as to the criminal law.
>
> This announcement is not intended to affect the use of precedent elsewhere than in this House.'

An explanatory note was also published with the Practice Statement (which is also sometimes referred to as the Practice Direction) which provides further information on the anticipated operation of the House of Lords:

Q

'**Explanatory note for press:**

Since the House of Lords decided the English case of *London Street Tramways* [*sic*] *v London County Council* in 1898, the House have considered themselves bound to follow their own decisions, except where a decision has been given *per incuriam* in disregard of a statutory provision or another decision binding on them.

The statement made is one of great importance, although it should not be supposed that there will frequently be cases in which the House thinks it right not to follow their own precedent. An example of a case in which the House might think it right to depart from a precedent is where they consider that the earlier decision was influenced by the existence of conditions which no longer prevail, and that in modern conditions the law ought to be different.

One consequence of this change is of major importance. The relaxation of the rule of judicial precedent will enable the House of Lords to pay greater attention to judicial decisions reached in the superior courts of the Commonwealth, where they differ from earlier decisions of the House of Lords. That could be of great help in the development of our own law. The superior courts of many other countries are not rigidly bound by their own decisions and the change in the practice of the House of Lords will bring us more into line with them.'

The key words in the Practice Direction are 'when it appears right to do so'. The House was very conscious of the need for caution in the exercise of its new power. This was felt to be especially important in cases where contracts, dealings with property, and financial arrangements had been made in reliance on previous House of Lords' decisions. The Law Lords also wished to avoid any reduction in the degree of certainty required in the sphere of criminal law where changes could cause an injustice. However, the House also recognised that there would be circumstances where modern conditions would require a change in the law, and that decisions which had been made in the past in response to factors which had since ceased to operate could now be overruled by the use of the Practice Statement.

The use of the Practice Statement

In practice, the Law Lords did indeed exercise caution in their use of this power, and, following the publication of the Practice Statement in 1966, two years passed before the House of Lords departed from one of its own previous decisions. The first case in which the authority of the Statement was invoked was that of *Conway v Rimmer* [1968] AC 910, HL in which the case of *Duncan v Cammell Laird & Co* [1942] AC 624, HL was overruled. Each of these cases concerned the extent to which the Crown could claim the right not to disclose information during a court case. The earlier case of *Duncan v Cammell Laird & Co* (1942) had been decided during the Second World War, and this had enabled the Government to claim 'public interest immunity', and thus avoid the need to comply with an order of the court requiring disclosure of certain documents. The different circumstances under which the case of *Conway v Rimmer* (1968) arose meant that the House of Lords removed this immunity from the Government. This case was therefore a good example of the way in which the Practice Statement could be used to adapt the law to changes in society.

However, this decision did not mean that a judicial 'free-for-all' would ensue and, in the intervening years, the House of Lords has continued to use its power in a relatively small number of cases. For example, in *Herrington v British Railways Board* [1972] 1 All ER 749, a rule which had been propounded in the earlier House of Lords' case of *Addie & Sons v Dumbreck* [1929] AC 358, HL was relaxed as a result of the Practice Statement. In *Addie & Sons v Dumbreck* (1929), the House had ruled that an occupier of property owed only a minimal duty of care to a trespasser, even where that trespasser happened to be a child. However, changes in society's opinion as to the appropriate duty owed in these circumstances led the Law Lords to formulate a duty on the part of an occupier to act humanely towards trespassers.

In *Murphy v Brentwood Borough Council* [1991] 1 AC 398, the House of Lords held, overruling the previous case of *Anns v Merton Borough Council* [1978] AC 728, that a local authority is not liable in tort for negligent inspection of building foundations, where the resulting defects are discovered before physical injury occurs. This was because the loss suffered is purely economic and, under the rule in *Anns v Merton Borough Council* (1978), a far too broad approach had been taken that had drawn the law wider than in any other areas of liability for 'pure economic loss' rather than for, say, physical damage to person.

In *Miliangos v George Frank (Textiles) Ltd* [1975] 1 All ER 1076, new developments in rules relating to the exchange rates for foreign currencies, and in particular the less favourable position of Sterling, led the House of Lords to change its own earlier ruling in the case of *Re United Railways of Havana & Regla Warehouses Ltd* [1960] 2 All ER 332, that damages awarded by an English court could only be awarded in Sterling. As a result of the case of *Miliangos v George Frank (Textiles) Ltd* (1975), damages may be awarded by a court in England based on the currency specified in the contract which gave rise to the dispute.

Cases such as these, in which the Practice Statement has been used to positive effect, indicate that the House will expect to see that broad issues of justice and public policy are involved before

altering a previous decision, and will not usually overturn a previous ruling simply because it is felt that the earlier decision was wrong. A good example of this line of reasoning can be seen in the case of *Jones v Secretary of State for Social Services* [1972] 1 All ER 145. This case concerned the interpretation of a statute, on which the House of Lords had previously given a ruling in the case of *Re Dowling* [1967] 1 AC 725. Despite the fact that four of the seven Law Lords who heard the *Jones* (1972) case felt that *Re Dowling* (1967) was wrongly decided, the House declined to depart from its earlier decision. Some of the reasons offered as justification for this decision were that no broad issues of justice or public policy or legal principle were involved; the case involved the interpretation of a statute and therefore any harmful consequences of the interpretation could be cured by further statutory provisions; and the need for finality in litigation.

The case of *R v Shivpuri* [1986] 2 All ER 334 proved to be an exception to the principles set out in the *Jones v Secretary of State for Social Services* (1972) case above. Here, the Lords took the unusual step of overruling a previous decision of their own which had been made only one year before. The case of *Anderton v Ryan* [1985] 2 All ER 355 was felt to have been wrongly decided, and to contain an error which distorted the law. The Law Lords felt that this situation needed to be remedied as quickly as possible by overruling the previous decision, despite the fact that this was a case which affected the criminal law and the interpretation of a statute, both factors which were thought to militate against the use of the Practice Statement. As Lord Bridge explained:

> J 'The Practice Statement is an effective abandonment of our pretention to infallibility. If a serious error embodied in a decision of this House has distorted the law, the sooner it is corrected the better.'

However, the Lords emphasised that this was an exceptional case, and that use of the Practice Statement generally would remain a rare occurrence. But, within a year, the House of Lords in *R v Howe* [1987] AC 417 overruled its own previous decision in *DPP for Northern Ireland v Lynch* [1975] 2 WLR 641. In *Howe* (1987) the House held that the defence of duress is not available to a charge of murder, even though, a year previously, it had said that it could be.

It is also clear that even though a case has been followed for a number of years, the House of Lords can and will overrule it 'when it appears right to do so'. The case of *MPC v Caldwell* [1982] AC 341 involved a charge of criminal damage. This offence is committed where a person destroys or damages property belonging to another, where the person intends to destroy or damage the property or is reckless about doing so. In the case of *Cunningham* [1957] 2 QB 396, the Court of Criminal Appeal had decided that a person acted 'recklessly' where they were aware of a risk and took the risk anyway. This is sometimes referred to as conscious or advertent risk-taking.

CASE EXAMPLE

MPC v Caldwell [1982] AC 341

The defendant, Caldwell, was a chef. He had an argument with the owner of the hotel where he worked, and in a drunken and angry state he set fire to the kitchens. He was charged with arson which is a form of criminal damage.

He could have been convicted using the *Cunningham* (1957) definition above, because drunkenness is no defence in these circumstances, but, nevertheless, the House of Lords decided to widen the *Cunningham* (1957) definition of 'reckless' to include not just thinking about a risk and taking it anyway, but failing to think about an obvious risk.

Later cases then had to answer the question: 'If the defendant could be convicted because he didn't think about an **obvious** risk, to whom must the risk be obvious?'. What if the defendant was blind, or very young, or suffering from a learning difficulty, and the risk was not obvious to him?

The Queen's Bench Divisional Court in *Elliott v C* [1983] 1 WLR 939 held that the answer to the question was 'Obvious to the reasonable person; that is, a sober and reasonable adult'.

CASE EXAMPLE

Elliott v C [1983] 1 WLR 939

C was a 14-year-old schoolgirl. She had learning difficulties and was in remedial class at school. One evening she stayed out all night and at 5 am she entered a garden shed, found white spirit there and poured it on to the carpet on the floor of the shed and threw two lit matches onto the spirit. The second match ignited, a fire immediately flared up out of control and she left the shed, which was destroyed. When interviewed later that day by the police she said she did not know why she had set fire to the shed but 'just felt like it'. She was charged with criminal damage (arson).

The magistrates found that the girl had given no thought at the time she started the fire to the possibility of there being a risk that this would happen, having regard to her age and understanding, and lack of experience of dealing with inflammable spirit and that she must have been exhausted at the time. However, the Divisional Court held that the risk of damage must have been obvious to a reasonably prudent man, even though on the facts of the particular case, the accused did not in fact, for some reason, appreciate the risk.

This case is generally considered to be harsh, if not completely wrong. However, despite a number of challenges, the case of *Caldwell* (1982) remained good law for 21 years until *R v G* [2003]

UKHL 50. Lord Bingham, with unanimous support, felt that conviction of a serious crime should depend on proof that the offender had a culpable or blameworthy state of mind. If the defendant genuinely did not perceive that risk, he may 'fairly be accused of stupidity or a lack of imagination', but that was insufficient for culpability. The need for the House to rectify this situation was 'compelling' and a matter of legal principle. The House used the 1966 Statement to overrule *Caldwell* (1982).

In the Practice Statement, the House of Lords emphasised that the practice of overruling previous decisions of the same court was not intended to affect the use of precedent in any other court. However, you will soon discover that Lord Denning, a former well-known Master of the Rolls, would have liked to extend the powers of the Court of Appeal in this direction, but was restrained by the House of Lords.

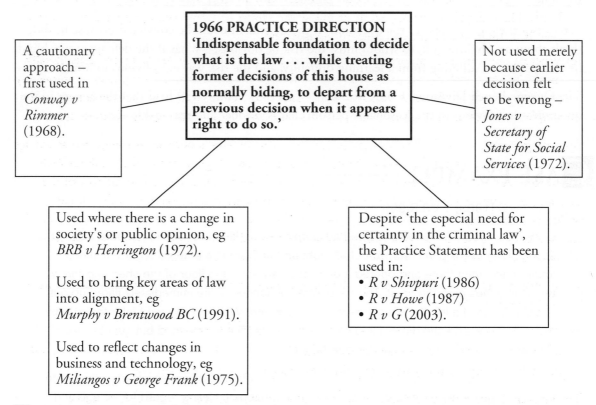

Figure 2.2 Precedent and the House of Lords

2.3.2 The Court of Appeal (Civil Division)

There are three main rules which apply to the Court of Appeal:

1. The Court of Appeal is bound by decisions of the House of Lords whether it agrees with them or not.

2. The decisions of the Court of Appeal itself are binding on the inferior courts in the hierarchy.

3. The Court of Appeal is normally bound by its own previous decisions. This is known as the 'self-binding rule', and means that unless one of the established exceptions to this rule applies, then the Court of Appeal will follow its own previous precedents.

The classic statement of the exceptions to the self-binding rule can be found in the case of *Young v Bristol Aeroplane Co Ltd* [1944] 2 All ER 293. Here, Lord Greene MR identified three situations in which it would be possible for the Court of Appeal to depart from its own previous decisions:

(a) Where previous decisions of the Court conflict with each other. In these circumstances the Court can decide which decision to follow and which to ignore (in practice, the Court of Appeal invariably follows the later of two conflicting decisions, but need not do so: *Great Peace Shipping v Tsavliris Salvage* [2002] 4 All ER 689).

(b) Where a previous decision of the Court conflicts with a subsequent decision of the House of Lords. Here, the Court of Appeal must follow the House of Lords' ruling rather than its own, even if it thinks the House of Lords' ruling is wrong.

(c) Where a previous decision of the Court appears to have been made *per incuriam*. This literally means 'through lack of care', which sounds as though it should enable later judges to ignore any previous precedent which seems to the later court to be wrong. The true position is not quite so simple, however, as the technical application of the *per incuriam* rule is actually quite narrow.

According to the case of *Morelle v Wakeling* [1955] 1 All ER 708, a decision was regarded as having been made *per incuriam* if the Court of Appeal was in a state of ignorance or forgetfulness with regard to a relevant part of statute law or a binding precedent and, as a result, some part of the decision, or some step in the reasoning, was found to be demonstrably wrong. In the case of *Williams v Fawcett* [1985] 1 All ER 787, however, the Court of Appeal felt that there were special features justifying an extension of this traditionally accepted form of the *per incuriam* rule above. Three of these features seem to be prominent in the judgment. They were:

1. the clarity with which the growth of the error could be detected if the previous decisions were read consecutively

2. the fact that the cases were concerned with the liberty of the subject and

3. that the cases were most unlikely to reach the House of Lords, which meant that there would be no further opportunity to correct the error which had crept into the law.

The rules in *Young v Bristol Aeroplane Co Ltd* (1944) above describe the currently accepted understanding of the doctrine of precedent as it relates to the Court of Appeal (Civil Division) where the European Convention on Human Rights is not concerned. However, you should be aware of the fact that, during the 1970s, the then Master of the Rolls, Lord Denning, challenged this accepted view of the role of the Court of Appeal. In a number of controversial cases he led a campaign, first, to establish that the Court of Appeal was not always strictly bound by House of Lords' decisions, and could even declare them to be wrongly decided using the doctrine of *per incuriam*. Secondly, he argued that the Court of Appeal should adopt the philosophy of the 1966

J

'. . . the rule as it had been laid down in the *Bristol Aeroplane* case had never been questioned . . . until, following on the announcement by Lord Gardiner LC in 1966 that the House of Lords would feel free in exceptional cases to depart from a previous decision of its own, Lord Denning MR conducted what may be described, I hope without offence, as a one-man crusade with the object of freeing the Court of Appeal from the shackles which the doctrine of *stare decisis* imposed on its liberty of decision by the application of the rule laid down in the *Bristol Aeroplane* case to its previous decisions; or, for that matter, by any decisions of this House itself of which the Court of Appeal disapproved . . .

In an appellate court of last resort a balance must be struck between the need on the one side for the legal certainty resulting from the binding effect of previous decisions and on the other side the avoidance of undue restriction on the proper development of the law.'

Lord Diplock continued that the Court of Appeal was and is not a court of final appeal. It is merely an intermediate appellate court. He said that the proper development of the law (his second point above) can be achieved by the Court of Appeal granting permission to appeal to the House of Lords. However, he pointed out, legal certainty would be at risk if the Court of Appeal was not bound by its own previous decisions. He concluded that:

J

'. . . the balance does not lie in the same place as in the case of a court of last resort. That is why Lord Gardiner LC's announcement about the future attitude towards precedent of the House of Lords in its judicial capacity concluded with the words: "This announcement is not intended to affect the use of precedent elsewhere than in this House." '

ACTIVITY

The Court of Appeal (Civil Division) is in the process of hearing appeals in the following five cases. Explain how the doctrine of precedent will apply in each case. In order to answer these questions, the traditional view of the doctrine of precedent must be adopted, Lord Denning's views having been rejected by the House of Lords.

CONTINUED ▶

- Case 1: There is a previous decision of the Court of Appeal (Case A), made in 1880, involving similar facts and legal issues. The Court of Appeal hearing Case 1 thinks that while Case A was correctly decided in 1880, the decision is outdated in today's social climate.

- Case 2: A previous case involving similar facts and legal issues was decided by the Court of Appeal in 1990 (Case B). The House of Lords has also made a ruling in a similar case (Case C) in 1993 but cases B and C conflict.

- Case 3: There are two previous Court of Appeal precedents relevant to the point in issue. Both were decided on the same day, by differently constituted Courts of Appeal, and these two decisions conflict with each other.

- Case 4: Case D was decided by the House of Lords in 1995. In 1996, the Court of Appeal decided Case E which conflicts with Case D, but Case D was not cited to the Court of Appeal in Case E.

- Case 5: Case F was decided by the House of Lords in 1995. In 1996, the Court of Appeal decided Case G which conflicts with Case F. Case F was cited to the Court of Appeal in Case G, but the Court of Appeal in Case G distinguished Case F. The Court of Appeal in Case 5 thinks the Court of Appeal in 1996 (Case G) was wrong to have distinguished Case F.

2.3.3 The Court of Appeal (Criminal Division)

The rules of precedent are in theory identical in the two divisions of the Court of Appeal, ie that the Court is bound by decisions of the House of Lords, and by its own previous decisions, subject to the exceptions outlined in the case of *Young v Bristol Aeroplane Co Ltd* (1944). While the rule regarding House of Lords' decisions remains the same, the self-binding rule is applied in a slightly different way in the Criminal Division. Case law indicates that the Court of Appeal (Criminal Division) may depart from its own previous decisions if it is satisfied that the law was misapplied or misunderstood, and that this power to deviate from the self-binding rule exists in addition to the exceptions set out in the *Young v Bristol Aeroplane Co Ltd* (1944) case.

As you will appreciate, the liberty of the individual is at stake in cases which are heard by the Court of Appeal (Criminal Division), and this is felt to be a more important factor than the consistency which is produced by rigid adherence to precedent. The danger of a wrongful conviction outweighs the need to follow the doctrine in its strict form. A slightly different view of precedent is therefore taken in such cases.

In *R v Taylor* [1950] 2 All ER 170, Lord Goddard CJ stated:

J   'This court, however, has to deal with questions involving the liberty of the subject, and if it finds, on reconsideration, that, in the opinion of a full court assembled for that purpose, the law has been either misapplied or misunderstood in a decision which it has previously given, and that, on the strength of that decision, an accused person has been sentenced and imprisoned it is the bounden duty of the court to reconsider the earlier decision with a view to seeing whether that person had been properly convicted.'

In *R v Simpson* [2003] EWCA Crim 1499, Lord Woolf CJ held that the Court of Appeal (Criminal Division), has a residual discretion to decide whether one of its own previous decisions should be treated as binding where there are grounds for saying that the previous case is wrong. He stated that the rules of precedent should be applied, bearing in mind that their objective is to assist the administration of justice and should not be regarded as so rigid that they cannot develop in order to meet the needs of contemporary society. While he endorsed a restrictive and cautious approach, he also recognised that a wrong decision in the Criminal Division could create greater problems than a wrong decision in the Civil Division, especially as, in practice, there is little prospect of obtaining leave to appeal to the House of Lords in a criminal matter.

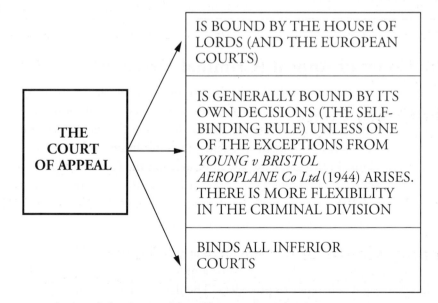

Figure 2.3 Precedent and the Court of Appeal

2.3.4 The Divisional Courts of the High Court

The Divisional Courts of the High Court are bound by decisions of the House of Lords and the Court of Appeal.

Decisions of the Divisional Courts are binding on inferior courts.

The Divisional Courts are normally bound by their own previous decisions, unless one or more of the three exceptions enunciated in the case of *Young v Bristol Aeroplane Co Ltd* (1944) applies. As in the Court of Appeal, there may be a greater degree of flexibility in this rule when the Divisional Court of the Queen's Bench Division considers appeals in criminal cases.

The similarity of the rules concerning precedent in the Court of Appeal and the Divisional Courts of the High Court can be explained in terms of function. The Divisional Courts are not generally courts of first instance: as with the Court of Appeal, they are appellate courts, and in certain circumstances they replace the Court of Appeal as the appropriate forum for appeal. In such cases, the next avenue of appeal is the House of Lords, which means that the Divisional Courts enjoy a great degree of authority and seniority. It is therefore logical for the same rules of precedent to be adopted here.

2.3.5 The High Court

The High Court is bound by decisions of those courts which are superior to it in the hierarchy.

Decisions of the High Court are binding on courts which are inferior to it in the hierarchy.

The High Court does not regard itself as bound by its own previous decisions, but they are of the strongest persuasive value.

2.3.6 The Crown Court

The Crown Court is bound by decisions of superior courts.

Its decisions are binding on those courts which are inferior to it in the hierarchy.

Decisions of the Crown Court are of persuasive, but not binding, authority for other judges in the Crown Court.

2.3.7 County Courts and Magistrates' Courts

These courts are bound by all superior courts. Their own decisions are not binding on any courts, not even on other courts at the same level in the hierarchy.

2.3.8 Other Courts

Both the European Court of Justice (the Court of Justice of the European Communities, to give it its full title) and the European Court of Human Rights do not bind themselves, but their decisions are binding on the courts in England.

The Judicial Committee of the Privy Council hears (among other things) appeals from Commonwealth countries. The Committee is composed of the Law Lords, ex-Law Lords and superior judges from Canada, Australia and New Zealand by invitation. As you can see, the composition of the Committee is impressive and although a decision (technically the advice) of the Committee is not binding on English courts – because the common law in the Commonwealth is not necessarily the same as in England – it is highly persuasive. Similarly, the Privy Council is not bound by the decisions of the House of Lords; in fact, the Committee is not strictly bound by even its own previous decisions, but it rarely departs from them.

2.4 The Human Rights Act 1998

Section 2 of the Human Rights Act (HRA) 1998 provides:

'Interpretation of Convention rights

2 (1) A court or tribunal determining a question which has arisen in connection with a Convention right must take into account any–

(a) judgment, decision, declaration or advisory opinion of the European Court of Human Rights,

(b) opinion of the Commission given in a report adopted under Article 31 of the Convention,

(c) decision of the Commission in connection with Article 26 or 27(2) of the Convention, or

(d) decision of the Committee of Ministers taken under Article 46 of the Convention, whenever made or given, so far as, in the opinion of the court or tribunal, it is relevant to the proceedings in which that question has arisen.'

This section has the potential radically to alter the operation of *stare decisis*. It has been held that the word 'must' in s 2(1) puts a duty on an inferior court to avoid (and impliedly overrule) the decision of a superior court where the lower court felt that the higher court's decision was incompatible with a decision of the European Court of Human Rights. While this new power of the lower court appears to be controversial because it gives a lower court the ability to avoid a superior court's decision, in reality it is not. The HRA 1998 is legislation and, as the primary source of law, must take precedence.

The case in question is the Court of Appeal's decision in *Mendoza v Ghaidan* [2004] UKHL 30; [2002] EWCA Civ 1533; [2003] 2 WLR 478.

CASE EXAMPLE

Mendoza v Ghaidan [2004] UKHL 30; [2002] EWCA Civ 1533; [2003] 2 WLR 478

Mr Mendoza had lived with his homosexual partner since 1972 and moved into a flat with him in 1983. The partner had a statutory tenancy on the flat. The relationship between Mr Mendoza and his partner was described as close, monogamous and loving. Essentially, they lived together as spouses, except for the fact that the relationship was a same-sex relationship. After the death of his partner, the landlord granted Mr Mendoza a different type of tenancy (an assured tenancy) which had less protection for the tenant.

The landlord had relied on the House of Lords' decision in *Fitzpatrick v Sterling* [2001] 1 AC 27 where it had been held that a homosexual partner in a long-term relationship was entitled to an assured tenancy as a member of the deceased's family, but could not obtain a statutory tenancy as these were available only to people living with the original tenant as his wife or her husband.

Mr Mendoza argued that his rights had been infringed under Art 8 (interest in home) and Art 14 (the right to exercise all of the Convention rights without discrimination) of the European Convention on Human Rights

The problem the Court of Appeal had to face, however, was that on the one hand *Fitzpatrick v Sterling* (2001) is a House of Lords' case and the Court of Appeal is bound by decisions of the House of Lords. On the other hand, it was clear that Mr Mendoza was being discriminated against under European Court of Human Rights case law (*Petrovic v Austria* (2001) 33 ECHR 14). While neither s 2 of the Human Rights Act 1998 nor the operation of *stare decisis* was mentioned by Buxton LJ in the case, he nevertheless found that the decision in *Fitzpatrick v Sterling* (2001) had infringed Art 14 and Mr Mendoza was granted a statutory tenancy. In effect, the Court of Appeal used the power under s 2 of the HRA 1998 to overrule a House of Lords' case to follow an ECHR case, but without clearly saying that s 2 HRA 1998 was being used. In June 2004, the House of Lords itself ([2004] UKHL 30) approved the decision in the Court of Appeal and thus implicitly approved the new operation of the doctrine, allowing the inferior court to overrule the decision of the superior court.

ACTIVITY

Practice essay title

'The literal translation of *stare decisis* (that all courts stand by all previous decisions) does not reflect the operation of judicial precedent in the twenty-first century.'

Discuss the validity of the above view.

2.5 The declaratory theory

The declaratory theory of judicial law-making was famously explained by William Blackstone, writing during the eighteenth century:

'[the judge] being sworn to determine, not according to his private sentiments . . . not according to his own private judgment, but according to the known laws and customs of the land: not delegated to pronounce a new law, but to maintain and expound the old one.'

Blackstone's Commentaries 69

Sir William Holdsworth in his article explained the theory thus:

'Cases do not make the law, but are only the best evidence of what the law is.'

'Case Law' (1934) 50 LQR 180

This view supposes that judges have no choice to make when deciding the outcome of a case. The law, in this regard, is seen as a web of legal principles that readily supply the answer (there is only one answer) to each problem that arises. Previous cases supply the evidence of the legal principles that have been adopted. This was Ronald Dworkin's view of the declaratory theory. An overruled case is regarded as never having been the law and it is said that the new (ie the correct) decision is not only to be applied from now on, but also retrospectively. Retrospectivity essentially means that the law as decided in 2005 will be applied to acts that took place in 1980. This retrospective effect is complicated. For example, consider a commercial contract that was made in 1993 for the supply of goods until 1999, on the basis of the law as it was understood to be in 1993. Consider further what might happen if that law was overruled in 1997. The terms of 1993 contract have to be interpreted after 1997 in a completely different light and this may affect the nature of the contractual relationship between the parties. The House of Lords has confirmed the retrospective nature of precedent in *Kleinwort Benson v Lincoln City Council* [1998] 4 All ER 513.

58

David Kairys has argued that judges do have a choice to make in their decision; but not an unfettered (free or unlimited) choice. The outcome of any particular case will be based upon those precedents that the judge believes to be correct, but also on his concept of what is socially and politically correct or justified. J A G Griffith (*The Politics of the Judiciary* (Fontana, 1991)) agrees with Kairys, but also argues that the judge's view of what is socially and politically correct is dictated by the narrow social background of the Judiciary (see Chapter 11). He contends that the judges are part of the 'Establishment' and their decisions in cases are pro-Establishment. Lord Reid, in a lecture in 1972, sided more with Kairys than Dworkin. He stated that the declaratory theory was a 'fairytale'; that judges do have choices; but 'where there is freedom to go in one direction or another . . . we should have regard to common sense, legal principle and public policy in that order'.

Lord Hobhouse, in *R v Governor of Brockhill Prison, ex p Evans (No 2)* [2001] 2 AC 19 at 48, said:

> **J** 'The common law develops as circumstances change and the balance of legal, social and economic needs changes. New concepts come into play; new statutes influence the non-statutory law. The strength of the common law is its ability to develop and evolve. All this carries with it the inevitable need to recognise that decisions may change. What was previously thought to be the law is open to challenge and review; if the challenge is successful, a new statement of the law will take the place of the old statement.'

While judges do now seem to recognise openly the need for the development of the common law, they also recognise that their job is not to act as legislators. In *C v DPP* [1995] 2 All ER 43, the House of Lords was asked to consider changing the law regarding childrens' criminal liability. There was a rebuttable common law presumption that 10–14 year old children were incapable of committing crime. This meant that a child aged 10–14 was presumed to be incapable of committing a crime unless the prosecution could prove otherwise. This would be called rebutting the presumption. The House of Lords refused to overrule the previous law and Lord Lowry (at 51) laid down guidelines for judicial law-making:

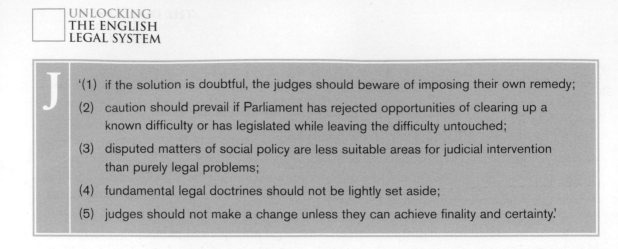

'(1) if the solution is doubtful, the judges should beware of imposing their own remedy;

(2) caution should prevail if Parliament has rejected opportunities of clearing up a known difficulty or has legislated while leaving the difficulty untouched;

(3) disputed matters of social policy are less suitable areas for judicial intervention than purely legal problems;

(4) fundamental legal doctrines should not be lightly set aside;

(5) judges should not make a change unless they can achieve finality and certainty.'

On the other hand, without referring to Lord Lowry's speech above, in *Fitzpatrick v Sterling Housing Association* [1999] 4 All ER 705, Lord Slynn said:

'It has been suggested that for your Lordships to decide this appeal in favour of the appellant would be to usurp the function of Parliament. It is trite that that is something the courts must not do. When considering social issues in particular judges must not substitute their own views to fill gaps . . . it would be a court's duty to give effect to it whatever changes in social attitudes a court might think ought to be reflected in the legislation. Similarly, if it were explicit or clear that the word must be given a very wide meaning so as to cover relationships for which a court, conscious of the traditional views of society might disapprove, the court's duty would be to give effect to it. It is, however, for the court in the first place to interpret each phrase in its statutory context. To do so is not to usurp Parliament's function; not to do so would be to abdicate the judicial function. If Parliament takes the view that the result is not what is wanted it will change the legislation.'

Where there is no binding precedent in a particular situation, judges still have to decide the outcome of a case. They cannot refuse to do so, and say it is a matter for Parliament and Parliament alone. It is generally accepted nowadays that judges do make law and the declaratory theory is seen as being unrealistic insofar as it suggests that judges have no choice to make when deciding cases. The system of precedent is certainly not so rigid as to prevent development of the law. For example, the House of Lords created new law in *Shaw v DPP* [1962] AC 220:

CASE EXAMPLE

Shaw v DPP [1962] AC 220

Shaw decided to fill what he perceived to be a gap in the market by publishing a directory of the names and addresses of prostitutes. Even though he had obtained advice from Scotland Yard that such activity would not be unlawful, he was subsequently convicted of the previously unknown offence of conspiracy to corrupt public morals

Most law students ask how Shaw could have been convicted of an offence that did not appear to have existed at the time he committed the act constituting the offence. Certainly, such an occurrence is both rare and highly controversial. If it were to occur today, there might be a successful appeal on the basis that the conviction breached Art 7 of the European Convention on Human Rights (no one shall be held guilty of any criminal offence on account of any act or omission which did not constitute a criminal offence under national or international law at the time when it was committed). However, the House of Lords insisted that even if the offence had not been prosecuted in that way previously, it did exist. The House referred to the old case of *R v Curl* (1727) 2 Stra 788. In that case the charge against the accused was that of publishing an obscene libel. The Court of King's Bench agreed with the argument submitted by the Attorney General:

J   'What I insist upon is that this is an offence at common law, as it tends to corrupt the morals of the King's subjects, and is against the peace of the King. . . . I do not insist that every immoral act is indictable, such as telling a lie, or the like; but if it is destructive of morality in general, if it does, or may, affect all the King's subjects, it then is an offence of a public nature.'

In *Shaw v DPP* (1962), Viscount Simonds agreed with this reasoning and at p 268 said:

J   '. . . there is in that court a residual power, where no statute has yet intervened to supersede the common law, to superintend those offences which are prejudicial to the public welfare. Such occasions will be rare, for Parliament has not been slow to legislate when attention has been sufficiently aroused. But gaps remain and will always remain since no one can foresee every way in which the wickedness of man may disrupt the order of society.'

The declaratory theory does still receive some attention: in *Re A (children) (conjoined twins: surgical separation)* [2000] 4 All ER 961, Ward LJ said at 968:

> 'This court is a court of law, not of morals, and our task has been to find, and our duty is then to apply the relevant principles of law to the situation before us – a situation which is quite unique.'

But such attention is not unanimous, as Lord Hoffmann stated in *Arthur J S Hall v Simons* [2000] 3 All ER 673:

> 'I hope that I will not be thought ungrateful if I do not encumber this speech with citations. The question of what the public interest now requires depends upon the strength of the arguments rather than the weight of authority.'

ACTIVITY

Practice essay title

'Blackstone's declaratory theory of law is just that; a theory. In practice judges do make law and the sooner we all accept that, the better.'

Discuss.

2.6 Avoiding precedents

2.6.1 Distinguishing

If a court can find sufficient differences between the material facts of a previous and a current case, then it may depart from the previous decision. It may also be that although a judge is bound by a precedent in a particular case, there are good reasons why the judge may wish not to follow it. In these circumstances it is likely that the judge will try to distinguish the precedent, so as to avoid having to follow the previous decision. This process of distinguishing cases is extremely important in practice, because it enables judges to develop the law, rather than being bound by precedent in every situation.

For example, read the facts and decisions of the two cases below and consider how a judge might distinguish the first (*King v Philips* [1953] 1 QB 429) in the second case (*Boardman v Sanderson* [1964] 1 WLR 1317).

CASE EXAMPLE

King v Philips [1953] 1 QB 429

A taxi driver reversed his taxi into a small boy on a tricycle. The boy and his tricycle luckily suffered only slight damage, but the boy's mother heard him scream and looked out of the upstairs window of their home which was about 70 to 80 yards away. She saw the tricycle under the taxicab but could not see the boy. He eventually ran home, but his mother had suffered nervous shock, a psychiatric injury, for which she claimed damages from the defendant.

The Court of Appeal held that the defendant was not liable to the mother because, on the facts, no 'hypothetical reasonable observer' could have anticipated that any injury, either physical or psychiatric, could have been caused to her by the backing of the taxi without due attention as to where it was going, and, accordingly, the driver owed no duty to the mother.

CASE EXAMPLE

Boardman v Sanderson [1964] 1 WLR 1317

The defendant ran his car wheel onto a young boy's foot. The boy screamed and his father heard the scream. The father ran to the scene, saw what had happened and suffered psychiatric shock. The defendant knew that the father was within earshot and was certain to come if his son screamed.

The Court of Appeal held that the father was entitled to damages for the shock he had suffered.

As you will have seen from the two sets of facts, the defendant in *Boardman v Sanderson* (1964) knew that the father was in the vicinity, which makes the case quite easy to distinguish from *King v Philips* (1953) where neither the taxi driver nor a 'hypothetical reasonable observer' would have foreseen any injury to the boy's mother. Where there is a significant difference between the facts of two cases, the previous case is distinguished in the present case.

A further example taken from the criminal law will also illustrate how cases can be distinguished. Consider how in the cases below, the third case (*R v Kendrick and Hopkins* [1997] 2 Cr App R 524) distinguished the second (*R v Mazo* [1997] 2 Cr App R 518), which had distinguished the first (*DPP v Gomez* (1993) 96 Cr App R 359):

CASE EXAMPLE

DPP v Gomez (1993) 96 Cr App R 359

Gomez worked as an assistant manager in a shop. A third party asked him if he would supply goods from the shop in exchange for two stolen cheques. Gomez went to the shop owner and asked him to authorise the supply of goods for the cheques but he did not inform the owner that the cheques were worthless. The owner agreed and the goods were supplied. Gomez was charged with theft.

For the defendant to be guilty of theft, the prosecution must prove that the defendant dishonestly appropriated property belonging to another, with the intention permanently to deprive the other of it. Gomez was convicted, but appealed against his conviction on the ground that while the contract of sale was voidable, the transfer to the third party was with the consent and express authority of the owner and, therefore, there was no 'appropriation'. The House of Lords rejected this argument, holding that an act which was authorised by the owner of goods may be an appropriation for the purposes of the Theft Act 1968, even though it was done with the owner's consent.

CASE EXAMPLE

R v Mazo [1997] 2 Cr App R 518

Mazo worked as a maid to Lady S. Over a two-year period, she cashed cheques totalling £37,000 made payable to her by Lady S. Mazo was charged with theft in relation to the cashing of the cheques. At her trial the prosecution case was that she had taken advantage of Lady S's mental incapacity. The jury convicted her.

Mazo appealed against her conviction on the ground that the transfers to her were valid gifts and that the trial judge had summed up incorrectly regarding Lady S's mental incapacity to make such gifts. Her appeal was allowed. The Court of Appeal held that while a transaction might be theft for the purposes of the Theft Act 1968 even if it was done with the owner's consent, the recipient of a valid gift could not be the subject of a conviction for theft. The court agreed that the jury had not been directed correctly about Lady S's mental incapacity.

CASE EXAMPLE

R v Kendrick and Hopkins [1997] 2 Cr App R 524

Kendrick and Hopkins ran a small residential home for the elderly where the victim, a lady aged 99 who was virtually blind, went to live in 1991. Kendrick and Hopkins took complete control of the victim's financial affairs, including writing cheques to themselves from her account, which they said were gifts from the victim. The appellants were charged with conspiracy to steal. The trial judge directed the jury in line with the law as represented by *DPP v Gomez* (1993) above. Kendrick and Hopkins were convicted.

They appealed on the ground that, under *R v Mazo* (1997), the judge should have directed the jury that the recipient of a valid gift could not be the subject of a conviction for theft. Therefore, they argued, the consent of the victim negated theft because the victim's mind had not been established to have been incapacitated. The Court of Appeal dismissed the appeals on the ground that it was not proper to read into the Theft Act 1968 the words 'without the consent of the owner'; and that there was nothing in the summing-up which would have resulted in the jury being confused as to whether the victim lacked the capacity to manage her affairs.

2.6.2 Reversing

Precedent may also be avoided by a superior court in the hierarchy reversing the decision of a court lower down in the hierarchy during the course of the same case. This will occur if, for example, the Court of Appeal has reached a particular decision in a particular case, but then the House of Lords reaches the opposite conclusion in the ensuing appeal in that case.

2.6.3 Overruling

The Court of Appeal and House of Lords also have the power to overrule the decision of a lower court, in a later, different, case. For example, the High Court may reach a decision in Case X, and that decision becomes a precedent for the future. Some time later, a similar case, Case Y, is heard by the High Court. Case X is used as a precedent, but the losing party appeals to the Court of Appeal. The Court of Appeal finds the original decision in Case X to have been erroneous (wrong), and overrules it.

The House of Lords overruled a very long-standing law in *R v R (Marital Exemption)* [1992] 1 AC 599.

CASE EXAMPLE

R v R (Marital Exemption) [1992] 1 AC 599

The defendant had married his wife in 1984, but they separated in 1989 and his wife returned to live with her parents. The parties had talked about divorcing. However, one evening, the defendant forced his way into his wife's parents' house and attempted to have sexual intercourse with her, in the course of which attempt he assaulted her. He was charged with attempted rape and assault. He was convicted.

He appealed on the ground that a husband could not be convicted of raping his wife (and therefore he could not be convicted of attempting to do so). The House of Lords recognised that, since the eighteenth century, there had been a rule of law that a wife was deemed to have consented irrevocably to sexual intercourse with her husband. Sir Matthew Hale's text, *History of the Pleas of the Crown*, published in 1736, had stated that:

> '. . . the husband cannot be guilty of a rape committed by himself upon his lawful wife, for by their mutual matrimonial consent and contract the wife hath given up herself in this kind unto her husband which she cannot retract.'

However, Lord Keith of Kinkel, who gave the leading speech of a unanimous House, went on to hold that:

'It may be taken that the proposition was generally regarded as an accurate statement of the common law of England [in 1736]. The common law is, however, capable of evolving in the light of changing social, economic and cultural developments. Hale's proposition reflected the state of affairs in these respects at the time it was enunciated. Since then the status of women, and particularly of married women, has changed out of all recognition in various ways which are very familiar and upon which it is unnecessary to go into detail. Apart from property matters and the availability of matrimonial remedies, one of the most important changes is that marriage is in modern times regarded as a partnership of equals, and no longer one in which the wife must be the subservient chattel [property] of the husband. Hale's proposition involves that by marriage a wife gives her irrevocable consent to sexual intercourse with her husband under all circumstances and irrespective of the state of her health or how she happens to be feeling at the time. In modern times any reasonable person must regard that conception as quite unacceptable.'

For the sake of accuracy, it is important to note that a judge distinguishes on the facts, but reverses or overrules a decision or judgment on the law. Also, note that distinguishing does not affect the validity of the precedent of the previous case. It is merely felt not to be relevant law on the given facts. An overruled case is regarded as never having been the law and it is not applied again in later cases. Although this last sentence might strike you as odd – men were not charged or were acquitted of raping their wives according to the law before *R v R* in 1992 – you will recognise the concept from the discussion of the declaratory theory from section 2.5 above.

ACTIVITY

Avoiding precedent – fill in the gaps.

1. In 1990, Betty Bloggs was convicted by the Crown Court of the murder of her husband, Alf. In her defence, Betty claimed that Alf had treated her brutally throughout their 20 years of marriage, and that this constituted provocation, even though there had been no violence between them immediately prior to the murder. The Crown Court judge had been persuaded by this argument, and regarded Betty's defence as correct in law. On appeal by the prosecution, however, the Court of Appeal (Criminal Division) held that this extension of the defence of provocation was incorrect. The decision of the Crown Court on this point of law was . . . . by the Court of Appeal.

2. In 1993, a similar case arose. Carrie Careful was charged with the murder of her husband, Denis. She pleaded a similar defence to that of Betty Bloggs. The Crown Court regarded itself as bound by the previous decision in the Court of Appeal. However, in Carrie's case, the court found that Denis had been violent towards her within an hour of the murder taking place. Because of this difference in the facts, the Crown Court was able to . . . . the case of Betty Bloggs, and did not follow it.

3. In 1994, Emily Earnest was charged with the murder of her husband, Fred, in circumstances identical to those in the Betty Bloggs case. Both the Crown Court and the Court of Appeal followed the precedent set in the Betty Bloggs case but, on appeal to the House of Lords, it was decided that this interpretation of the law was completely incorrect, and the Betty Bloggs case was . . . .

2.7 Pros and cons of precedent

Finally, it is important to notice some of the arguments in favour of the doctrine of precedent as it is operated in the English legal system, and also to be aware of some of the drawbacks; not all lawyers (and not even all judges) agree with a strict application of the principle of *stare decisis*.

It is true that the doctrine of precedent is efficient because it enables judges to avoid having to solve the same legal problem more than once, and thus may save a considerable amount of judicial

time and energy. A further advantage is that this system lends some degree of predictability to legal decision-making. This is of great importance to lawyers when attempting to advise their clients as to the likely outcome of litigation. When a particular factual situation or legal principle has featured in a previous court case, the lawyer is able to assess the case before him in the light of the previous decision, and guide the client according to whether the outcome is likely to be in the client's favour or not. Another argument in favour of a strict application of the doctrine is that use of previous precedents satisfies the requirements of justice, ie that people be treated alike in like circumstances. Thus, a case heard in the High Court in Manchester, to which a precedent of the Court of Appeal is applicable, will, by the application of that precedent, be dealt with in the same way as a similar case being heard by the High Court in Nottingham. This means that the doctrine can be regarded as being certain and consistent. There are ways, however, for precedents to be avoided, so there is an element of flexibility too.

Critics have nevertheless argued that this system is unconstitutional because it allows judges to change the law, rather than for law reform to be for Parliament alone within the separation of powers doctrine (see Chapter 1 at section 1.2). Alternatively, other critics have pointed out that *stare decisis* can lead to judicial laziness and as it may discourage members of the Judiciary from taking responsibility for thinking through solutions to legal problems. Certainly, because the doctrine is essentially backward-looking, it may stifle creativity in decision-making, and may lead to stagnation in the law. Related to this latter point is the criticism that, unless a case arises which allows a court the opportunity to amend a previous decision by not following the precedent, the law cannot develop and respond to changes in social circumstances. Legal change could therefore become dependent upon those who have the money to be able to afford to pursue litigation.

Further reading

Slapper, G and Kelly, D, *The English Legal System* (7th edn, Cavendish, 2004) Chapter 5.3.

Smith, Bailey and Gunn on the Modern English Legal System (4th edn, Sweet & Maxwell, 2002), Chapters 7 and 8.

Summary

Court	Is the court bound by a higher court?	Does the court bind any lower courts?	Is the court bound by its own previous decisions?
ECJ	n/a	Yes. The system of *stare decisis* means that all courts are bound	The ECJ does not regard itself as bound by its own previous decisions
Privy Council	Strictly no, but it is rare for it to depart from a House of Lords' decision	No, but it is strongly persuasive	Generally, no
House of Lords	Yes, on matters of EU law, it is bound by the decisions of the ECJ	Yes	Before 1966, it was bound. Since the Practice Statement 1966, it can depart from its own decisions when it appears right to do so
Court of Appeal (Civil Division)	Yes	Yes	It is normally bound unless the three rules from *Young v Bristol Aeroplane Co Ltd* (1944) are relevant. Note the effect of the Human Rights Act 1998 if European Convention rights are involved in the case (*Mendoza v Ghaidan* (2003))
Court of Appeal (Criminal Division)	Yes	Yes	Generally operates in the same way as the Civil Division, but the approach adopted in *R v Taylor* (1950) (approved and applied in *Gould*) are also relevant
Divisional Courts	Yes	Yes	Treated as the Court of Appeal because they have appellate jurisdiction
High Court	Yes	Yes	Previous decisions are strongly persuasive. It may overrule its own previous decisions, but this is rare
Crown Court	Yes	Yes	Persuasive only
County Court	Yes	n/a	No
Magistrates' Court	Yes	n/a	No

■ *Figure 2.4 The doctrine in practice*

chapter 3 STATUTORY INTERPRETATION ■

3.1 Introduction

In Chapter 1 we looked at the enactment of statutes by Parliament and also the making of secondary legislation such as statutory instruments. In each year approximately 60 Acts of Parliament are passed and, in addition, about 3,000 statutory instruments become law. With so much legislation being written down each year, it would appear that judges only have to apply the law. In fact it is said that the role of Parliament is to **make** the law and the role of the judges is to **apply** the law. However, the division between making and applying is not as straightforward as this. Many of the disputes that come before the courts concern the meaning of words in an Act or secondary legislation. In such cases judges may well often have to decide on which of two possible meanings should be used or even whether they should 'fill in the gaps' where an Act does not make it clear whether a certain situation should be covered.

3.1.1 The need for statutory interpretation

There are many reasons why the meaning of legislation may be unclear and the judges, therefore, have to interpret it. The main reasons are:

1. Failure of legislation to cover a specific point

The legislation may have been drafted in great detail, with the draftsman trying to cover every possible contingency. Despite this, situations can arise which were not specifically covered. The question then is whether the courts should interpret the legislation so as to include the situation which is omitted from it, or whether they should limit the legislation to the precise points listed by Parliament. This has led to the biggest dispute in how legislation should be interpreted. What may be termed 'active' judges take the view that they should 'fill in the gaps' while passive judges think that this should be left to Parliament as it is not the role of a judge to make law.

The passive line of reasoning can be seen in the following case:

CASE EXAMPLE

London & North Eastern Railway Co v Berriman [1946] 1 All ER 255

Mr Berriman was a railway worker who was hit and killed by a train while he was doing maintenance work, oiling points on a railway line. A regulation made under the Fatal Accidents Act stated that a look-out should be provided for men working on or near the railway line 'for the purposes of relaying or repairing' it. Mr Berriman was not relaying or repairing the line; he was maintaining it. His widow tried to claim compensation for his death because the railway company had not provided a look-out man while Mr Berriman had to work on the line, but the court ruled that the relevant regulation did not cover maintenance work and so Mrs Berriman's claim failed.

The court looked only at the specific words in the regulations. It was not prepared to look at any broad principle that the purpose of making a regulation that a look-out man should be provided was to protect those working on railway lines. Under this view it could be argued that it did not matter whether oiling points was maintenance rather than repair work. Men doing either were equally in need of protection. The different attitudes towards statutory interpretation are discussed further at section 3.4.

2. A broad term

In order to avoid the problems of having to list all possible contingencies, legislation may use words designed to cover several possibilities. But a word or words with a wide meaning can lead to problems as to what exactly they cover. In the Dangerous Dogs Act 1991 there is a phrase 'any dog of the type known as the pit bull terrier'. This seems a simple phrase but it has led to problems. What is meant by 'type'? Does it mean the same as 'breed'? In *Brock v DPP*, *The Times*, 23rd July 1993 this was the key point in dispute. The Queen's Bench Divisional Court decided that 'type' had a wider meaning than 'breed'. It could cover dogs who were not pedigree pit bull terriers, but had a substantial number of the characteristics of such a dog.

3. Ambiguity

Ambiguity occurs where a word or phrase has more than one meaning. It may not be clear which meaning should be used. Section 57 of the Offences Against the Person Act 1861 made it an offence to 'marry' while one's original spouse was still alive (and there had been no divorce). In *R v Allen* (1872) LR 1 CCR 367 it was accepted that the word 'marry' can mean to become legally married to the other person or in a more general way it can mean that the person takes part or 'goes through' a ceremony of marriage. This was important because, if only the first meaning was accepted, the offence of bigamy could never be committed since a person who is still married to another person cannot legally marry anyone else (see section 3.2.2 for further discussion).

4. A drafting error

It is possible that the Parliamentary Counsel who drafted the original Bill may have made an error which has not been noticed by Parliament; this is particularly likely to occur where the Bill is amended several times while going through Parliament.

5. New developments

New technology may mean that an old Act of Parliament does not apparently cover present-day situations. This was seen in the case of *Royal College of Nursing v DHSS* [1981] 1 All ER 545 where medical science and methods of producing an abortion had changed since the passing of the Abortion Act in 1967. This case is discussed more fully at section 3.2.3. It was also seen in *R (Quintavalle) v Secretary of State for Health* [2003] UKHL 13 where scientific advances made it possible to create human embryos by cell nuclear replacement. This had not been foreseen when the Human Fertilisation and Embryology Act 1990 was passed. In such cases the problem for the courts is whether to extend the Act to cover the new development. There is an exercise on this case in Appendix 1.

6. Changes in the use of language

The meaning of words can change over the years. Sometimes it is necessary to interpret an Act of Parliament enacted in the 1800s. Language used then can have different meanings to those of today. An example is the case of *Cheeseman v DPP*, *The Times*, 2nd November 1990 in which the meaning of the word 'passengers' was important to the case. The Act which had to be considered by the court dated from 1847 and so the court looked at the *Oxford English Dictionary* for that date to check on the meaning. The meaning given to the word then was 'a passer-by or through'. This is completely different to today's meaning of the word as someone who is carried in vehicle, train, plane or ship (see section 3.2.1 for further consideration of this case).

So it can be seen that legislation which appears to be simply expressed can lead to a disputed case in the courts in which the interpretation of words or a phrase is crucial to the outcome of the case. The method that judges use is also critical as the decision of an activist judge may well be different from that of a passive judge in the same case.

3.1.2 Applying the law

Even where the judge is applying the law in a passive manner, there are still many points which they will consider. These are known as aids to interpretation. An interesting example of this was seen in *DPP v Bull* [1994] 4 All ER 411 where the words in s 1(1) of the Street Offences Act 1959 had to be considered by the courts. This section states:

's 1(1) It shall be an offence for a common prostitute to loiter or solicit in a public street or public place for the purposes of prostitution.'

The word which caused difficulty in this section was 'prostitute'. This is a word which most people would say was easily understandable. You probably can give a definition for it. You can look it up in a dictionary. It might also be interesting to ask other people how they would define it. So why was there a problem of interpretation in *DPP v Bull* (1994)?

CASE EXAMPLE

DPP v Bull [1994] 4 All ER 411

Bull was a male prostitute charged with an offence against s 1(1) of the Street Offences Act 1959. The case was heard by a stipendiary magistrate at Wells Street Magistrates' Court. The magistrate dismissed the case on the ground that the words 'common prostitute' applied to female prostitutes only. The prosecution appealed by way of case stated and the Queen's Bench Divisional Court had to decide whether the words were meant to apply to women only or could also cover male prostitutes.

The prosecution counsel in the case put forward six reasons why the court should decided that 'prostitute' could apply to both males and females. This points were listed by Lord Justice Mann in his judgment.

J 'The submission for the appellant was that s 1(1) of the 1959 Act is unambiguous and is not gender specific. Our attention was drawn to the following six factors which were relied upon:

   (i) The phrase in s 1(1) "a common prostitute" was linguistically capable of including a male person. The *Oxford English Dictionary* (1989) includes within the possibilities for "prostitute", "a man who undertakes male homosexual acts for payment".

   (ii) Lord Taylor has recently said in *R v McFarlane* [1994] 2 All ER 283:

   > "both the dictionary definitions and the cases show that the crucial feature in defining prostitution is the making of an offer of sexual services for reward."

   (iii) Section 1(2) and (3) of the 1959 Act refer respectively to "a person" and "anyone".

   (iv) In contrast s 2(1) refers specifically to "a woman". . . .

   (v) Since 1967 male prostitution has been in certain circumstances not unlawful and accordingly in the new environment it is open to the court to interpret s 1(1) of the 1959 Act as being applicable to prostitutes who are male, "even if this was not the original intention of the provision". . . .

   (vi) Where Parliament intends to deal with gender specific prostitution it uses specifically the words "woman", "girl" or "her" . . .'.

CONTINUED ▶

However, the court rejected all these arguments and preferred the point put by the defendant's lawyer. This was also explained by Lord Justice Mann:

J   Mr Fulford's [counsel for Bull] main submission was that the court should avail itself of the report which led to the 1959 Act and of the parliamentary debate upon the Bill for the Act . . . Section 1(1) of the Act was as a result of a recommendation in the *Report of the Committee on Homosexual Offences and Prostitution* [the Wolfenden Report Cmnd 247, 1957]. The relevant chapter of the report leaves me in no doubt that the committee was only concerned with the female prostitute. . . . It is plain that the "mischief" that the Act was intended to remedy was a mischief created by women.'

So the decision of the court was that 'prostitute' in the Street Offences Act 1959 only applied to female prostitutes. But to reach that decision the court had considered a number of points.

This is an example of applying the law. In other cases the judges may actually create law. An example of this is considered next.

3.1.3 Judicial law-making

In *Mendoza v Ghaidan* [2002] EWCA Civ 1533 the Court of Appeal (Civil Division) had to consider the wording of the Rent Act 1977. The relevant part of the Act was paras 2 and 3 of Sch 1 to the Rent Act 1977 as amended which read:

S   's 2(1)   The surviving spouse (if any) of the original tenant, if residing in the dwelling-house immediately before the death of the original tenant, shall after the death be the statutory tenant if and so long as he or she occupies the dwelling-house as his or her residence.

(2)   For the purposes of this paragraph, a person who was living with the original tenant as his or her wife or husband shall be treated as the spouse of the original tenant.

3(1)   Where paragraph 2 above does not apply, but a person who was a member of the original tenant's family was residing with him in the dwelling-house at the time of and for the period of two years immediately before his death then, after his death, that person . . . shall be entitled to an assured tenancy of the dwelling-house by succession.'

The point involved in *Mendoza v Ghaidan* (2002) was whether there could be the transfer of a statutory tenancy to a same-sex partner. The wording of paras 2 and 3 appears to make it quite clear that a same-sex partner only qualifies by virtue of being a member of the family under para 3(1) and so is entitled to only an assured tenancy. This was the decision which had been reached by the House of Lords in the earlier case of *Fitzpatrick v Sterling Housing Association* [2001] 1 AC 27. The Court of Appeal reconsidered the law because of the effect of the Human Rights Act 1998 and decisions of the European Court of Human Rights. They had to decide whether this provision of the Rent Act 1977 infringed Art 14 (on discrimination) of the European Convention on Human Rights. The Court of Appeal held that the wording did appear to breach the Convention. Giving judgment, Buxton LJ said:

> **J** 'In order to remedy this breach of the Convention the court must, if it can, read the Schedule so that its provisions are rendered compatible with the Convention rights of the survivors of same-sex partnerships. The width of this duty, imposed by section 3 of the Human Rights Act 1998, has been emphasised by Lord Steyn in *R v A* [2001] 2 WLR 1546.
>
> That duty can be properly discharged by reading the words "as his or her wife or husband" to mean "as <u>if they were</u> his or her wife or husband". That wording achieves what is required in the present case, and does not open the door to lesser relationships (such as, for instance, sisters sharing a house, or long-term lodgers) because those relationships do not enjoy the marriage-like characteristics that for instance Lord Nicholls discerned in *Fitzpatrick*'.

So in *Mendoza v Ghaidan* (2002) the judges were prepared to read words into the Rent Act 1977 to achieve the result they desired. In the case of *Fitzpatrick v Sterling Housing Association* (2001) the House of Lords had not been prepared to do this. The Lords thought that the 1977 Act was clear and that only a husband or a wife was entitled to be a statutory tenant. In fact, it is almost certainly true that Parliament, when passing the Act, did intend that only a husband or wife was entitled to a statutory tenancy. The case also raises an interesting comparison to *DPP v Bull* (1994). In *Mendoza v Ghaidan* (2002) it could be argued that the words 'husband' and 'wife' are gender-specific, unlike the word 'prostitute' considered in *DPP v Bull* (1994) which is gender-neutral. However, the Court of Appeal was prepared to ignore this, as Buxton LJ went on to say:

> **J** 'It is quite true, as Mr Small pointed out, that the words "husband" and "wife" are in their natural meaning gender-specific. They are also, however, in their natural meaning limited to persons who are party to a lawful marriage. Parliament, by paragraph 2(2), removed that last requirement. And Parliament having swallowed the camel of including unmarried partners within the protection given to married couples, it is not for this court to strain at the gnat of including such partners who are of the same sex as each other.'

In fact, the Court of Appeal could have held that the words were limited to their natural gender-specific meanings. It could then have declared that the Rent Act 1977 was incompatible with human rights and so left it to Parliament to amend the Act. This route would have been the passive one. Instead, the Court of Appeal chose to be more active and create law.

3.1.4 Interpretation or construction?

Many old textbooks write about the construction of statutes. Is this the same as interpretation? Well, no, 'interpretation' really means making out the meaning of the words, while 'construction' is what happens when judges resolve any ambiguities or uncertainties. This means that every time there is a dispute as to what an Act means the court has to interpret it, ie decide what the meaning is. However, it is only if that meaning is not clear from the actual words, because, for example, there are uncertainties or ambiguities, that the court will have to construct the statute. 'Construct' in this sense means build up the meaning. This was made very clear in a judgment in *Franklin v Attorney General* [1973] 1 All ER 879 when Lawson J said:

> J
>
> 'I approach the answer to the question in two stages. Stage one is this: whether the meaning of the Cyprus Act 1960 in this respect is clear and unambiguous, and if so, what does it mean? At this stage I look at the words of the enactment as a whole, including the Schedule, and I use no further aids, no further extrinsic aids in order to reach a conclusion as to the clear and unambiguous meaning of the words . . . If I find that the answer on the first stage in my inquiry is that the meaning of the Act in this respect is ambiguous, then I have to go on to the second stage and consider two possible different meanings . . . Now if I get to this second stage, then in my judgment, and then only, am I entitled to look at extrinsic aids, such as the long title, the headings, the side-notes, other legislation; then only am I entitled to resort to maxims of construction.'

Although 'interpretation' and 'construction' have different meanings, today it is more usual to refer only to 'interpretation' in a wider sense covering both meanings.

3.1.5 Parliamentary definitions

In order to help with the understanding of a statute, Parliament sometimes includes sections defining certain words used in that statute. Such sections are called interpretation sections. In the Theft Act 1968, for example, the definition of 'theft' is given in s 1, and then sections 2–6 define the key words in that definition.

In some Acts where Parliament wants to make sure that a particular word covers a wider than usual range, this can be made clear in the Act. For example, in the Theft Act 1968 an important element in the offence of burglary is that the defendant has to enter a building or part of a building as a trespasser. The Act does not define 'building' but instead gives an extended meaning to it, to include inhabited places such as houseboats or caravans, which would otherwise not be included in the offence. This is set out in s 9(4) of the Theft Act 1968:

's 9(4) References . . . to a building shall apply also to an inhabited vehicle or vessel, and shall apply to any such vehicle or vessel at times when the person having a habitation is not there as well as at times when he is.'

To help the judges with general words, Parliament has also passed the Interpretation Act 1978 which sets down some general rules for interpretation. Among these are the rules that in any Act, unless the contrary appears, 'he' includes 'she', and singular includes plural. This rule does not apply to Acts setting out sexual offences, so the provisions of the Interpretation Act 1978 could not be used in *DPP v Bull* (1994).

3.2 The three 'rules'

As we have seen, despite various parliamentary aids, there may still be problems in deciding exactly what a particular Act refers to or what precisely it covers. Judges have coped with this problem over the centuries by developing the three so-called 'rules' of interpretation. These are:

- the literal rule
- the golden rule
- the mischief rule.

These rules take different approaches to interpretation and some judges prefer to use one rule, while other judges prefer another rule. This means that in English law the interpretation of a statute may differ according to which judge is hearing the case. However, once an interpretation has been laid down, it may then form a precedent for future cases under the normal rules of judicial precedent. Since the three rules can result in very different decisions, it is important to understand them. However, they do not have to be used and, in more recent times, judges have tended to use two main approaches instead of the supposed 'rules'. These are:

- the literal approach
- the purposive approach.

3.2.1 The literal rule

Under this rule courts will give words their plain, ordinary or literal meaning, even if the result is not very sensible. This idea was expressed by Lord Esher in *R v Judge of the City of London Court* [1892] 1 QB 273 when he said:

> **J** 'If the words of an Act are clear then you must follow them even though they lead to a manifest absurdity. The court has nothing to do with the question whether the legislature has committed an absurdity.'

This does not seem to be a very constructive attitude towards applying words in legislation. Parliament would certainly not have intended the effect of any Act to be absurd. However, it does mean that judges are not imposing their ideas of what they think the law should be; they are leaving it to Parliament to make the law. The reason for using the literal rule was explained rather better by Lord Bramwell in *Hill v East and West India Dock Co* (1884) 9 App Cas 448 when he said:

> **J** 'I should like to have a good definition of what is such an absurdity that you are to disregard the plain words of an Act of Parliament. It is to be remembered that what seems absurd to one man does not seem absurd to another . . . . I think it is infinitely better, although an absurdity or an injustice or other objectionable result may be evolved as the consequences of your construction, to adhere to the words of an Act of Parliament and leave the legislature to set it right than to alter those words according to one's notion of an absurdity.'

The literal rule developed in the early nineteenth century and has been the main rule applied by the courts ever since then. It has been used in many cases, even though the result may in some cases create an absurdity. This is illustrated in the following case:

CASE EXAMPLE

Whiteley v Chappell (1868) 4 LR QB 147:

The defendant was charged under a section which made it an offence to impersonate 'any person entitled to vote'. The defendant had pretended to be a person whose name was on the voters' list, but who had died. The court held that the defendant was not guilty since a dead person is not, in the literal meaning of the words, 'entitled to vote'.

Another case in which the use of literal rule made the law as Parliament had intended it virtually unenforceable was *Fisher v Bell* [1960] 3 All ER 731. That case involved the interpretation of s 1(1) of the Restriction of Offensive Weapons Act 1959. This section stated:

's 1(1) Any person who manufactures, sells or hires or offers for sale or hire or lends or gives to any other person –

(a)   any knife which has a blade which opens automatically by hand pressure applied to a button, spring or other device in or attached to the handle of the knife, sometimes known as a 'flick knife' . . . shall be guilty of an offence . . .'

In *Fisher v Bell* (1960) the defendant was a shop-keeper who had displayed a flick knife marked with a price in his shop window but had not actually sold any. He was charged under s 1(1) of the 1959 Act and the court had to decide whether he was guilty of offering the knife for sale. There is a technical legal meaning in contract law of 'offer'. This has the effect that displaying an article in a shop window is not an offer; it is only an invitation to treat. The Court of Appeal held that under the literal legal meaning of 'offer', the shop-keeper had not made an offer to sell and so was not guilty of the offence. Parliament immediately changed the law to make it clear that displaying a flick knife in a shop window was an offence.

Yet another case which may be considered to have led to an absurd result is *Cheeseman v DPP, The Times*, 2nd November 1990:

CASE EXAMPLE

Cheeseman v DPP, The Times, 2nd November 1990

The defendant was charged with wilfully and indecently exposing his person in a street to the annoyance of passengers contrary to s 28 of the Town Causes Act 1847. Members of the public had complained of the behaviour of a man in a public lavatory. Police officers were stationed in the lavatory following these complaints in order to catch the offender. They witnessed the defendant masturbating and they arrested him. The defendant's conviction was quashed by the Queen's Bench Divisional Court because the police officers were not 'passengers' within the meaning of s 28.

The whole case rested on the meaning of the word 'passengers' and, as already explained at section 3.1, the meaning in 1847 was 'a passer by or through; a traveller (usually on foot); a wayfarer'. Although the behaviour had occurred in a public lavatory rather than the street, that did not prevent the defendant from being guilty as s 81 of the Public Health Amendment Act 1902 had extended the meaning of the word 'street' in s 28 of the Town Causes Act 1847 to include any place of public resort under the control of the local authority.

The judges in the Divisional Court pointed out that before the meaning of 'street' was enlarged in 1907 the old dictionary definition of 'passenger' was not hard to apply: It

CONTINUED ▶

clearly covered anyone using the street for ordinary purposes of passage or travel. the problem was that the dictionary definition could not be so aptly applied to a place of public resort such as a public lavatory. However, the judges thought that on a common-sense reading and when applied in context, 'passenger' had to mean anyone resorting in the ordinary way to a place for one of the purposes for which people would normally resort to it. Applying this to the case, they held that the two police officers were not 'passengers' because they had been stationed in the public lavatory in order to catch the person committing acts which had given rise to earlier complaints. They were not resorting to that place of public resort in the ordinary way but were there for a special purpose.

The literal rule is also criticised because it can lead to what are considered harsh decisions, as in *London & North Eastern Railway Co v Berriman* (1946) (see section 3.1) where a railway worker was killed while doing maintenance work on a railway line. His widow tried to claim compensation because no look-out man had been provided. The court took the words 'relaying' and 'repairing' in their literal meaning and said that oiling points was maintaining the line and not relaying or repairing, so that Mrs Berriman's claim failed.

With decisions such as those above it is not surprising that Professor Michael Zander has denounced the literal rule as being mechanical and divorced from the realities of the use of language. The Law Commission, which produced a report *The Interpretation of Statutes* in 1969, also thought that the literal rule creates problems. It wrote:

> 'To place undue emphasis on the literal meaning of words of a provision is to assume an unattainable perfection in draftsmanship; it presupposes that the draftsmen can always choose words to describe the situations intended to be covered by the provision which will leave no room for a difference of opinion as to their meaning. Such an approach ignores the limitations of language, which is not infrequently demonstrated even at the level of the House of Lords when Law Lords differ as to the so-called "plain meaning" of words.'

In fact, many words have more than one meaning, as can be seen by looking up words in a dictionary. Since the literal rule cannot always provide clarity, other methods of interpretation have been created by the judges.

3.2.2 The golden rule

This rule is a modification of the literal rule. The golden rule starts by looking at the literal meaning but the court is then allowed to avoid an interpretation which would lead to an absurd result. The first use of the name 'golden rule' is thought to have been in *Mattison v Hart* (1854) 14 CB 357 when Jervis CJ said:

> J 'We must, therefore, in this case have recourse to what is called the golden rule of
> construction, as applied to Acts of Parliament, viz, to give the words used by the
> legislature their plain meaning unless it is manifest from the general scope and
> intention of the statute, injustice and absurdity would result.'

Although this says that the plain meaning of the words should be applied (ie the literal rule), it
does seem to allow quite wide deviation from the literal rule. This is because it can be done where
there is 'injustice or absurdity'. The rule was more closely defined in *Grey v Pearson* (1857) 6 HL
Cas 61 by Baron Parke when he stated:

> J 'The grammatical and ordinary sense of the words is to be adhered to, unless that
> would lead to some absurdity, to some repugnance or inconsistency with the rest of
> the instrument, in which case the grammatical and ordinary sense of the words may
> be modified, so as to avoid the absurdity and inconsistency, but no further.'

Again it is stressed that the literal rule is the starting point but instead of the wide term 'injustice'
the use of the golden rule is restricted to where there is absurdity, repugnance or inconsistency with
the rest of the Act. In the twentieth century judges had two views on how far the golden rule
should be used. The first is very narrow and is shown by Lord Reid's comments in *Jones v DPP*
(1962) when he said:

> J 'It is a cardinal principle applicable to all kinds of statutes that you may not for any
> reason attach to a statutory provision a meaning which the words of that provision
> cannot reasonably bear. If they are capable of more than one meaning, then you can
> choose between those meanings, but beyond this you cannot go.'

So under the narrow application of the golden rule the court may only choose between the possible
meanings of a word or phrase. If there is only one meaning, then that must be taken. This narrow
view can be seen in practice in *R v Allen* (1872) LR 1 CCR 367 where s 57 of the Offences Against
the Person Act 1861 made it an offence to 'marry' while one's original spouse was still alive (and
there had been no divorce). The word 'marry' can mean to become legally married to the other
person or in a more general way it can mean that the person takes part or 'goes through' a
ceremony of marriage. The court decided that in the Offences Against the Person Act 1861 the
word had this second meaning of going through a ceremony of marriage. This was because a

person who is still married to another person cannot legally marry anyone else so if the first meaning of being legally married was applied then there would be the absurd situation that no one could ever be guilty of bigamy.

The second and wider application of the golden rule is where the words have only one clear meaning, but that meaning would lead to a repugnant situation. In *Grey v Pearson* (1857) repugnancy was specifically mentioned. This allows the courts more freedom to modify the words of the legislation in order to avoid the problem. A very clear example of this was the case of *Re Sigsworth* [1935] Ch 89:

CASE EXAMPLE

Re Sigsworth [1935] Ch 89

A son had murdered his mother. The mother had not made a will, so normally her estate would have been inherited by her next-of-kin according to the rules set out in the Administration of Justice Act 1925. This meant that the murderer son would have inherited as her 'issue'. There was no ambiguity in the words of the Act, but the court was not prepared to let a murderer benefit from his crime, so it was held that the literal rule should not apply, the golden rule would be used to prevent the repugnant situation of the son inheriting. Effectively, the court was writing into the Act that the 'issue' would not be entitled to inherit where they had killed the deceased.

This use of the golden rule is more in line with the modern purposive approach and decisions such as *R v Registrar General, ex p Smith* [1991] 2 All ER 88 (see section 3.3). The golden rule also allows the courts to modify words of a statute when it is necessary to avoid an absurdity or repugnant situation. This happened in *Adler v George* [1964] 2 QB 7 in which there was a prosecution under the Official Secrets Act 1920 for an offence of obstructing HM Forces 'in the vicinity of' a prohibited place. The defendants in the case had obstructed HM Forces but **in** a prohibited place. The Divisional Court read the Act as being '**in or** in the vicinity of' to avoid the absurdity of being able to convict someone who was near (in the vicinity of) of a prohibited place but not being able to convict someone who carried out the obstruction in the place.

3.2.3 The mischief rule

This rule gives a judge more discretion than the other two rules. The definition of the rule comes from *Heydon's Case* (1584) Co Rep 7a, where it was said that there were four points the court should consider. These, in the original language of that old case, were:

82

J

'1st What was the Common Law before the making of the Act.

2nd What was the mischief and defect for which the Common Law did not provide.

3rd What remedy the Parliament hath resolved and appointed to cure the disease of the commonwealth.

And, 4th The true reason of the remedy; and then the office of all Judges is always to make such construction as shall suppress the mischief, and advance the remedy.'

So under this rule the court should look to see what the law was before the Act was passed in order to discover what gap or 'mischief' the Act was intended to cover. Then the court should interpret the Act in such a way that the gap is covered. This is clearly a quite different approach to the literal rule.

An example of a case in which the mischief rule was used is *Smith v Hughes* [1960] 2 All ER 859. In this case the court had to interpret s 1(1) of the Street Offences Act 1959 which said 'it shall be an offence for a common prostitute to loiter or solicit in a street or public place for the purpose of prostitution'.

CASE EXAMPLE

Smith v Hughes [1960] 2 All ER 859

Six women had been convicted under s 1(1) of the 1959 Act and in each case they argued on appeal that they were not 'in a street or public place' as required by the Act for them to be guilty. One woman had been on a balcony and the others had been at the windows of ground-floor rooms, with the window either half-open or closed. In each case the women were attracting the attention of men by calling to them or tapping on the window. The court decided that they were guilty.

In this case the court did not use the plain, ordinary grammatical meaning of the words 'in a street or public place'. Instead the judges looked to see what mischief the act was aimed at. This was explained by Parker LCJ when he said:

J

'For my part I approach the matter by considering what is the mischief aimed at by this Act. Everybody knows that this was an Act to clean up the streets, to enable people to walk along the streets without being molested or solicited by common prostitutes. Viewed in this way it can matter little whether the prostitute is soliciting while in the street or is standing in the doorway or on a balcony, or at a window, or whether the window is shut or open or half open; . . . '

A similar point arose in *Eastbourne Borough Council v Stirling*, *The Times*, 16th November 2000, where a taxi driver was charged with 'plying for hire in any street' without a licence to do so. His vehicle was parked on a taxi rank on a station forecourt. He was found guilty as, although he was on private land, he was likely to get customers from the street. The court referred to *Smith v Hughes* (1960) and said that it was the same point. A driver would be plying for hire in the street when his vehicle was positioned so that the offer of services was aimed at people in the street.

An interesting point shown by *Smith v Hughes* (1960) is that the same judge may choose to use the literal rule in one case and the mischief rule in another. Parker LCJ, who gave the judgment in *Smith v Hughes* (1960), also gave the judgment in *Fisher v Bell* (1960) where he choose to use the literal rule. This has prompted the comment that judges choose whichever rule gives the result that they wish to achieve in the case.

Another case in which the mischief rule was used is *Royal College of Nursing v DHSS* [1981] 1 All ER 545. However, in this case there was disagreement among the judges in the House of Lords as to the method of interpretation to be used.

ASE EXAMPLE

Royal College of Nursing v DHSS [1981] 1 All ER 545

This case concerned the wording of the Abortion Act 1967, which provided that no criminal offence was committed 'when a pregnancy is terminated by a registered medical practitioner'. When the Act was passed in 1967 the procedure for carrying out an abortion was such that only a doctor (a registered medical practitioner) could do it. However, by 1980, improvements in medical technique meant that pregnancy could be terminated by inducing premature labour with drugs. The first part of the procedure for this was carried out by a doctor, but the second part could be performed by nurses without a doctor present. The Department of Health and Social Security issued a circular giving advice that it was legal for nurses to carry out the second part of the procedure, provided that the termination had been decided upon by a registered medical practitioner, initiated by him and he remained responsible throughout the process for its overall conduct, though he did not have to be present throughout. The Royal College of Nursing sought a declaration that the circular was wrong in law.

At first instance the judge refused the declaration and held that the advice in the circular did not involve the performance of any unlawful act by nurses. The Court of Appeal reversed this decision but on appeal to the House of Lords the majority (3) of the judges reinstated the decision of the judge at first instance. They held that the procedure was lawful under the Abortion Act 1967. However, the other two judges in the House of Lords dissented, holding that the procedure was not lawful. Of the three judges in the majority Lord Diplock clearly based his judgment on the mischief rule. He said:

CONTINUED ▶

J 'The Abortion Act 1967 which it falls to this House to construe is described in its long title as "An Act to amend and clarify the law relating to termination of pregnancy by registered medical practitioners . . .". Whatever may be the technical imperfections of its draftsmanship, however, its purpose in my view becomes clear if one starts by considering what was the state of the law relating to abortion before the passing of the Act, what was the mischief that required amendment, and in what respect was the existing law unclear . . . My Lords, the wording and structure of the section are far from elegant, but the policy of the Act, it seems to me, is clear. There are two aspects to it: the first is to broaden the grounds upon which abortions may be lawfully carried obtained; the second is to ensure that the abortion is carried out with proper skill and in hygienic conditions.'

So Lord Diplock relied on the fact that the mischief Parliament was trying to remedy was the unsatisfactory state of the law before 1967, as a result of which there were a large number of illegal abortions (often called 'back-street abortions') which were carried out in unhygienic conditions. In some cases this led to the death of the woman whose pregnancy was terminated. He also relied on the policy of the 1967 Act (and therefore the policy of Parliament) which was to broaden the grounds for abortion and ensure that they were carried out with proper skill in hospital. Lord Keith of Kinkel also relied on the policy of the Act. He pointed out:

J '"Termination of pregnancy" is an expression commonly used . . . to describe in neutral and unemotive terms the bringing about of an abortion. So used, it is capable of covering the whole process designed to lead to that result, and in my view it does so in the present context . . . This conclusion is the more satisfactory as it appears to me to be fully in accordance with that part of the policy and purpose of the Act which was directed to securing that socially acceptable abortions should be carried out under the safest conditions attainable.'

An interesting point about Lord Keith's judgment is that he was prepared to put a broad literal meaning on the words 'termination of pregnancy', so that he felt that both the literal meaning and the policy view gave the same result in the case. The other judge who held that the drug-induced method of terminating a pregnancy which was carried out by nurses was lawful was Lord Roskill. He came to this conclusion based on the factual situation that the steps taken by a nurse in giving the drugs were lawful 'provided that the entirety of the treatment for the termination of the pregnancy and her participation in it is at all times under the control of the doctor even though the doctor is not present throughout the entirety of the treatment'.

CONTINUED ▸

The two dissenting judges took the literal view and said that the words of the Act were clear and that terminations could only be carried out by a registered medical practitioner. Lord Edmund-Davies stated that to read the words 'terminated by a registered medical practitioner' as meaning 'terminated by treatment for the termination of pregnancy in accordance with recognised medical practice' was redrafting the Act 'with a vengeance'.

This case is an example of how, even judges in the House of Lords cannot agree on the method of interpretation to be used. At the Court of Appeal it also is another example that judges are inconsistent in their approach to which rule they use. This was shown by the fact that Lord Denning, usually noted for using a more purposive approach and 'filling in the gaps' (see section 3.5), decided that the procedure was unlawful. He based this decision on the literal meaning of the Act, saying:

> **J** 'If the Department of Health want the nurses to terminate a pregnancy, the Minister should go to Parliament and get the statute altered. He should ask them to amend it by adding the words "or by a suitably qualified person in accordance with the written instructions of a registered medical practitioner". I doubt whether Parliament would accept the amendment. It is too controversial. At any rate that is the way to amend the law.'

One of the questions with the mischief rule is what can the court look at to discover the mischief which Parliament was trying to put right. As seen in Lord Diplock's judgment in the *Royal College of Nursing v DHSS* (1981) case, the courts can look at the rest of the Act. Lord Diplock specifically referred to the long title of the Act. It is also allowable to consider outside factors such as the social or other conditions which led to the passing of the Act. The extent to which other outside (extrinsic) aids can be used is considered at section 3.7.

The case of *Royal College of Nursing v DHSS* (1981) also raises the question of whether the mischief rule and the more modern purposive approach are the same. Certainly Lord Diplock appeared to combine the two, but it can also be said that the purposive approach goes beyond looking at the mischief which the Act was passed to cover (see section 3.3 for further discussion of the purposive approach).

ACTIVITY

Read the facts of the following case.

R v Maginnis [1987] 1 All ER 907

The case involved the wording of s 5 of the Misuse of Drugs Act 1971 which states:

 's 5 . . . it is an offence for a person to have a controlled drug in his possession, whether lawful or not, with intent to supply it to another . . .'

The police had found a package of cannabis in Maginnis's car. He told the police that the package was not his but had been left in his car by a friend to be collected by the friend later. The defendant was convicted of the offence and appealed on the ground that his intention to return the drug to its owner could not amount to an intention to 'supply' the drug within the meaning of s 5 of the Act.

Consider the word 'supply' and explain how the case could have been decided using:

1. the literal rule
2. the golden rule
3. the mischief rule.

3.3 The purposive approach

This goes beyond the mischief rule in that the court is not just looking to see what the gap was in the old law; the judges are deciding what they believe Parliament meant to achieve. The champion of this approach in English law was Lord Denning. His attitude towards statutory interpretation is shown when he said in the case of *Magor and St Mellons v Newport Corporation* [1950] 2 All ER 1226:

> J 'We sit here to find out the intention of Parliament and carry it out, and we do this better by filling in the gaps and making sense of the enactment than by opening it up to destructive analysis.'

However his attitude was criticised by judges in the House of Lords when they heard the appeal in the case. Lord Simonds called Lord Denning's approach 'a naked usurpation of the legislative function under the thin disguise of interpretation' and pointed out that 'if a gap is disclosed the remedy lies in an amending Act'. Another judge, Lord Scarman, said:

> **J** 'If Parliament says one thing but means another, it is not, under the historic principles of the common law, for the courts to correct it. The general principle must surely be acceptable in our society. We are to be governed not by Parliament's intentions but by Parliament's enactments.'

This speech shows the problem with the purposive approach. Should the judges refuse to follow the clear words of Parliament? How do they know what Parliament's intentions were? Opponents of the purposive approach say that it is impossible to discover Parliament's intentions; only the words of the statute can show what Parliament wanted. Despite opposition to the approach it is being used more and more often by the courts. An example is *R v Registrar General, ex p Smith* [1991] 2 All ER 88 in which the court had to consider s 51 of the Adoption Act 1976 which states:

 's 51(1) Subject to subsections (4) and (6), the Registrar-General shall on an application made in the prescribed manner by an adopted person a record of whose birth is kept by the Registrar-General and who has attained the age of 18 years supply to that person . . . such information as is necessary to enable that person to obtain a certified copy of the record of his birth.'

Sub-section (4) says that before supplying that information the Registrar General has to inform the applicant about counselling services available. Sub-section (6) states that if the adoption was before 1975 the Registrar General cannot give the information unless the applicant has attended an interview with a counsellor.

CASE EXAMPLE

R v Registrar General, ex p Smith [1991] 2 All ER 88

The case involved an application by Charles Smith for information to enable him to obtain his birth certificate. Mr Smith had made his application in the correct manner and was prepared to see a counsellor. On a literal view of the 1976 Acts the Registrar General had to supply him with the information, since the Act uses the phrase 'shall . . . supply'. The problem was that Mr Smith had been convicted of two murders and was detained in Broadmoor as he suffered from recurring bouts of psychotic illness. A psychiatrist thought that it was possible he might be hostile towards his natural mother. This posed a difficulty for the court; should they apply the clear meaning of the words in this situation?

The judges in the Court of Appeal decided that the case called for the purposive approach, saying that, despite the plain language of the Act, Parliament could not have intended to promote serious crime. So, in view of the risk to the applicant's natural mother if he discovered her identity, they ruled that the Registrar General did not have to supply any information.

Another example of the use of the purposive approach is *Jones v Tower Boot Co Ltd* [1997] IRLR 168 in which the Court of Appeal had to interpret s 32(1) of the Race Relations Act 1976. This section states that:

's 32(1) Anything done by a person in the course of employment shall be treated for the purposes of this Act . . . as done by his employer as well as by him, whether or not it was done with the employer's knowledge or approval.'

CASE EXAMPLE

Raymondo Jones worked for Tower Boot as a machine operative for one month. During this time he was subjected to a number of unpleasant incidents of racial harassment by fellow workers. These included his arm being burnt by a hot screwdriver, being whipped with a piece of welt, having metal bolts thrown at his head. He was also repeatedly called names such as 'chimp', 'monkey' and 'baboon'. It was clear that this was racial harassment by the fellow workers, but the point to be decided was whether the employers were liable for the acts of these employees.

The words 'course of employment' were the critical ones. In the law of tort this phrase has a well-established legal meaning, with the nub of the test being 'whether the unauthorised wrongful act is so connected with that which he was employed to do as to be a mode of doing it'. The employers argued that this literal meaning of 'course of employment' should be used. This would mean that they were not liable for the racial harassment, as burning and whipping another person could not be considered as an improper mode of performing authorised tasks. The Court of Appeal held that the employers were liable for the racial harassment. Lord Justice Waite considered the principles of statutory interpretation and said:

J 'Two principles are in my view involved. The first is that a statute is to be construed according to its legislative purpose, with due regard to the result which it is the stated or presumed intention of Parliament to achieve and the means provided for achieving it (the "purposive construction"); and the second is that words in a statute are to be given their normal meaning according to the English language unless the context indicates that such words have to be given a special or technical meaning as a term of art (the "linguistic construction").'

He pointed out that the Race Relations Act 1976 and the Sex Discrimination Act 1975 broke new ground in seeking to work upon the minds of men and women and affect their attitude to the social consequences of differences between the sexes or distinction of skin

CONTINUED ▸

colour. He felt that the general thrust of the Race Relations Act 1976 was to educate, persuade and, where necessary, coerce people into eliminating discrimination. He went on to say:

> J
>
> 'Since the getting and losing of work, and the daily functioning of the workplace, are prime areas for potential discrimination on grounds of race or sex, it is not surprising that both Acts contain specific provisions to govern the field of employment. Those provisions are themselves wide-ranging . . . There is no indication that Parliament intended in any way to limit the general thrust of the legislation.
>
> A purposive construction accordingly requires s 32 of the Race Relations Act 1976 to be given a broad interpretation. It would be inconsistent with that requirement to allow the notion of the "course of employment" to be construed in any sense more limited than the natural meaning of those everyday words would allow . . .'

The use of the purposive approach was particuarly important as, if the literal interpretation were taken, it would allow racial harassment on the scale that was suffered by the complainant to 'slip through the net of employer responsibility'. Lord Justice Waite thought that it would be wrong to apply a common law principle which had evolved in another area of the law to deal to deal with vicarious responsibility for a wrong doing of a wholly different kind. If the literal interpretation were taken it would seriously undermine the Discrimination Acts and 'flout the purpose which they were passed to achieve'.

More recently, in *R (Quintavalle) v Secretary of State* [2003] UKHL 13 the House of Lords used the purposive approach in deciding that organisms created by cell nuclear replacement (CNR) came within the definition of 'embryo' in the Human Fertilisation and Embryology Act 1990. Section 1(1)(a) of this Act states that 'embryo means a live human embryo where fertilisation is complete'. CNR was not possible in 1990 when the Act was passed and the problem is that fertilisation is not used in CNR. Lord Bingham said:

> J
>
> '[T]he court's task, within permissible bounds of interpretation is to give effect to Parliament's purpose . . . Parliament could not have intended to distinguish between embryos produced by, or without, fertilisation since it was unaware of the latter possibility.'

The House of Lords followed Lord Wilberforce's judgment in *Royal College of Nursing of the United Kingdom v Department of Health and Social Security* (1981) when he said:

> **J** 'In interpreting an Act of Parliament it is proper, and indeed necessary, to have regard to the state of affairs existing, and known by Parliament to be existing, at the time. It is a fair presumption that Parliament's policy or intention is directed to that state of affairs. . . . [W]hen a new state of affairs, or a fresh set of facts bearing on the policy, comes into existence, the courts have to consider whether they fall within the Parliamentary intention. They may be held to do so, if they fall within the same genus of facts as do those to which the express policy has been formulated. They may also be held to do so if there can be detected a clear purpose in the legislation which can only be fulfilled if the extension is made.'

3.3.1 European influence

The purposive approach is the one preferred by most European countries when interpreting their own legislation. It is also the approach which has been adopted by the European Court of Justice in interpreting European Union law. In fact, the Treaty of Rome sets out general principles but without explicit details. Lord Denning said of the Treaty in *Bulmer (HP) Ltd v J Bollinger* SA [1974] 2 All ER 1226:

> **J** 'It lays down general principles. It expresses its aims and purposes. All in sentences of moderate length and commendable style. But it lacks precision. It uses words and phrases without defining what they mean. An English lawyer would look for an interpretation clause, but he would look in vain. There is none. All the way through the Treaty there are gaps and lacunae. These have to be filled in by the judges . . .'

Since the United Kingdom became a member of the European Union in 1973 the influence of the European preference for the purposive approach has affected the English courts in two ways. First, they have had to accept that, at least for law which has been passed as a result of having to conform to a European law, the purposive approach is the correct one use. This was laid down by the European Court of Justice in *von Colson v Land Nordrhein-Westfalen* (Case 14/83) [1984] ECR 1891; [1986] 2 CMLR 430 when it held that:

> **J** '[I]n applying the national law and in particular the provisions of a national law specifically introduced in order to implement [the Directive], national courts are required to interpret their national law in the light of the wording and the purpose of the Directive.'

This use of the purposive approach to interpret national legislation in the light of an EU directive can be seen in *Pickstone v Freemans plc* [1988] 2 All ER 803. This case involved the interpretation of the Equal Pay Act 1970 which had been amended by adding a new subsection (s 1(2)(c)), in order to implement the Equal Pay Directive (75/117/EEC). This subsection allowed a claim for equal pay based on the fact that the applicant was doing 'work of equal value' to someone of the opposite sex, even though they were not doing the same job. However, the subsection also stated that if there was a someone of the opposite sex doing 'like work' to the applicant, then no claim could be brought under s (1)(2)(c).

CASE EXAMPLE

Pickstone v Freemans plc [1988] 2 All ER 803

Women warehouse operatives were paid the same as male warehouse operatives. However, Ms Pickstone claimed that their work was of equal value to that done by a male warehouse checker, who was paid £4.22 more a week than they were. Their employers argued that as the women were employed on 'like work' to male warehouse operatives then they could not bring a claim under s (1)(2)(c) of the 1970 Act for work of equal value. This was the literal interpretation of the 1970 Act. The House of Lords decided that the literal approach would have left the United Kingdom in breach of its treaty obligations to give effect to EU Directives. So it used the purposive approach and held that Ms Pickstone was entitled to claim on the basis of work of equal value even though there was a male employee doing the same work as her.

The second effect of using the purposive approach for European Union law is that, as judges are having to use the purposive approach for EU law, they are becoming more accustomed to it and, therefore, more likely to apply it to English law.

3.4 Literal approach versus purposive approach

This conflict between the literal approach and the purposive approach is one of the major issues in statutory interpretation. There is still no consensus on which approach should be used. Should judges examine each word and take the words literally or should it be accepted that an Act of Parliament cannot cover every situation and that meanings of words cannot always be exact?

The case of *Cheeseman v DPP* (1990) (see section 3.2.1) illustrates this. In that case the court took the words literally. However, it can be argued that the purposive approach should have been used as the defendant was 'wilfully and indecently exposing his person in a street' and that he was caught doing that. Is it important whether the police officers were 'passengers'? After all they had been sent there because of previous complaints about this type of behaviour. Also, the defendant presumably thought they were ordinary members of the public. It can be argued that the whole purpose of the Act was to prevent this type of behaviour.

In 1969 the Law Commission recommended in its report, *The Interpretation of Statutes,* Law Com No 21, 1969, that legislation should be passed to harmonise the methods of interpretation used by the judges. They put forward draft clauses for this purpose. The most important one stated:

'cl (b)   The principles of interpretation would include:

(i)   the preference of a construction which would promote the general legislative purpose over one which would not;

(ii)   the preference of a construction which is consistent with the international obligations of the United Kingdom over one which is not.'

Parliament did not act on this recommendation and there is still no legislation which sets out which method of interpretation should be preferred. However, judges are using the purposive approach more readily. In *Notham v London Borough of Barnet* [1978] 1 All ER 1243 Lord Denning quoted from the Law Commission report when he said:

> J   'The literal method is now completely out of date . . . In all cases now in the interpretation of statutes we adopt such a construction as will "promote the general legislative purpose" underlying the provision . . . Whenever the strict interpretation of a statute gives rise to an absurd and unjust situation, the judges can and should use their good sense to remedy it – by reading words in, if necessary – so as to do what Parliament would have done had they had the situation in mind.'

The use of the purposive approach has been strengthened by the decision in *Pepper (Inspector of Taxes) v Hart* [1993] 1 All ER 42. In this case the House of Lords accepted that it was permissible to look at the records of parliamentary debate in *Hansard* in order to discover Parliament's intention when enacting the relevant legislation (see section 3.7.2 for further discussion on this). In *Pepper v Hart* (1993) Lord Griffiths stated:

> J   'The days have long passed when the courts adopted a strict constructionist view of interpretation which required them to adopt the literal meaning of the language. the courts now adopt a purposive approach which seeks to give effect to the true purpose of legislation and are prepared to look at much extraneous material that bears on the background against which the legislation was enacted.'

Yet, despite claims that the purposive approach is now the preferred method, there are still cases in which the courts use the literal approach. An example is the following case:

CASE EXAMPLE

Cutter v Eagle Star Insurance Co Ltd [1998] 4 All ER 417

The claimant was sitting in the front passenger seat of his friend's car, parked in a multi-storey car park. Inflammable gas leaked inside the car from a can of lighter fuel, so that when the driver returned to the car and lit a cigarette, the gas was ignited and the claimant was injured. The claimant sued the driver for negligence and won the case. However, the driver had no money and could not pay the damages. So the claimant tried to claim the money from the driver's insurance company, Eagle Star. The driver's insurance policy provided cover against any liability for death or bodily injury to any person arising out of the use of his car on a 'road'. The Road Traffic Act 1988 defines 'road' as 'any highway and any other road to which the public has access'.

The House of Lords accepted that the true purpose of the Road Traffic Act 1988 was to protect the public from dangers arising from the use of motor vehicles. However, it applied the literal meaning of 'road' and held that the insurance policy did not cover an event occurring in a car park.

Lord Clyde said:

J

'It may be perfectly proper to adopt even a strained construction to enable the object and purpose of legislation to be fulfilled. But it cannot be taken to the length of applying unnatural meanings to familiar words . . . This must be particularly so where the language has no evident ambiguity or uncertainty about it . . . Against the employment of a broad approach to express the purpose of the Act must be put the undesirability of adopting anything beyond a strict construction of provisions which have penal consequences.'

So, the rejection of the purposive approach was based on three main points. First, that 'unnatural meanings' should not be applied to ordinary words. Next, that the purposive approach should not be used where the words in the act are not ambiguous or uncertain. Finally, that where the legislation created a criminal offence, it was undesirable to use a broad approach.

ACTIVITY

Practice essay title

The rules and approaches to statutory interpretation allow the courts too much discretion in the way they interpret the law.

Discuss.

■ Key facts chart on approaches and 'rules' of statutory interpretation

KEY FACTS

Rule/Approach	Comment	Cases
The literal rule	Uses plain ordinary, grammatical meaning of words Avoids judicial law-making BUT Assumes 'unattainable prefect in draftsmanship' May lead to absurd decision May lead to injustice	*Whiteley v Chappell* (1868) *Fisher v Bell* (1960) *London & NE Railway Co v Berriman* (1946)
The golden rule	Starts from literal approach but avoids absurdity or repugnance or inconsistency Court can modify words or write in words BUT what is an absurdity? Limited in scope	*R v Allen* (1872) *Re Sigsworth* (1935) *Adler v George* (1964)
The mischief rule	Looks at the gap in the previous law and interprets the words so as to 'advance the remedy' The Law Commission favoured this rule Nearest to the purposive approach	*Smith v Hughes* (1960) *Eastbourne BC v Stirling* (2000) *Royal College of Nursing v DHSS* (1981)
The literal approach	Takes the literal meaning of words (see literal rule above)	
The purposive approach	Looks for the intention of Parliament BUT allows for judicial law-making	*R v Registrar General, ex p Smith* (1991) *Jones v Tower Boot Co* (1997) *R (Quintavalle) v Secretary of State* (2003)

3.5 Rules of language

Even the literal rule does not take words in complete isolation. It is common sense that the other words in the Act must be looked at to see if they affect the word or phrase which is in dispute. In looking at the other words in the Act, the courts have developed a number of minor rules which can help to make the meaning of words and phrases clear where a particular sentence construction has been used. There are three main rules of language. They are:

- the *ejusdem generis* rule
- *expressio unius est exclusio alterius* (the mention of one thing excludes others)
- *noscitur a sociis* (a word is known by the company it keeps).

3.5.1 The *ejusdem generis* rule

This states that where there is a list of words which is followed by general words, then the general words are limited to the same kind of items as the specific words. This is easier to understand by looking at cases. In *Powell v Kempton Park Racecourse* [1899] AC 143 the defendant was charged with keeping a 'house, office, room or other place for betting'. He had been operating betting at what is known as Tattersall's Ring, which is outdoors. The House of Lords decided that the general words 'other place' had to refer to indoor places since all the words in the list were indoor places, and so the defendant was not guilty.

A more modern case illustrating the use of the *ejusdem generis* rule is *Wood v Commissioner of Police of the Metropolis* [1986] 2 All ER 570. The Divisional Court held that in s 4 of the Vagrancy Act 1824 the words 'any gun, pistol, hanger, cutlass, bludgeon, or other offensive weapon' did not include a piece of glass. The general words 'other offensive weapon' had to be interpreted in the light of the list of items and all these were items made or adapted for the purpose of causing injury. A piece of glass had not been made for that purpose.

There must be at least two specific words in a list before the general word or phrase for this rule to operate. In *Allen v Emmerson* [1944] KB 362 the Divisional Court had to interpret the phrase 'theatres and other places of amusement' and decide if it applied to a funfair. As there was only one specific word 'theatres', it was decided that a funfair did come under the general term 'other places of amusement' even though it was not of the same kind as theatres.

3.5.2 *Expressio unius est exclusio alterius* (the express mention of one thing excludes others)

Where there is a list of words which is not followed by general words, then the Act applies only to the items in the list. In *Tempest v Kilner* (1846) 3 CB 249 the court had to considered whether the Statute of Frauds 1677, which required a contract for the sale of 'goods, wares and merchandise' of more than £10 to be evidenced in writing, applied to a contract for the sale of stocks and shares. The list 'goods, wares and merchandise' was not followed by any general words, so the court held that only contracts for those three types of things were affected by the statute; because stocks and shares were not mentioned, they were not caught by the statute.

3.5.3 *Noscitur a sociis* (a word is known by the company it keeps)

This means that the words must be looked at in context and interpreted accordingly. It involves looking at other words in the same section or at other sections in the Act. Words in the same section were important in *Inland Revenue Commissioners v Frere* [1965] AC 402, where the section set out rules for 'interest, annuities or other annual interest'. The first use of the word 'interest' on its own could have meant any interest paid, whether daily, monthly or annually. Because of the words 'other annual interest' in the section, the court decided that 'interest' only meant annual interest.

Other sections of an Act were considered by the House of Lords in *Bromley London Borough Council v Greater London Council* [1982] 1 All ER 129. The issue in this case was whether the GLC could operate a cheap fare scheme on its transport systems, where the amounts being charged meant that the transport system would run at a loss. The decision in the case revolved around the meaning of the word 'economy' in the Transport (London) Act 1969. The House of Lords looked at the whole Act and, in particular, at another section which imposed a duty to make up any deficit as far as possible. As a result, it decided that 'economy' meant running on business lines and ruled that the cheap fares policy was not legal since it involved deliberately running the transport system at a loss and this was not running it on business lines.

Another case in which the wording of other sections of the Act was important is the following:

CASE EXAMPLE

Harrow London Borough Council v Shah and Shah [1999] 3 All ER 302

The defendants owned a newsagent's business where lottery tickets were sold. They had told their staff not to sell tickets to anyone under 16 years old. They also told their staff that if there was any doubt about a customer's age, the staff should ask for proof of age, and if still in doubt should refer the matter to the defendants. One of their staff sold a lottery ticket to a 13-year-old boy without asking for proof of age. The salesman mistakenly believed the boy was over 16 years old. The first defendant was in a back room of the premises at the time: the other was not on the premises. Both defendants were charged with selling a lottery ticket to a person under 16, contrary to s 13(1)(c) of the National Lottery Act 1993.

The wording in s 13(1)(c) provides that 'Any other person who was a party to the contravention shall be guilty of an offence'. It does not have any provision for a due

CONTINUED ▶

> diligence defence (ie that the defendant has taken all possible care to prevent the offence occurring). The Divisional Court compared s 13(1)(c) with s 13(1)(a) which does contain a 'due diligence' defence. Because of this the court held that a defendant could be guilty under s 13(1)(c) even though they had taken all reasonable care to prevent the offence from occurring.

3.6 Presumptions

The courts will also make certain presumptions or assumptions about the law, but these are only a starting point. If the statute clearly states the opposite then the presumption will not apply and it is said that the presumption is rebutted. The most important presumptions are:

1. A presumption against a change in the common law

In other words, it is assumed that the common law will apply unless Parliament has made it plain in the Act that the common law has been altered. An example of this occurred in *Leach v R* [1912] AC 305, where the question was whether a wife could be made to give evidence against her husband under the Criminal Evidence Act 1898. Since the 1898 Act did not expressly say that this should happen it was held that the common law rule that a wife could not be compelled to give evidence still applied. If there had been explicit words saying that a wife was compellable then the old common law would not apply. This is now the position under s 80 of the Police and Criminal Evidence Act 1984, which expressly states that in a crime of violence one spouse can be made to give evidence against the other spouse.

2. A presumption that *mens rea* is required in criminal cases

The basic common law rule is that no one can be convicted of a crime unless it is shown that they had the required intention to commit it. In *Sweet v Parsley* [1970] AC 132 the defendant was charged with being concerned with the management of premises which were used for the purposes of smoking cannabis. The facts were that the defendant was the owner of premises which she had leased out and the tenants had smoked cannabis there without her knowledge. She was clearly 'concerned in the management' of the premises and cannabis had been smoked there, but because she had no knowledge of the events she had no *mens rea*. The key issue was whether *mens rea* was required; the Misuse of Drugs Act 1971 did not say there was any need for knowledge of the events. The House of Lords held that the defendant was not guilty as the presumption that *mens rea* was required had not been rebutted.

In *B (a minor) v DPP* [2000] 1 All ER 833 the House of Lords again stressed the presumption that *mens rea* was required in criminal offences when Lord Nicholls said:

> **J** 'The common law presumes that, unless Parliament indicated otherwise, the appropriate mental element is an unexpressed ingredient of every statutory offence.'

3. A presumption that the Crown is not bound by any statute unless the statute expressly says so

4. A presumption that legislation does not apply retrospectively

This means that no Act of Parliament will apply to past happenings; each Act will normally only apply from the date it comes into effect. However, since this is only a presumption, Parliament can enact legislation with a retrospective effect if it expressly states this in the Act. There are very few Acts where Parliament has stated that there is retrospective effect. Examples are the War Damage Act 1965 and the War Crimes Act 1991.

3.7 Intrinsic and extrinsic aids

There are certain ways in which the courts can try to discover the intention of Parliament and certain matters which they can look at in order to help with the interpretation of a statute.

3.7.1 Intrinsic aids

These are matters within the statute itself that may help to make its meaning clearer. The court can consider the long title, the short title and the preamble, if any. Older statutes usually have a preamble which sets out Parliament's purpose in enacting that statute. Modern statutes either do not have a preamble or contain a very brief one. For example, the Theft Act 1968 states that it is an Act to modernise the law of theft. The long title may also explain briefly Parliament's intentions. An unusual approach was taken in the Arbitration Act 1996 where a statement of the principles of the Act is set out in s 2. This is a new development in statutory drafting and one that could both encourage and help the use of the purposive approach.

The other useful internal aids are any headings before a group of sections, and any Schedules attached to the Act. There are often also marginal notes explaining different sections but these are not generally regarded as giving Parliament's intention as they will have been inserted after the parliamentary debates and are only helpful comments put in by the printer.

3.7.2 Extrinsic aids

These are matters which are outside the Act and it has always been accepted that some external sources can help explain the meaning of an Act. These undisputed sources are:

* previous Acts of Parliament on the same topic
* the historical setting

- earlier case law

- dictionaries of the time.

So far as other extrinsic aids are concerned, attitudes have changed. Originally the courts had very strict rules that other extrinsic aids should not be considered, however, for the following three aids the courts' attitude has changed. These three main extrinsic aids are:

1 *Hansard* – the official report of what was said in Parliament when the Act was debated.

2 Reports of law reform bodies such as the Law Commission which led to the passing of the Act.

3 International Conventions, Regulations or Directives which have been implemented by English legislation.

All of these are considered separately in the next three sections.

3.7.3 The use of *Hansard*

Until 1992 there was a firm rule that the courts could not look at what was said in the debates in Parliament. Some years earlier, Lord Denning had tried to attack this ban on *Hansard* in *Davis v Johnson* [1978] 1 All ER 1132, which involved the interpretation of the Domestic Violence and Matrimonial Proceedings Act 1976. He admitted that he had indeed read *Hansard* before making his decision, saying:

> J 'Some may say – and indeed have said – that judges should not pay any attention to what is said in Parliament. They should grope about in the dark for the meaning of an Act without switching on the light. I do not accede to this view.'

This was in the Court of Appeal and when the case was appealed to the House of Lords, it disapproved of Lord Denning's view. Lord Scarman explained the Lords' reasons by saying:

> J 'Such material is an unreliable guide to the meaning of what is enacted. It promotes confusion, not clarity. The cut and thrust of debate and the pressures of executive responsibility . . . are not always conducive to a clear and unbiased explanation of the meaning of statutory language.'

However, in *Pepper (Inspector of Taxes) v Hart* (1993) the House of Lords relaxed the rule and accepted that *Hansard* could be used in a limited way. This case was unusual in that seven judges heard the appeal, rather than the normal panel of five. Those seven judges included the then Lord Chancellor, Lord Mackay, who was the only judge to disagree with the use of *Hansard*. The majority ruled that *Hansard* could be consulted.

CASE EXAMPLE

Pepper (Inspector of Taxes) v Hart [1993] 1 All ER 42

Malvern College, an independent school for boys, allowed sons of teachers to be educated at the college for one-fifth of the fees charged to other people. This concession was a taxable benefit and the teachers had to pay tax on it. The question was exactly how the calculation of the amount to be taxed should be done. Under the applicable Finance Act this had to be done on the 'cash equivalent' of the benefit. Section 63 of the Finance Act defined 'cash equivalent' as 'an amount equal to the cost of the benefit' and further defined the 'cost of the benefit' as 'the amount of any expense incurred in or in connection with its provision'. This was ambiguous as it could mean either:

(a) the marginal (or additional) cost to the employer of providing it to the employee (this on the facts was nil) or

(b) the average cost of providing it to both the employee and the public (this would involve the teachers having to pay a considerable amount of tax).

The tax inspector took the view that (b) was the correct interpretation but the teachers challenged this.

The case went on appeal to the House of Lords where it was submitted that it should be possible to look at *Hansard* to see what had been said about this point when Parliament was considering the Finance Act. One of the arguments against looking at *Hansard* was that this would infringe s 1, art 9 of the Bill of Rights 1688. This, in its original spelling, states:

's 1 of article 9 That the freedome of speech and debates or proceedings in Parlyament ought not to be impeached or questioned in any court or place out of Parlyament.'

All seven judges in the House of Lords stated that there was no infringement of s 1, art 9 of the Bill of Rights 1688. The courts would be looking at *Hansard* in order to try to implement what was said there. They would not be 'questioning' the debates. Lord Browne-Wilkinson in his judgment summarised the other reasons which had been put forward against the use of *Hansard*. He identified the following points:

• the prohibition on using *Hansard* preserved the 'constitutional proprieties' under which Parliament creates the law and the judges merely apply it

• the prohibition avoided the practical difficulty of an expensive researching of parliamentary materials

CONTINUED ▸

- *Hansard* does not provide the citizen with an accessible and defined text regulating his legal rights and

- in many cases it is unlikely that *Hansard* will provide any helpful guidance.

The majority of the Law Lords rejected all these arguments. However, Lord Mackay thought that the expense of researching *Hansard* was a good reason for ruling against its use, particularly as in many cases there would be no useful material in *Hansard*. But the other six Law Lords ruled that *Hansard* could be referred to. However, they put limitations on its use, as set out by Lord Browne-Wilkinson in his judgment:

J   'The exclusionary rule should be relaxed so as to permit reference to parliamentary materials where; (a) legislation is ambiguous or obscure, or leads to an absurdity; (b) the material relied on consists of one or more statements by a minister or other promoter of the Bill together if necessary with such other parliamentary material as is necessary to understand such statements and their effect; (c) the statements relied on are clear. Further than this I would not at present go.'

So *Hansard* may be considered, but only where the words of the Act are ambiguous or obscure or lead to an absurdity. Even then, *Hansard* should only be used if there was a clear statement by the Minister introducing the legislation, which would resolve the ambiguity or absurdity. In fact, in *DPP v Bull* (1994) (see section 3.1.2) the court said that it had not looked at *Hansard* because the legislation was not 'ambiguous, obscure nor productive of absurdity'.

The only time that a wider use of *Hansard* is permitted is where the court is considering an Act that introduced an international Convention or European Directive into English law. This was pointed out by the Queen's Bench Divisional Court in *Three Rivers District Council v Bank of England (No 2)* [1996] 2 All ER 363. In such a situation it is important to interpret the statute purposively and consistently with any European materials and the court can look at Ministerial statements, even if the statute does not appear to be ambiguous or obscure.

Since 1993, *Hansard* has been referred to in a number of cases. Lord Mackay's predictions on cost have been confirmed by some solicitors, with one estimating that it had added 25 per cent to the bill. On other occasions it is clear that *Hansard* has not been helpful or that the court would have reached the same conclusion in any event. Pre-*Pepper v Hart* (1993), Vera Sachs did a study of 34 cases and found that reference to *Hansard* would not have helped in these cases. She pointed out:

'In every case studied the disputed clause was either undebated or received obscure and confusing replies from the Minister.'

V Sachs, 'Towards Discovering Parliamentary Intent', 1982 Scat LR 143

Professor Michael Zander conducted a study of House of Lords' decisions which had been made after November 1992 (when *Pepper v Hart* (1993) allowed reference to *Hansard*). He found that there were virtually no cases in which the court's decision had been influenced by reading *Hansard*. He found that virtually all cases fell into one of three categories:

1. there was no ambiguity or other reason for consulting *Hansard* or

2. *Hansard* was consulted but it was of no assistance or

3. the comments by the Minister confirmed the view that the court had already taken of the matter.

Professor Zander wrote:

> 'Thus even in cases where the court agrees to look at *Pepper v Hart* material, it appears to be exceedingly rare that the material affects the outcome. When considering the balance of advantage flowing from the decision one also has to put into the scale not only the considerable number of cases where the court refuses even to look at the material, but the presumably much greater number of cases where *Hansard* has been scoured by the lawyers in vain. . . . In short, it seems that the Lord Chancellor, Lord Mackay, who, as has been seen, dissented in *Pepper v Hart* mainly out of concern that the costs of the reform would outweigh the likely benefits, was probably right.'

M Zander, The Law-Making Process (5th edn, Butterworths, 1999), p 155

In *Wilson v First County Trust (No 2)*, [2003] UKHL 40 the Speaker of the House of Commons and the Clerk of the Parliament were joined in the case to make representations on the use of *Hansard* for the purpose of deciding compatibility of an Act with the European Convention on Human Rights. This was the first time that officers of Parliament had sought to be heard on the use of *Hansard* in the courts. It was submitted by counsel for the Speaker that the courts should not treat speeches made in Parliament, whether by Ministers or others, as evidence of the policy consideration which led to legislation taking a particular form. He further argued that there were no circumstances in which it was appropriate for a court to refer to *Hansard* in order to decide whether an enactment was compatible with the European Convention.

The House of Lords rejected these arguments and held that *Hansard* could be consulted even where the question of compatibility with Convention rights was an issue. Lord Nicholls said:

> **J** 'The courts would be failing in the discharge of the new role assigned to them by Parliament if they were to exclude from consideration relevant information whose only source was a Ministerial statement in Parliament or an explanatory note prepared by his department while the Bill was proceeding through Parliament.
>
> By having such material the court would not be questioning proceedings in Parliament or intruding improperly into the legislative process or ascribing to Parliament the views expressed by a Minister. The court would merely be placing itself in a better position to understand the legislation.'

However, the Lords pointed out that the occasions when resort to *Hansard* was necessary would seldom arise. In fact, they held that it was not necessary to refer to *Hansard* in this case.

3.7.4 Law reform reports

The courts used to hold that reports by law reform bodies should not be considered by the courts. However this rule was relaxed in the *Black Clawson* case in 1975 (*Black-Clawson International Ltd v Papierwerke etc AG* [1975] 1 All ER 810) when it was accepted that such a report should be looked at to discover the 'mischief' or gap in the law which the legislation based on the report was designed to deal with. An example of a case in which the court looked at a report is *DPP v Bull* (1994) (see section 3.1.2). Here, the court considered the Wolfenden Report, *Report of the Committee on Homosexual Offences and Prostitution*, Cmnd 247 (1957). This made it clear that the 'mischief' which had been identified was that of women loitering or soliciting for the purposes of prostitution: the report did not identify any problem caused by male prostitutes. Accordingly the court held that s 1(1) of the Street Offences Act 1959 applied only to women prostitutes.

In the *Black-Clawson* (1975) case, although all five judges in the House of Lords agreed that reports could be considered to identify the mischief Parliament had intended to deal with, they were divided on whether they could go further and use the report to find the intention of Parliament. However, by 1993 the Lords appear to have accepted that reports could be used to look for the intention of the legislature. This is shown by Lord Browne-Wilkinson in *Pepper v Hart* (1993) when he said:

> **J** 'Given the purposive approach to construction now adopted by the courts in order to give effect to the true intentions of the legislature, the fine distinction between looking for the mischief and looking for the intention in using words to provide the remedy are technical and inappropriate.'

Although all the Law Lords had agreed in *Black-Clawson* (1975) that reports could be considered to identify the mischief Parliament had intended to deal with, there have been cases since then in which the courts have not consulted the relevant report. For example, in *Anderton v Ryan* [1985] 2 All ER 355 the House of Lords did not consult the Law Commission's report *Criminal Law: Attempt and Impossibility in Relation to Attempt, Conspiracy and Incitement,* Law Com No 102 (1980). As a result, they came to a decision which was severely criticised by both practising and academic lawyers. The Lords themselves accepted that they had made a bad error and they corrected it in the following year in *R v Shivpuri* [1986] 2 All ER 334 when they overruled *Anderton v Ryan* (1985).

Another case in which the relevant report was not considered by the House of Lords was *Metropolitan Police Commissioner v Caldwell* [1981] 1 All ER 961. In this case the House of Lords did not look at the report by the Law Commission (*Report on Offences of Damage to Property,* Law Com No 29 (1970)) which led the passing of the Criminal Damage Act 1971. In this report the Law Commission had pointed out the old-fashioned use of the word 'maliciously' in the old Acts where the word was meant to mean that the defendant either intended to do the damage or knew that he was taking a risk that it would be damaged. The Commission proposed that it should be replaced by the phrase 'intending or being reckless'. This was the wording used in both the draft Bill and the final Act. It was clear that the Law Commission meant 'reckless' to cover situations where the defendant had realised that there was a risk but had gone on to take that risk. This is known as 'subjective recklessness'.

However in *Caldwell* (1981), when the word 'reckless' in the Criminal Damage Act 1971 was considered by the House of Lords, it ruled that it covered not only subjective risk-taking but also situations where a reasonable person would have realised the risk but the defendant had not given any thought to the possibility of there being any risk (an objective test). This decision was criticised but it remained in force for over 20 years until the House of Lords reconsidered the matter in *R v G* [2003] UKHL 50 and overruled *Caldwell* (1981), holding that in that case the Law Lords had 'adopted an interpretation of section 1 of the 1971 Act which was beyond the range of feasible meanings'. In *R v G* (2003) the Lords emphasised the meaning that the Law Commission had intended and which Parliament must also have intended. Lord Bingham said:

> J '[S]ection 1 as enacted followed, subject to an immaterial addition, the draft proposed by the Law Commission. It cannot be supposed that by "reckless" Parliament meant anything different from the Law Commission. The Law Commission's meaning was made plain both in its Report (Law Com No 29, 1970) and in Working Paper No 23 which preceded it. These materials (not, it would seem, placed before the House in *R v Caldwell*) reveal a very plain intention to replace the old expression "maliciously" by the more familiar expression "reckless" but to give the latter expression the meaning which *R v Cunningham* [1957] 2 QB 396 had given to the former. . . . No relevant change in the *mens rea* necessary for the proof of the offence was intended, and in holding otherwise the majority misconstrued section 1 of the Act.'

3.7.5 International Conventions

We have already seen that where a national law is passed to give effect to a European Union treaty or other law, the courts will look at the original EU law when deciding on interpretation. This is also the position where a national law has been passed in order to give effect to any international treaty or Convention. In *Salomon v Commissioners of Customs and Excise* [1967] 2 QB 116 the Court of Appeal looked at an international Convention because it thought that English law should be interpreted in such a way as to be consistent with international law.

In *Fothergill v Monarch Airlines Ltd* [1980] 2 All ER 696 the House of Lords decided that the original Convention should be considered as it was possible that in translating and adapting the Convention to our legislative process, the true meaning of the original might have been lost. The House of Lords in that same case went further and also held that an English court could consider any preparatory materials or explanatory notes published with an international Convention. The reasoning behind this was that other countries allowed the use of such material, known as *travaux préparatoires*, and it should therefore be allowed in this country in order to get uniformity in the interpretation of international rules.

■ Key facts chart on aids to interpretation

KEY FACTS

Aid	Comment	Cases
Rules of language	Looks at phrases and other words in the Act	
1. *Ejusdem generis*	General words which follow a list are limited to the same kind	*Powell v Kempton Park* (1899)
2. *Expressio unius est exclusio alterius*	The express mention of one thing excludes others	*Tempest v Kilner* (1846)
3. *Noscitur a sociis*	A word is known by the company it keeps	*IRC v Frere* (1965)
Interpretation Act 1978	Makes general rules so that unless the contrary is stated in an Act: • 'he' includes 'she' • singular includes plural etc	

CONTINUED ▶

KEY FACTS

Aid	Comment	Cases
Intrinsic aids	Matters within the Act, especially: • short title, long title and preamble • definition sections	
Extrinsic aids	*Hansard* Law reform reports International Conventions	*Pepper v Hart* (1993) *Black-Clawson case* (1975) *Fothergill v Monarch Airlines Ltd* (1980)

3.8 The effect of the Human Rights Act 1998

Section 3 of the Human Rights Act (HRA) 1998 says that, so far as it is possible to do so, legislation must be read and given effect in a way which is compatible with the rights in the European Convention on Human Rights. This applies to any case where one of the rights is concerned, but it does not apply where there is no involvement of human rights.

A good example of the difference the HRA 1998 has made to interpretation is *R v Offen* [2000] 1 WLR 253. This case considered the meaning of the word 'exceptional' in the Crime (Sentences) Act 1997 where any offender committing a second serious offence had to be given a life sentence unless there were 'exceptional circumstances'. Before the HRA 1998 came into force the Court of Appeal in *R v Kelly* [2000] QB 198 had said that 'exceptional' was an ordinary English adjective, saying:

J 'To be exceptional a circumstance need not be unique or unprecedented or very rare; but it cannot be one that is regularly or routinely or normally encountered.'

This led to a strict approach where offenders were given life sentences even when the earlier crime had been committed a long time ago and the second offence was not that serious of its type. In *Offen* (2000), which was decided after the HRA 1998 came into force in October 2000, the Court of Appeal said that this restricted approach in *Kelly* (2000) could lead to the sentence being arbitrary and disproportionate and a breach of both Arts 3 and 5 of the European Convention on Human Rights. In order to interpret the Crime (Sentences) Act 1997 in a way which was compatible with the Convention, it was necessary to consider whether the offender was a danger to

107

the public. If he was not, then he was an exception to the normal rule in the 1997 Act, and this could be considered exceptional circumstances so that a life sentence need not be given.

Another example of the effect of the HRA 1998 on interpretation is *Mendoza v Ghaidan* [2002] EWCA Civ 1533 (see section 3.1.3). In this case the Court of Appeal ignored a House of Lords' judgment which had been made prior to the implementation of the HRA 1998 and read the words 'as his or her wife or husband' in the Rent Act 1977 to mean 'as **if they were** his or her wife or husband' in order to interpret the 1977 Act in accordance with the European Convention on Human Rights. In 2004 the House of Lords confirmed the Court of Appeal's decision in this case.

ACTIVITY

Self-assessment questions

1. Explain how the literal rule operates.

2. Explain how the golden rule modifies the literal rule.

3. How does the mischief rule operate?

4. Give two case examples of the operation of:

    (a) the literal rule

    (b) the golden rule

    (c) the mischief rule.

5. What is the purposive approach?

6. What are the advantages and disadvantages of this approach to statutory interpretation?

7. What is meant by 'intrinsic aids'?

8. What limitations are placed on referring to parliamentary debates in *Hansard*?

9. Explain the advantages and disadvantages of looking at parliamentary debates in *Hansard*.

10. When will a court look at the report of a law reform body as an aid to statutory interpretation?

Further reading

Jenkins, J C, '*Pepper v Hart*: A Draftsman's Perspective' (1994) 15 Stat LR 23, 25.

Leitch, W A, 'Interpretation and the Interpretation Act 1978' (1980) Stat LR 5.

Williams, G, 'The Meaning of Literal Interpretation' [1981] NLJ 1128, 1149.

chapter 4 CIVIL COURTS ■

4.1 Introduction to the courts system

Although the main focus of this chapter is on civil courts, it is necessary to understand some basic points and to put the whole matter into context. The introductory points considered are:

- the differences between civil and criminal cases
- whether a court is a superior or an inferior court
- appellate courts and trial courts
- the differences between courts and tribunals.

4.1.1 Civil and criminal cases

When looking at the court structure, it is important to understand that civil and criminal cases are dealt with differently. This stems from the fact that the purposes of civil and criminal law are different.

Civil law

Civil law is concerned with rights and duties between individuals. When there is a breach of a right or a failure of duty then the aim of the civil law is to put the parties into the position they would have been in if there had been no breach or failure. This is not always possible; for example in negligence cases where the claimant has been left paralysed or with other permanent injuries. In such cases the court awards damages (a sum of money) as compensation. Apart from trying to correct past breaches, the courts, in some cases, may be asked to make an order to prevent a future breach of a right. For example, where trespass or harassment is likely to occur in the future, the courts can grant an injunction forbidding this.

Civil law has many different branches. The main areas that are likely to lead to court cases are contract law, the law of tort, family law, the law of succession, company law, employment law and land law. However, there are also many other specialist areas, varying from copyright and patents to marine law, on which the courts may be required to adjudicate. This book does not deal with the actual legal rules of any of the areas, only with the system for dealing with disputes.

As civil law involves regulating disputes between private individuals and businesses, it is also called private law. Civil cases are started by the person or business complaining of the breach or failure.

Criminal law

Criminal law sets out what behaviour is forbidden by the State, at risk of punishment. So the purpose of criminal cases is to decide if the defendant is guilty of such behaviour and, if so, to impose a suitable penalty. A person who commits a crime is said to have offended against the State and the State, therefore, has the right to prosecute him. This is so even though there is often an individual victim of a crime as well. For example, if a defendant commits the crime of burglary by breaking into a house and stealing, the State prosecutes the defendant for that burglary, although it is also possible for the victim to bring a private prosecution if the State does not take proceedings. However, if there is a private prosecution, the State still has the right to intervene and take over the matter. Also, at the end of the case, if the defendant is found guilty, the court will punish the defendant for the offence, because he has broken the criminal law set down by the State. The victim will not necessarily be given any compensation, since the case is not viewed as a dispute between the burglar and the householder. However, the criminal courts have the power to order that the offender pays the victim compensation and can make such an order as well as punishing the offender.

Distinctions between criminal cases and civil cases

There are many differences between criminal cases and civil cases. Important ones are:

- the courts in which the trial takes place
- the way of starting a case and the procedure of the case
- the standard of proof
- the outcome of the case.

First, the cases take place in different courts. In general, criminal cases will be tried in either the magistrates' court or the Crown Court, while civil cases are heard in the High Court or the County Court. However, some civil matters, especially family cases, can be dealt with in the magistrates' court.

The person starting the case is given a different name: in criminal cases they are referred to as the prosecutor, while in civil cases they are usually called the claimant. As already stated, the criminal case is taken on behalf of the State, and the main prosecution body is the Crown Prosecution Service which is responsible for conducting cases. There are, however, other State agencies which may prosecute certain types of crime, such as the Serious Fraud Office, which prosecutes very complex fraud cases, or the Commissioners for Customs and Excise, who can prosecute smuggling cases. Civil cases are started by the person making the claim.

A very important difference is the standard to which the case has to be proved. Criminal cases must be proved 'beyond reasonable doubt'. This is a very high standard of proof, and is necessary since a conviction could result in a defendant serving a long prison sentence. Civil cases have to be proved only 'on the balance of probabilities', a lower standard in which the judge decides who is most

110

likely to be right. This difference in the standard to which a case has to be proved means that even though a defendant in a criminal case has been acquitted, a civil case based on the same facts against that defendant can still be successful. Such situations are not common, but have happened.

The outcome of a civil case is that judgment will be given in favour of one of the parties. If this is the claimant, then the court will then decide on the remedy to which that person is entitled. This will vary with the type of case. It may be a sum of money, an injunction, rescission of a contract or a declaration. In a criminal case, if the defendant is found guilty then the court has to decide on the most suitable penalty. This may be a custodial sentence, a community sentence, a fine or a discharge.

As can be seen, the terminology used in civil and criminal cases is different. A civil case is started by a claimant, whereas there is a prosecutor in criminal cases. In a civil case it is correct to speak of the defendant being sued, but in a criminal case the defendant is charged with or accused of a crime. The outcome of a civil case is that judgment is given for or against the claimant. Alternatively, this can be expressed by saying that the defendant has been found liable or not liable. In a criminal case the verdict is that the defendant is guilty or not guilty. In a civil case the defendant may be ordered to pay damages, whereas in a criminal case the defendant may be fined. The damages are payable to the claimant but the money from a fine in a criminal case goes to the State.

■ Key facts chart on differences between civil and criminal cases

KEY FACTS

	Civil cases	Criminal cases
Purpose of the case	To enforce rights	To decide if the criminal law has been broken
Person starting case	The individual whose rights have been affected	Usually the State, through the Crown Prosecution Service
Legal name for that person	Claimant	Prosecutor
Courts hearing cases	County Court High Court	Magistrates' Court Crown Court
Standard of proof	The balance of probabilities	Beyond reasonable doubt

KEY FACTS

	Civil cases	Criminal cases
Person(s) making the decision	Judge Jury for a few cases (mainly defamation)	Magistrates in Magistrates' Court Jury in Crown Court
Decision	Judgment for the claimant (or defendant)	Guilty or not guilty
Powers of the court	Award damages Order an injunction Make a declaration Special remedies for contract law: • specific performance • rescission • rectification	Pass sentence: • prison • community sentence • fine • discharge May also order compensation to be paid to the victim

4.1.2 Superior courts and inferior courts

Another distinction is between superior courts and inferior courts. The House of Lords, the Court of Appeal, the High Court and the Crown Court are superior courts, while the County Court and the magistrates' court are inferior courts. This distinction is important for two reasons. The first is that inferior courts have limited jurisdiction. They hear the less serious cases. Secondly, inferior courts are subject to the supervisory prerogative jurisdiction of the High Court. This means that the High Court can quash a decision of an inferior court if it was made in breach of the rules of natural justice or where the court did not have power to deal with that particular type of case. On this second point the Crown Court is in an unusual position. It is an inferior court but for some matters it is subject to supervision by the High Court. This is set out in the Supreme Court Act 1981.

 's 29(3) In relation to the jurisdiction of the Crown Court, other than its jurisdiction in matters relating to trial on indictment, the High Court shall have all such jurisdiction to make orders of mandamus, prohibition or certiorari as the High Court possess in relation to the jurisdiction of an inferior court.'

So, for anything other than matters related to trial on indictment, the High Court has supervisory powers over the Crown Court. This includes decisions on the granting of bail or where the Crown Court is hearing an appeal from the magistrates' court.

4.1.3 Appellate courts and trial courts

The courts in which the initial trial of a case takes place are known as courts of trial or courts of first instance. Courts which hear appeals are called appellate courts. Many courts have both first instance and appellate jurisdiction.

County Courts hear civil cases at first instance but since the Woolf Reforms (see section 4.3) they also have appellate jurisdiction. This is because the appeal route for small claims cases and fast-track cases heard at first instance by a District Judge in the County Court is to a Circuit Judge in the same County Court.

Although the High Court is the court of first instance for major civil case, it also sits as an appeal court. In particular, appeals on fast-track cases heard at first instance by a Circuit Judge in the County Court are heard by a single judge in the High Court. In addition, all the divisions of the High Court have appellate jurisdiction when two or three judges sit as a Divisional Court. The Queen's Bench Divisional is the most important of the Divisional Courts. For more information on appeals, see Chapter 6.

The Court of Appeal and the House of Lords are only appellate courts. They do not hear any cases at first instance.

4.1.4 Courts and tribunals

The systems of courts and tribunals are distinct. Separate tribunals have been set up to deal with specific rights given by the State to individuals. For example, employment tribunals hear cases where failure to pay wages, unfair dismissal or discrimination against an employee is alleged. Tribunals are considered more fully at section 4.5.

However, there can be confusion because in a general sense a court can be called a tribunal. This is obvious when the dictionary definition of 'tribunal' is considered:

> 'a judgment-seat: a court of justice or arbitration: a body appointed to adjudicate
> in some matter or to enquire into some disputed question'.

It is important to be able to distinguish between a court and a tribunal, as the rules on contempt of court apply only to courts. The actual name given to the tribunal or court is not a totally reliable guide. For example, despite its name, the Employment Appeal Tribunal is a court for the purposes of contempt of court. The problem of how to identify what is a court was considered in *Attorney General v British Broadcasting Corporation* [1980] 3 All ER 161 where the House of Lords held that a local valuation court was not a court even though it had the word 'court' in its title.

Lord Scarman said:

> **J** 'I would identify a court in (or 'of') law, ie a court of judicature, as a body established to exercise, either generally or subject to defined limits, the judicial power of the state. In this context judicial power is to be contrasted with legislative and executive (ie administrative) power. If the body under review is established for a purely legislative or administrative purpose, it is part of the legislative or administrative system of the state, even though it has to perform duties which are judicial in character.'

The functions of the local valuation court were administrative rather than judicial. Similarly, in *General Medical Council v British Broadcasting Corporation* [1998] 3 All ER 426, the Court of Appeal held that the Professional Conduct Committee of the General Medical Council is not a court. The committee does have a judicial function but this is to exercise the self-regulatory power of the medical profession to maintain professional standards. The Committee is not exercising the judicial power of the State.

This concept of a court exercising the judicial power of the State is now incorporated into s 19 of the Contempt of Court Act 1981.

4.2 Civil courts of trial

The system of civil courts that now operates in England and Wales is based on the system set up in the nineteenth century. However, there have been many modifications to jurisdiction and procedure, especially in the late twentieth century. The courts where cases are tried at first instance are the High Court and the County Court.

The High Court was created as part of the Supreme Court of Judicature in 1873.

In the High Court there are three divisions:

- Chancery Division
- Queen's Bench Division
- Family Division.

These divisions stem from the Judicature Act 1873 which set up the Supreme Court of Judicature. Originally there were five divisions but by 1880 these had been reduced to three. The third division in 1880 was named the Probate, Divorce and Admiralty Division (PDA). The name of this division was changed to the Family Division in 1971 under the Administration of Justice Act 1970. At the same time the work of the old PDA Division was re-allocated with the Family Division keeping the increasing area of divorce and family law and non-contentious probate, while the admiralty part of its jurisdiction was given to the Queen's Bench Division and disputed probate cases were allocated to the Chancery Division.

The High Court as a whole has jurisdiction to hear any civil case. However, each division has been given jurisdiction to hear certain types of cases so that judges with the relevant specialist knowledge can deal with them.

The modern County Courts were created by the County Courts Act 1846 to hear small cases. Initially the limit on its jurisdiction to hear claims was £20. This was raised at intervals to reflect inflation so that by 1981 the limit was £5,000. In 1991 this upper limit was removed, so that in theory the County Court can hear cases of any value.

We will now go on to consider the present-day jurisdiction of the three divisions of the High Court and the County Court in more detail.

4.2.1 Queen's Bench Division

This is the biggest Division of the High Court. Its main jurisdiction is to try cases involving the law of contract and tort. In addition, it has three special courts attached to it. These are the Commercial Court, the Admiralty Court and the Technology and Construction Court.

The Queen's Bench Division is the only division in which cases can still be tried by a jury sitting with the judge. Even in this division this is now a rare occurrence, with only a very small number of jury trials each year. For further information on the use of juries in civil cases, see Chapter 8.

Commercial Court

This court has specialist judges to deal with insurance and banking and other commercial matters, for example the problems of the Lloyd's 'names' for the losses caused by large insurance claims. In this court a simplified speedier procedure is used and the case may be decided on documentary evidence.

Admiralty Court

This, as its name implies, deals with matters relating to shipping. The two most common matters dealt with are damage to cargo and collision of ships. The judge in the Admiralty Court sits with two lay assessors, who are chosen from Masters of Trinity House, and who are there to advise the judge on questions of seamanship and navigation.

Technology and Construction Court

The Queen's Bench Division also administers the Technology and Construction Court which hears cases which are technically complex. This includes building and engineering disputes and computer litigation. Cases can be referred to it by either the Queen's Bench Division or the Chancery Division.

4.2.2 Chancery Division

The principal business of this division consists of corporate and personal insolvency disputes, the enforcement of mortgages, partnership disputes, intellectual property rights, copyright and patent, disputes relating to trust property, disputed probate cases and administration of the estates of deceased persons. There is also a special Companies Court in the division which deals mainly with winding up companies. Juries are never used in the Chancery Division and cases are heard by a single judge.

4.2.3 Family Division

This division has jurisdiction to hear a wide range of matters connected with the family. This includes all matrimonial cases, including divorce and declarations for nullity of marriage, and related issues such as disputes over matrimonial property. It also hears wardship and adoption cases and all proceedings relating to children under the Children Act 1989. As well, it has jurisdiction over any proceedings under the Child Abduction and Custody Act 1985. It also grants probate in non-contentious probate cases.

4.2.4 County Court

There are about 220 County Courts around England and Wales. These have jurisdiction to hear:

- claims based on the law of contract
- claims based on the law of tort
- claims for the recovery of land, eg landlord and tenant disputes
- matters connected to trusts, mortgages and dissolution of partnerships: for all these there is a financial limit of in that the amount of the fund or the value of the property involved cannot exceed £30,000
- contentious probate proceedings where the net value of the estate is less than £30,000
- proceedings under the Children Act 1989.

In addition, some County Courts have been given jurisdiction to hear petitions for divorce or nullity of marriage and all related matters. A small number of County Courts also have admiralty jurisdiction for claims up to £5,000 (£15,000 in salvage cases).

There are limitations on the jurisdiction of the County Court. The first limitation, for certain types of cases, is financial. This can be seen in the above list. However, where the parties agree that the County Court should have jurisdiction then it is possible for larger claims to be dealt with here. Otherwise the case will have to be dealt with in the High Court which has unlimited jurisdiction. In fact, all claims for less than £15,000 have to be started in the County Court. In addition, personal injury cases of less than £50,000 must be started in the County Court, but where the claim is for more than £50,000 it should be tried in the High Court unless it is more suitable for trial in a County Court.

The second limitation is geographical. A claim can be started in any County Court but if it is defended it is usually transferred to the County Court for the district in which the defendant's address for service is situated.

There is also a limitation in that defamation cases must be started in the High Court although it is then possible for such cases to be transferred for trial to the County Court where suitable.

4.2.5 Small claims

In 1973 a new procedure for small claims was started within the County Court. This was a more informal hearing which encouraged parties to take the case without the help of lawyers. Initially the limit on small claims was £75, but by 1979 it had increased to £500 and, by 1991, £1,000.

The small claims procedure allows the District Judge to be flexible in the way he deals with each case. To achieve this, District Judges are encouraged to be more inquisitorial and given training in how to handle small claims cases, so that they will take an active part in the proceedings, asking questions and making sure that both parties explain all their important points. Litigants are encouraged to take their own case so that costs are kept low. However, it is possible to have a lawyer to represent you at a small claims hearing but the winner cannot claim the costs of using a lawyer from the losing party.

4.2.6 The track system

The Woolf Report (see section 4.4) recommended that civil cases should be allocated to one of three tracks. These are based on the value of the amount claimed. The three tracks now are:

- small claims cases with a limit of £5,000
- fast-track cases from £5,000 to £15,000
- multi-track cases over £15,000.

Small claims track

This track kept the same principles as the earlier small claims court. However, the general limit now is £5,000, but parties with a larger claim can have their case dealt with as a small claims case if they agree. The limit for personal injury and housing cases is lower, at £1,000. All small claims cases are dealt with in the County Court. Where possible, the case is dealt with at one hearing with no pre-trial hearing. The judge has flexibility to run the proceedings in the way he thinks is the most suitable for each case.

Fast-track cases

The limits on these cases are normally £5,000 to £15,000 but cases for a greater value can be dealt with in this way if they are straightforward. In addition, claims which are for less than £15,000 may be dealt with as multi-track cases if they are thought to be too complex for the fast-track system. All fast-track cases are dealt with in the County Court. The aim is that all fast-track cases

should be heard within 30 weeks of the case being set down for trial. The length of the hearing should be no more than one day. To save cost and delay, only one joint expert witness is allowed. There are also fixed costs for hearings.

Multi-track cases

These are for claims over £15,000 or for complex cases for a lesser amount. These can be started and heard in either the County Court or the High Court. The emphasis in multi-track cases is on case management by the judge. This should mean that issues are identified and the judge can set timetables for any pre-trial procedure that is necessary.

Allocation of cases to the tracks

The allocation of each case to its proper track is based on answers given by the parties to an allocation questionnaire (Form N150). Once a defence is filed, the court sends this questionnaire to both parties. The main consideration in allocating a case to a track is the amount of the claim, but the allocation judge will also consider the complexity of the facts of the case, whether there are difficult issues of law involved, the amount of oral evidence, the time the hearing is likely to take and the wishes of the parties.

4.2.7 Transfer of cases between the County Court and the High Court

All small claims and fast-track cases must be started in the County Court and will be tried there. However, as we have seen, multi-track cases can be started in either the High Court or the County Court. There are various rules about when cases should be transferred. Section 40 of the County Courts Act 1984 allows defamation claims and other contract and tort cases to be transferred from the High Court to the County Court. Under r 30.3 of the Civil Procedure Rules (CPR) the following criteria are considered:

(i) the financial value of the claim and the amount in dispute, if different

(ii) whether it would be more convenient or fair for hearings (including the trial) to be held in some other court

(iii) the availability of a judge specialising in the type of claim in question

(iv) the complexity of the facts, legal issues, remedies or procedures involved

(v) the importance of the outcome of the claim to the public in general and

(vi) the facilities available at the court where the claim is being dealt with and whether they may be inadequate because of any disabilities of a party or potential witness.

In addition, a Practice Direction has been issued under Pt 29 of the CPR, stating that certain types of proceedings are particularly suitable for trial in the High Court and, therefore, should not normally be transferred to a County Court. These are cases involving:

(i) professional negligence

(ii) fatal accidents

(iii) allegations of fraud or undue influence

(iv) defamation

(v) malicious prosecution or false imprisonment

(vi) claims against the police

(vii) contentious probate claims.

This Practice Direction does not totally prevent the transfer of such cases to the County Court, especially where the parties agree to the trial taking place in the County Court.

Amount claimed	Where case is started	Where case is tried
Up to £5,000 BUT personal injury cases and housing cases only up to £1,000	County Court	County Court Small claims track
Between £5,000 and £15,000 AND personal injury cases and housing cases from £1,000	County Court	County Court Fast track
Over £15,000 or complex cases of less value Exceptions: personal injury cases up to £50,000 Defamation cases	County Court or High Court County Court only High Court only	County Court or High Court Usually tried in court where case was commenced BUT cases for less than £25,000 are likely to be transferred to the County Court AND cases over £50,000 are likely to be transferred to High Court County Court can hear any value (even over £50,000) with the agreement of the parties

Figure 4.1 Starting and trying cases in the civil courts

ACTIVITY

Explain where the claims in the following situations may be started and tried.

1. A month ago Selina bought a washing machine for £350. It has developed several minor faults including a leak. Selina has complained to the store where she bought the machine. They have offered to replace it with another machine of the same model, but they refuse to refund her money. Selina wants to return the machine and claim its cost. Advise Selina as to which court she must start proceedings in and to which track the case is likely to allocated.

2. Tyler was seriously injured when a car mounted a pavement and hit him as he was waiting for a bus. He estimates his claim as being for about £85,000. Advise him as to which court(s) he may commence his claim in, the track to which it is likely to be allocated and in which court(s) it may be tried.

3. Victoria suffered minor injuries when a car in which she was a passenger crashed. She has been told that she is likely to get £12,000 in damages. Advise her as to which court she must start proceedings in and the track to which her case is likely to be allocated.

4. Wallace wishes to sue a local newspaper for defamation. He is prepared to limit his claim to £20,000. Advise him as to which court(s) he may commence his claim in, the track to which it is likely to be allocated and in which court(s) it may be tried.

5. Yves has had an extension built onto his house. The work has been done so badly that the foundations of the original house have been damaged and it has cost Yves £30,000 to put them right. Advise him as to which court(s) he may commence his claim in, the track to which it is likely to be allocated and in which court(s) it may be tried.

4.3 Problems in the civil justice system

During the second half of the twentieth century it was felt that taking a case to court was very expensive. There were also excessive delays, so that the average wait from issuing a claim in the County Court to the trial was three years, while for the High Court it was five years. Between 1950 and the year 2000, this problem of delay was considered on six occasions by different committees. These were:

- the Evershed Committee (1953)
- the Winn Committee (1968)
- the Cantley Committee (1979)
- the Civil Justice Review (1988)

- the Heilbron–Hodge Committee (1993) and
- the Woolf Review (1995–96).

The first three reports led to minor changes but these had little effect on the problems of delay and cost. The last three led to more major changes. In particular, the Woolf Report instituted the three-track system and a complete new set of Civil Procedure Rules. This has led to a change in attitude of litigants and lawyers, from an adversarial stance of the two parties in a case to a more co-operative one.

4.3.1 The Civil Justice Review

The Civil Justice Review produced five consultation papers on different types of civil claim, covering personal injuries, small claims, the Commercial Court, enforcement of debt and housing cases.

The Review thought that delay was a matter of public concern for the following reasons:

 (i) it caused personal stress, anxiety and financial hardship to claimants and their families

 (ii) these pressures often led claimants to accept low settlement offers

(iii) delay reduced the availability of evidence and eroded the reliability of the evidence which was available

(iv) delay meant that compensation was delayed until long after it was needed

 (v) it lowered public estimation of the legal system.

A major recommendation of the Civil Justice Review was that there should be no upper limit on the jurisdiction of the County Court. This was given effect through s 1 of the Courts and Legal Services Act 1990 which gave the Lord Chancellor power to confer jurisdiction on the County Courts and to allocate business between the High Court and the County Courts. And in 1991 the Lord Chancellor exercised this power to remove the upper limit on the County Court.

The Civil Justice Review also proposed various changes to combat delay, but virtually none of them were adopted immediately after the Review. Some of them on the timetable of cases were repeated in the Woolf Report and subsequently brought into effect. These were:

- laying down and enforcing a strict timetable for larger cases
- giving court administrators targets for trials
- the court taking control of the timetable.

4.3.2 The Heilbron–Hodge Committee

The Heilbron Committee was set up by the Law Society and the Bar Council. The fact that the legal professions took this step underlines the dissatisfaction with the civil justice system. The Heilbron Committee, which reported in 1993, started with the concept that:

> **Q** 'It is axiomatic that in any free and democratic society all citizens should be equal before the law. This means that all litigants, rich and poor, however large or however small is the subject matter of their litigation, should have access to a fair and impartial system of disputes resolution.'

The Committee thought that the existing court procedures were 'unnecessarily technical, inflexible, rule-ridden, formalistic and often incomprehensible to the ordinary litigant'. They also pointed out that fear of the cost of litigation deterred people from using the courts, and that most people want their dispute resolved rather than have their 'day in court'.

One of the Committee's main recommendations was that the court should take over control of cases. It said:

> **Q** 'Litigants and their lawyers need to have imposed upon them, within sensible procedural time-frames, an obligation to prosecute and defend their proceedings with efficiency and despatch. Therefore, once the process of the court is invoked, the court should have a more active and responsible role over the progress and conduct of cases.
>
> *Civil Justice on Trial – the Case for Change* (1992), p 6, para 1.8(ii)

Many of their recommendations were aimed at simplifying procedures and some of these were put into effect by Practice Directions which were issued to all three divisions of the High Court in 1995.

Other recommendations were more far-reaching. These included a recommendation that the Queen's Bench Division and the Chancery Division of the High Court should be merged into one single division, but this solution was not adopted. Other recommendations were that more High Court judges should be appointed; this was aimed both at avoiding the long waiting time for a case to be heard and at the over-use of Deputy High Court judges. This recommendation was implemented by the Lord Chancellor's Department and over the period from 1993 to 2003 the number of High Court judges was increased from 60 to 73.

4.4 The Woolf Report

This enquiry was headed by Lord Justice Woolf. It started its deliberations in 1994 with an Interim Report being published in 1995 and a final report in 1996. It built on many of the recommendation of the Civil Justice Review and the Heilbron–Hodge Report. As in that report, Lord Woolf highlighted the lack of court control over cases when he wrote in his report:

> **Q** 'In particular there is no clear judicial responsibility for managing individual cases or for the overall administration of the civil courts.'
>
> Interim Report of the Woolf Report *Inquiry into Civil Justice, Access to Justice* (1995), p 7, para 1

Lord Woolf also considered whether the High Court and the County Court should be amalgamated to form one civil court but concluded that this was not necessary provided that there was flexibility between the courts. He said:

> **Q** '6. I have therefore considered whether to recommend the unification of the two courts. This would be an advance since it would produce a single, vertically integrated court. However, very much the same result could be achieved if the movement towards aligning the jurisdiction of the county courts and the High Court was continued and the powers of Circuit judges were to be extended. This would make it generally unnecessary to identify the criteria which mark the boundary between the jurisdiction.'
>
> Interim Report of the Woolf *Inquiry into Civil Justice, Access to Justice* (1995)

The Interim Report proposed:

- extending small claims up to £3,000; this was brought into effect immediately and later extended to £5,000
- a new fast track for straightforward cases up to £10,000; when the track system came into force in 1999, some four years after the Interim Report, the upper limit was set at £15,000
- a new multi-track for cases over £10,000 (£15,000) with capping of costs
- encouraging the use of ADR
- giving judges more responsibility for managing cases
- more use of information technology
- simpler documents and procedures.

The final Woolf Report *Access to Justice* was published in July 1996. This extended the ideas of the interim report and set out key objectives which were:

- parties to be encouraged to explore alternatives to a court resolution of a dispute
- a single set of rules governing proceedings in the High Court and the County Court

- a shorter timetable for cases to reach court and for length of trials
- more affordable litigation.

4.4.1 The track system

The track system was a key component of the Woolf Report. The intention of it is that cases should be dealt with in a way that is proportionate to the value of the claim and the importance of the issues in the case. Prior to the Woolf reforms it was found that for smaller claims the costs of cases were often higher that the value of the claim. By increasing the limit on the amount that could be dealt with as a small claim and introducing the fast track for intermediate value claims it was hoped that the cost would be considerably reduced.

The emphasis on case management in multi-track was also aimed at reducing cost and delay. Lord Woolf pointed out:

<table>
<tr>
<td>**Q**</td>
<td>"14. The new multi-track will itself straddle the High Court and the county courts. Within it cases will be handled by High Court judges, Circuit judges, Masters and District judges. The courts, through the procedural judges, will have responsibility for ensuring that cases are dealt with at the appropriate level.'</td>
</tr>
</table>

4.4.2 Civil procedure

The Woolf Report led to a completely new set of Civil Procedure Rules (CPR). These form a single procedural code so that the same rules apply in both the High Court and the County Court. The general objectives in making or altering the CPR are set out in s 1(3) of the Civil Procedure Act 1997 as amended by the Courts Act 2003. This states that:

's 1(3) Any power to make or alter Civil Procedure Rules is to be exercised with a view to securing that–

(a) the system of civil justice is accessible, fair and efficient, and

(b) the rules are both simple and simply expressed.'

Within the CPR, r 1.1 sets out that the overriding objective of the CPR is to enable courts to deal with cases justly. Rule 1.2 explains that this includes:

(a) ensuring that the parties are on an equal footing

(b) saving expense

(c) dealing with the case in ways which are proportionate to:

- the amount of money involved

- the importance of the case
- the complexity of the issues and
- the financial position of each party

(d) ensuring that it is dealt with expeditiously and fairly and

(e) allotting to it an appropriate share of the court's resources, while taking into account the need to allot resources to other cases.

4.4.3 Case management

As already seen, case management is an important feature in multi-track cases. Rule 1.4 of the CPR sets out what is involved in case management:

'r 1.4 (1) The court must further the overriding objective by actively managing cases.

(2) Active case management includes:

(a) encouraging the parties to co-operate with each other in the conduct of the proceedings;

(b) identifying the issues at an early stage:

(c) deciding promptly which issues need full investigation and trial and accordingly disposing summarily of the others;

(d) deciding the order in which issues are to be decided;

(e) encouraging the parties to use an alternative dispute resolution procedure if the court considers that appropriate and facilitating the use of such procedure;

(f) helping the parties settle the whole or part of the case;

(g) fixing timetables or otherwise controlling the progress of the case;

(h) considering whether the likely benefit of taking a particular step justify the cost of taking it;

(i) dealing with the case without the parties needing to attend court;

(j) making use of technology; and

(k) giving directions to ensure that the trial of a case proceeds quickly and efficiently.'

This is a very comprehensive list which allows judges to decide what is necessary for each particular case and giving wide powers to ensure that cases are dealt with properly.

4.4.4 Pre-action protocols

In order to make sure that parties have taken all necessary steps before staring a case, pre-action protocols for different types of claim have been produced, giving very clear guidance on what a

claimant needs to do. If a claimant does not adhere to these pre-action protocols then they may not be awarded their full costs at the end of the case, even though they win the case.

4.4.5 Encouraging ADR

Rule 1.4(2)(e) of the CPR states that the court must encourage the parties to use an alternative dispute resolution (ADR) procedure if the court considers that appropriate and, if so, facilitate the use of such procedure. Although the rule only states that the court should encourage ADR, the courts have taken a tough line. In *R (Cowl and others) v Plymouth City Council* [2001] EWCA Civ 1935 the Court of Appeal held that judicial review proceedings about the closure of an old people's home should be allowed to go ahead if a significant part of the issues could be resolved by ADR. Lord Woolf, giving judgment, said:

> **J** 'the importance of this appeal is that it illustrates that, even that disputes between public authorities and members of the public for whom they are responsible, sufficient attention is paid to the paramount importance of avoiding litigation whenever that is possible'.

He stated that if necessary the court might have to hold, on its own initiative, an inter-parties hearing in which the parties could explain what steps they had taken to resolve the dispute without involvement of the court. This placed the lawyers on both sides under a heavy obligation to use ADR unless it really proved impossible.

The Court of Appeal showed the same tough attitude to the use of ADR instead of litigation in *Dunnett v Railtrack plc (in administration)* [2002] EWCA Civ 303; [2002] 2 All ER 850 where the court applied cost penalties for a failure to use ADR. What had happened was that the claimant had been granted leave to appeal, but in giving leave the trial judge advised both parties that they should consider the use of ADR. The defendant declined to mediate. On the hearing of the appeal the claimant's appeal was dismissed but the defendant was not awarded costs, because of their refusal to try ADR. Brooke LJ said:

> **J** 'It is hoped that publicity will draw the attention of lawyers to their duties to further the overriding objective . . . and to the possibility that, if they turn down out of hand the chance of alternative dispute resolution when suggested by the court, as happened on this occasion, they may have to face uncomfortable cost consequences.'

This case was the first time that a successful party was refused costs because they declined to mediate.

In *Cable & Wireless plc v IBM United Kingdom Ltd* (2002) EWHC 303 the judge held that a contractual term providing for mandatory ADR in the event of a dispute was capable of being enforced by a stay of any proceedings. However, this could only happen if there was sufficient certainty as to what type of ADR procedure should be used. The court stressed the overriding objective of the CPR and also the encouragement of ADR in case management under r 1.4(2)(e).

This very hard line on the use of ADR was considered as going beyond 'encouraging' ADR. Indeed, Khawar Qureshi, in an article 'Doors of the High Court are opened by fewer and fewer', *The Times*, 27th April 2004, pointed out that it could violate Art 6 of the European Convention on Human Rights – the right to a fair trial. The matter was considered further by the courts in the conjoined appeals of *Halsey v Milton Keynes General NHS Trust* and *Steel v Joy and another* [2004] EWCA Civ 576. In this case the Law Society was joined as an interested party and put forward arguments on the point of when ADR should be used. The Court of Appeal stressed the distinction between encouraging mediation strongly and ordering it and said that:

> **J** '. . . to oblige truly unwilling parties to refer their disputes to mediation would be to impose an unacceptable obstruction on their right of access to the courts.'

Lord Justice Lawton set out the relevant factors to be considered in deciding whether to impose a costs penalty for refusal to try ADR. He started by pointing out that an order to deprive a successful party of some or all of his costs because that party had refused to agree to ADR was an exception to the general rule that costs should follow the event. The burden was on the unsuccessful party to show why there should be a departure from the general rule. Relevant factors to be considered in such cases were:

- the nature of the dispute: some cases were unsuitable for ADR; these included cases where there was a point of law or interpretation in issue, claims involving fraud and cases where there was a claim for an injunction
- the merits of the case: where a party reasonably believes that they have a watertight case then they may be justified in refusing to use ADR
- previous attempts to settle by other methods: although parties should realised that mediation often succeeded where other attempts to settle had failed
- the cost of mediation: this is particularly important where the amount being claimed is relatively small
- delay: if mediation was suggested late in the case and would have the effect of delaying the trial then that was a good reason for refusing ADR
- whether mediation had a reasonable prospect of success.

So, the present position is that the court will continue to strongly encourage the use of ADR, while recognising that there are circumstances in which a refusal to attempt ADR is justified.

4.4.6 Strict timetables

One of the key points of case management is that the courts should set timetables for the parties, and that these timetables should be strictly enforced. This has been done with a strictness that sometimes seems out of proportion.

CASE EXAMPLE

Vinos v Marks and Spencer plc [2001] 3 All ER 784

The claimant had suffered injuries at work. His solicitor negotiated with the defendants over a long period of time but no settlement was reached. A week before the expiry of the limitation period for issuing proceedings the solicitor issued a claim, but because of an oversight did not serve it on the defendants until nine days after the four-month period set out in the Civil Procedure Rules for serving claims. The claimant applied for an extension of time to serve the proceedings. The Court of Appeal refused to give this.

It is noticeable in this case that the Court of Appeal was not prepared to apply r 3.10 of the CPR which provides that 'where there has been an error of procedure such as failure to comply with a rule or practice direction (a) the error does not invalidate any step taken in the proceedings unless the court so orders; and (b) the court may make an order to remedy the error'. The Court of Appeal held that the general words of this rule did not allow it to extend the period for service.

Later in the same year (2001) the Court of Appeal made another strict decision on time limits in *Godwin v Swindon Borough Council* [2001] EWCA Civ 1478; [2001] 4 All ER 641.

CASE EXAMPLE

Godwin v Swindon Borough Council [2001] EWCA Civ 1478; [2001] 4 All ER 641

The claim form actually arrived at the defendants in time but the 'deeming' provision in r 6.7(1) of the CPR meant that it was deemed to have arrived three days late. Even though there was evidence that it had arrived in time, the court ruled that the service of the claim was out of time and refused to remedy the situation. Again, the court refused to use other provisions in the CPR which would have allowed the case to go ahead. In particular, the court refused to use r 6.9 of the CPR which gives the court power to dispense with service altogether, as it felt that that would condone the failure to comply with the express terms of the rule about service.

In the next year the same point about service occurred in *Anderton v Clwyd County Council* [2002] EWCA Civ 933; [2002] 3 All ER 813 which involved five separate appeals on the point. The

Court of Appeal again held that the deemed date of service under r 6.7(1) of the CPR could not be rebutted by evidence that the claim form had in fact been received earlier (and within the time for service). However, unlike in the case of *Godwin v Swindon Borough Council* (2001), they were prepared to use their power under r 6.9 of the CPR to dispense with service altogether. The court held that this could be done in exceptional circumstances where there had been an attempt to serve within the time limit, even though this was not successful.

However, in *Cranfield v Bridgegrove Ltd* [2003] EWCA Civ 656; [2003] 3 All ER 129, where the same point was again considered by the Court of Appeal, the court held that the principle established in *Godwin* (2001) was important. The court would only exercise its power to dispense with service under r 6.9 of the CPR in truly exceptional cases. The court would not normally exercise its discretion where there had been late service. So it can be seen that the time limits set down in the CPR are enforced very strictly.

4.4.7 Judgment in default and summary judgment

In cases where the defendant fails to file either an acknowledgement of service or a defence within the time limits, the claimant can normally ask the court to give judgment in the case in his favour. This is known as a default judgment. This means that the case ends at this point with a judgment for the claimant. However, the default judgment can be set aside if it was obtained in breach of the technical rules or if the defendant can show that he has a real prospect of successfully defending the claim or if it appears to the court that there is some other good reason why the default judgment should be set aside.

Summary judgment

This is where the defendant has both acknowledged service and filed a defence within the correct time limits, but the defence does not reveal a real defence. In such cases the court has power to give summary judgment for the claimant (Pt 24 of the CPR). This can be done where the claimant applies for summary judgment or where the court identifies the case as being one where there is no real defence. The test applied by the court is whether the defendant has a real prospect of success.

It is also possible for the court to strike out a claim if it discloses no reasonable grounds for bringing the case.

4.4.8 Part 36 offers to settle

Under the CPR both the defendant and the claimant can make an official offer to settle the case. Prior to the Woolf reforms, only the defendant could do this by making a payment into court. If the claimant was then awarded less than the amount paid in, the claimant had to pay the defendant's costs of the case. Part 36 allows the court more discretion on what costs order should be made where there has been a Pt 36 offer.

Part 36 offers have proved popular with both claimants and defendants and frequently lead to the case been settled.

4.4.9 Are the Woolf reforms a success?

Lord Woolf thought that a civil justice system should:

- be just in the results it delivers
- be fair in the way it treats litigants
- offer appropriate procedures at a reasonable cost
- deal with cases at a reasonable speed
- be understandable to those who use it
- provide as much certainty as the nature of particular cases allows
- be effective, adequately resourced and organised.

In fact, the great majority of civil legal disputes do not even get as far as lawyers, let alone into the courts. In 1984 the Oxford Socio-Legal Centre published research into personal injury cases (D Harris *et al, Compensation and Support for Illness and Injury* (Clarendon Press, 1984). This study was based on a national household survey which produced a random sample of 1,711 victims of accidents who had suffered some impairment for at least two weeks after their accident. Only 26 per cent of these had even considered claiming damages. Fourteen per cent had actually consulted a solicitor and most of these (12 per cent of the original sample some 182 cases) had received damages. Of the 12 per cent where damages were obtained, in two in five cases a claim had been issued in the courts, but there was a court hearing in only five cases. This represented 2.7 per cent of the 182 who obtained damages, but only 0.2 per cent of the total sample of 1,711.

In 1999 Hazel Genn published a study (*Paths to Justice* (Hart Publishing, 1999)) in which she had surveyed 4,125 randomly selected adults to find out what experience they had had of any legal problems. She found that two out of every five people had experienced a problem which could have led to litigation. About 60 per cent of these tried to resolve the problem with advice; about one-third tried to resolve it without advice; and about 5 per cent did nothing. Although people sought advice, they were unlikely to use the courts to resolve their dispute. Only two out of ten cases used legal proceedings or contacted an Ombudsman. In many of these cases the people in the survey had had cases taken against them. So very few of those in the survey actually took proceedings.

If the civil justice system was cheaper, quicker and simpler, one would expect that more people would be prepared to consider litigation if they could not achieve a satisfactory conclusion to their dispute by other means.

Fewer cases

In fact the number of cases heard at first instance has decreased. This trend started following the Civil Justice Review 1985 and the Courts and Legal Services Act 1990 which made major changes to the distribution of work between the High Court and the County Court. The trend has continued following the Woolf reforms.

Year	1990	1994	1998	1999	2000	2001	2002	2003
Number of cases commenced in Queen's Bench Division	350,000	157,453	114,984	72,161	26,876	21,613	18,624	14,191
Number of money claims commenced in the County Court	3,034,923	2,487,377	2,010,606	1,760,308	1,631,966	1,502,879	1,395,754	1,354,446

Figure 4.2 Number of cases commenced in the Queen's Bench Division and the County Court

There was a slight increase in County Court claims in the early 1990s, with the removal of the upper limit in that court. However, as the table in Figure 4.2 shows, the overall trend is for fewer and fewer cases to be started.

This can be interpreted in two opposing ways. The first is that more cases are settled through negotiation and so fewer cases are started in the courts. This view would suggest that the Woolf reforms have been a success, as one of the changes in 'culture' that Lord Woolf wanted to bring about was that disputants should view litigation as a last resort and disputes should be settled by non-court means. The second point of view is that there are fewer cases because people increasingly perceive court proceedings as being slow, costly and complex. If this is the reason for the reducing numbers of cases then the Woolf reforms have failed in their objectives.

Research

There has been relatively little research into the effect of the Woolf reforms. The only substantial study carried out is *More Civil Justice? The impact of the Woolf reforms on pre-action behaviour* by Tamara Goriely, Richard Moorhead and Pamela Abrams (May 2002) which was published jointly by the Law Society and the Civil Justice Council. This study concentrated on pre-action behaviour and pre-action protocols and was based on interviews with 54 solicitors dealing with personal injury cases, clinical negligence cases or housing repair cases. The study found that in all three markets claimant work was concentrated in fewer, more specialist solicitor firms. This was mainly the result of Legal Services Commission policy rather than the Woolf reforms.

The study focused on fast-track cases. It showed:

- a less adversarial culture
- a greater willingness to 'put cards on the table'
- Part 36 offers are popular
- insurance companies are more prepared to settle

BUT

- in personal injury cases front-loading of work means that costs have gone up

131

- generally the ratio of costs to damages remains the same as pre-Woolf – 68 per cent

- delay has not improved because solicitors do more work before opening proper negotiations (because of the tight timetables once cases are started)

- overall the average time for settlement in personal injury cases was 13 months (similar to pre-Woolf) but the minimum time is longer, mainly because getting medical reports takes longer than before.

The study also found that there were problems in other areas, in particular inconsistent case management by judges and difficulties with conditional fee agreements.

A study, *Further funding: A continuing evaluation of the Civil Justice Reforms* (LCD, August 2002) stated that the time between issue and hearing for small claims had risen slightly but 'may now be falling'. On costs the study concludes that there is 'conflicting evidence' and many of the claims for more expense are 'anecdotal'.

Suzanne Burn considered all the available evidence in *The Woolf Reforms in Retrospect* (2003) Legal Action (8). She points out that it is difficult to isolate 'the Woolf factor' because there are a number of other factors that came into effect either at the same time as the Woolf reforms or within a short time afterwards. These include:

- the withdrawal of legal aid from certain types of civil claim, in particular personal injury cases

- the widening of the scope of conditional fee agreement together with the ability to recover success fees and insurance premiums (see Chapter 7 for detailed information)

- the introduction of tougher standards and controls by both the Law Society and the Legal Services Commission

- the implementation of the Human Rights Act 1998 in October 2000.

With the overlapping effects of these other changes and also the fact that there is only limited empirical research, Burn points out that measuring the success or otherwise of the Woolf Reforms is difficult. However, she does state:

> 'Certainly the total volume of litigation has fallen since April 1999. But this was a well-established trend going back many years. The rate of settlement between issue and trial has also increased . . . and anecdotally the number of fast track trials, in particular, has dropped sharply in many courts. But the time taken for cases to get to trial has surprisingly improved very little post-April 1999 . . . A factor in this is almost certainly the continuing under-resourcing of many County Courts which causes delays in issuing, allocation, listing and production of orders.'

Burn also highlights other areas where there are still problems. These include the fact that the new Civil Procedure Rules are very lengthy and too many amendments have been issued – some 32 amendments in four years, at the time Burn was writing. There is also the fact that small claims listings seem to have suffered as priority has been given to fast-track and multi-track conferences and trials. Increases in court fees and problems in the enforcement of judgments may also have played a part in reducing the number of small claims cases. In multi-track cases some practitioners told Burn that they had doubts about the usefulness of case management, with some claiming that case management 'takes extra time and cost, but adds little value'. The main complaints were that conferences were not arranged efficiently and judges often had not read the papers in advance.

Lack of IT

Lord Woolf's recommendations included that more use should be made of IT to make the court system more efficient. Burn feels very strongly that 'the lack of investment in the civil courts, particularly the County Courts is greatly handicapping the development of an accessible, efficient, modern civil justice system in England and Wales'.

This point was also made by Lord Justice Brooke in May 2003. In a speech at a seminar in Leeds he said:

> 'Far and away our greatest need is to introduce software systems which will enable court staff and judges to manage court business better in the civil and family courts. Today the courts are not networked . . . we are miles behind most government departments and modern private sector businesses . . . At present we rely on paper filing systems. It is not always easy to retain and motivate staff when files go missing, or get into a muddle quite so often. Nowadays court users have every reason to complain about some of the delays and inefficiencies that occur.'

Critics

One of the main critics of the Woolf reforms throughout has been Professor Zander. From 1995 onwards he has published articles and essays pointing out likely problems in the approach taken by Lord Woolf. See *The Woolf Report: Forwards or Backwards for the new Lord Chancellor* (1997) 16 Civil Justice Quarterly Review, pp 208–227. With evidence now emerging that the reforms have not been as successful as hoped, Zander wrote that he:

> 'remains of the view that on balance the disadvantages of the reforms outweigh the advantages. He believes that if Lord Woolf had presented his package of reforms with an admission that, in addition to the great upheaval involved, they would end by costing most litigants more, that they would not greatly reduce delays (if at all) and that they would hugely increase uncontrollable judicial discretion, it is doubtful whether they would have been implemented.'

M Zander, *Cases and materials on the English Legal System* (9th edn, LexisNexis Butterworths, 2003), p 135

4.5 Enforcement of judgment

When the court awards damages to the claimant, payment of those damages is due immediately unless the court has order payment by instalments or postponed payment for some reason, possibly pending an appeal. One of the main problems in litigation is that if the other party does not pay, it is left to the claimant to take steps to enforce the judgment; the courts will not intervene unless the claimant initiates enforcement proceedings. However, the court does have various powers which can be used.

Oral examination

If the other party is an individual it is likely that the claimant will have no knowledge of his financial resources. In order to try to discover what assets the debtor has, the claimant can apply to the court for an order that the judgment debtor be orally examined before the court about his means. This allows both a court official and the applicant to cross-examine the debtor to try to discover if he is working and, if so, who his employers are and whether he owns property or has a bank account or any investments. Once this information is known it is easier to decide the most appropriate way of enforcing the judgment.

Warrant of execution

This is where the claimant applies for an order that the court enforcement officer seize goods belonging to the debtor and then sell them to raise money to pay the judgment. This is the most common way of trying to enforce a judgment.

Attachment of earnings

If the debtor is working in regular employment, then it is possible to have an order made under the Attachment of Earnings Act 1971. This orders the debtor's employer to deduct money from the debtor's wages each week and send that money to the court. The court will decide a figure for the 'protected earnings' of the debtor, and the employer can only deduct from above that figure so that the debtor is left with enough money for essential living expenses.

Third-party debt orders

Where the debtor has a bank account or a savings account, or where the debtor is owed money by a third party, the claimant can ask the court to order the other party to pay enough of that money to the court to satisfy the judgment.

Bankruptcy proceedings

If the judgment is for more than £750 and a warrant of execution has already been issued without success, then the claimant may apply for the debtor to be declared bankrupt. If this occurs the debtor's assets are divided among his creditors in proportion to the amount owed to them.

Unpaid judgments

Despite all these methods of enforcement, some judgments will remain unpaid. Indeed, the claimant may well have incurred extra court costs in trying to enforce the judgment. This is particularly true of small claims. There is a register in which judgments which have not been paid can be entered. The judicial statistics show that, in 2002, 814,824 County Court judgments were entered. Only 146,325 had been paid in full by the end of the year, with another 75,212 being cancelled. These figures show that the majority of successful claimants do not receive the full amount of damages awarded to them.

John Baldwin in his report, *Evaluating the effectiveness of enforcement procedures in undefended claims in the civil courts*, made the following points about the problems with enforcement:

- it was the most critical issue confronting the civil courts at the time of his report (March 2003)
- the system needs to be overhauled otherwise public confidence in the civil courts will be undermined
- the key to improving enforcement is to ensure that courts have adequate information about the financial circumstances of defendants.

The Government has consulted widely on the problem of enforcement and issued a White Paper, *Effective enforcement*, in March 2003. This suggested that there should be a register of judgment debts which included both High Court and County Court judgments. This was put into force by s 98 of the Courts Act 2003. The White Paper also stated that it is important to improve the quality and quantity of information available on which creditors can base their decisions on which is the best method of enforcement to use in any particular case. This would also make it possible to identify at an earlier stage those debtors who do not have the resources with which to pay the debt and so help creditors to avoid wasting money trying to enforce a judgment. To enable the necessary information to be obtained it is proposed to introduce a data disclosure order. When a creditor applies to the court for such an order, the court will seek information from third parties such as the Inland Revenue, financial institutions and credit reference agencies. This will provide much wider and more accurate information about the defendant's financial position than the current method which relies on the information given by the defendant.

ACTIVITY

Self-assessment questions

1. Identify five differences between civil and criminal cases.
2. What is meant by a court of first instance?
3. Name the three divisions of the High Court.
4. Name the tracks in civil cases and give the financial limits of each.

CONTINUED ▶

5. What report published in 1996 led to major changes in the civil justice system, including the establishing of the track system?

6. What were the key objectives set out in that report?

7. Explain what is involved in case management.

8. What are the advantages and disadvantages of pre-action protocols?

9. What has been the courts' approach to time limits in cases?

10. In what ways is enforcement going to be improved?

4.6 Tribunals

Tribunals operate alongside the court system and have become an important and integral part of the legal system. They have been referred to as the third pillar of the legal system – the administrative justice pillar: the civil justice system and the criminal justice system being the other two pillars. It should be noted that the parties in tribunal cases cannot go to court to resolve their dispute. This is different to the use of alternative dispute resolution procedures (ADR) where the parties decide to use ADR instead of using the courts (see section 4.7). For tribunal cases the appropriate tribunal must be used.

It was mainly the development of the welfare state after 1945 that led to the creation of administrative tribunals. It was necessary to have a system that gave people a way of challenging administrative decisions made, usually by government departments, and thus allow individuals to have full access to the various rights given them under the welfare state and other legislation. There are also what are known as domestic tribunals which are set up by private bodies to resolve their own internal disputes. These are explained in section 4.6.6.

4.6.1 Administrative tribunals

These are tribunals that have been created by statute. As already stated, their main function is to resolve disputes between private individuals and government departments, usually in respect of a decision made by a department. This gives individuals a way of ensuring that any rights which have been granted through social, welfare, employment and other legislation are protected. There are many different rights. These may be related to social security, such as the right to a mobility allowance for those who are too disabled to walk more than a very short distance. Or they may be related to employment, for example the right to a payment if one is made redundant from work. There are also rights in education such as the right not to be excluded unnecessarily from school. There are also rights which are part of our basic human rights, for example the right not to be discriminated against because of one's sex, race or disability or the right not to be held in a mental hospital unnecessarily or the right of immigrants to have a claim for political asylum heard. Others are concerned with more technical points, such as the level of compensation payable when land has been compulsorily purchased; or appeals against the refusal to grant a licence in respect of chemical weapons. These are just a few examples; there are many more.

Since tribunals have been set up as the welfare state has developed, new developments will often result in the creation of a new tribunal. For example, following the Child Support Act in 1995, the Child Support Appeals Tribunal was created. Also the development of new techniques in fertilisation of human cells led to the need to regulate what could be done and the Human Fertilisation and Embryology Authority was set up to hear appeals on decisions in respect of this. There are now over 70 different types of tribunal and many of these will have panels sitting at several places around the country. There are over 2,000 tribunals in total and they hear about one million cases each year.

4.6.2 Composition and procedure

Since the different tribunals have been set up at different times over a number of years, they do not all operate in the same way. The Council on Tribunals has issued model rules for tribunals to follow but, despite this, there are differences between tribunals both in the size of panel and in the procedure used.

Panels

In many tribunals the decision is made by a single person. However, in other tribunals there is a panel of three; a legally qualified chairman and two lay members who have expertise in the particular field of the tribunal. For example, the lay members of an Industrial Injuries Tribunal would be medically qualified while those on an Employment Tribunal hearing an unfair dismissal claim would be representatives of organisations for employers and employees respectively. Surveyors sit on the Lands Tribunal and tax experts sit as Special Commissioners of income tax. The Leggatt Report 2001 (see section 4.6.4) thought lay members, whether they had expert knowledge or not, should sit as part of a tribunal panel only if they have a particular function to fulfil.

Procedure

The procedure for each type of tribunal also tends to vary but there are common elements in that the system is designed to encourage individuals to bring their own cases and not use lawyers. Generally there are no formal rules of evidence and procedure but the rules of natural justice apply. This means that both parties must be given an equal chance to state their side. Employment Tribunals are the most formal and their procedure is similar to that of a court. Other tribunals operate in a more informal way, but the variation in procedure can be confusing. The Leggatt Report found that:

Q	'1.23 At the hearings, users can experience some quite old-fashioned processes. Examples include a legal representative reading out in full a paper submission which is already in front of all the parties; witnesses

CONTINUED ▶

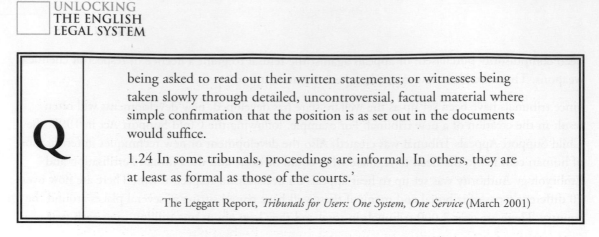

> being asked to read out their written statements; or witnesses being taken slowly through detailed, uncontroversial, factual material where simple confirmation that the position is as set out in the documents would suffice.
>
> 1.24 In some tribunals, proceedings are informal. In others, they are at least as formal as those of the courts.'
>
> The Leggatt Report, *Tribunals for Users: One System, One Service* (March 2001)

As applicants at tribunals are encouraged to bring the cases themselves without the use of lawyers, legal aid is not normally available for most tribunal hearings, but there are some exceptions where it is, such as for an application to the Mental Health Review Tribunal where the applicant's liberty is in question.

4.6.3 Advantages and disadvantages of tribunals

Tribunals were set up to prevent the overloading of the courts with the extra cases that social, employment and other rights claims would generate. In 1979 the Benson Commission on Legal Services pointed out the importance of the role of tribunals in this respect as it heard six times the number of cases dealt with by the courts. This trend has continued with the largest numbers of cases being in respect of immigration and employment. In 2002 the Judicial Statistics show that there were over 84,000 appeals to the Immigration Adjudicators. Other tribunals have a much smaller workload, for example the Transport Tribunal which hears appeals and application in respect of licences for heavy goods operators and public service vehicles received only 280 cases in 2002.

For the applicant in tribunal cases the advantages are that such cases are dealt with more cheaply, more quickly, and more informally than they would be if there were a court hearing. There is also the fact that the panel is often composed of a mix of legal expertise and lay expertise in the field concerned. However all these claims need to be evaluated.

Cost-effectiveness

As applicants are encouraged to represent themselves and not use lawyers, it is true to say that tribunal hearings do not normally involve the costs associated with court hearings. It is also rare for an order for costs to be made by a tribunal, so that an applicant need not fear a large bill if they lose the case. However, applicants who are not represented have a lower chance of winning their case than those who are represented, so the saving on the cost of a lawyer may not be that cost effective. Hazel Genn, in *The Effectiveness of Representation at Tribunals* (1989), found that the success rate for those with lawyers was 49 per cent, while for those without lawyers it was 28 per cent. She also discovered that applicants lost most often when they appeared without representation against a legally represented respondent. She found that representation had an effect on the amount awarded in successful cases. The mean amount of award made in her study was £1,084 in cases where the applicant had legal representation, but only £449 in cases where the applicant received no advice from any source.

Speedy hearings

This was one of the original advantages of tribunal hearings but it is no longer true to say that cases will be dealt with speedily. Successive reports by the Council on Tribunals have highlighted delays. These are caused by the vast volume of work that tribunals now face, together with the fact that any lay members sit only part-time. The use of lay members creates a particular problem if the case is complex and likely to last several days as it can lead to proceedings being spread over separate days several weeks apart. An extreme example of delay was seen in the case of *Darnell v United Kingdom*, *The Times*, 24th November 1993 in which a doctor who was dismissed in 1984 started proceedings for unfair dismissal. The final decision in those proceedings was made nine years later in 1993 by the Employment Appeal Tribunal. In the meantime the doctor had complained to the European Court of Human Rights over the delay and this complaint was upheld.

Simple procedure

It is true that there is a more informal hearing than in court. In addition, most cases are heard in private. These comments do not apply to Employment Tribunals which are open to the public and tend to be more formal. The procedure is also relatively flexible and the tribunals are not bound by strict rules of evidence. However, for individuals presenting their own cases the venue is unfamiliar and the procedure can be confusing. The Leggatt Report highlighted the point that users may be disconcerted if the proceedings are totally unstructured, because they are then uncertain when to bring in particular points.

Where applicants are not represented the chairman is expected to take an inquisitorial role and help to establish the points that the applicant wishes to make. This ideal is not always achieved, as shown by research into social security cases carried out by Baldwin, Wikeley and Young in their study, *Judging Social Security*, published in 1992. They found that of the hearings they attended, the chairman's handling of the case could be described as 'good' or 'excellent' in 57 per cent of cases and 'adequate' in a further quarter of cases. However, in one-sixth of cases the chairman's conduct was open to serious criticism. This type of criticism has also been levelled at Employment Tribunals. In these cases an applicant in person may often find themselves opposed by a lawyer representing the employer, and so it is even more important that the proceedings should be kept simple and that the chairman should act inquisitorially to redress the balance.

The problem of the unrepresented applicant comes about because legal aid is not available for most tribunals. This may put an applicant at a disadvantage if the other side (often a government department or an employer) uses a lawyer.

Impartiality

There used to be a criticism that the chairmen of tribunals were not sufficiently impartial as they were in many cases appointed by the Minister of the government department against whom the case was being brought. This problem was highlighted by the Franks Committee (1957) which

recommended that all appointments should be impartial. Now the system is that the Council on Tribunals recommends potential chairmen to the Lord Chancellor. The Lord Chancellor then decides which people will be placed on a panel of chairmen for tribunal hearings. Despite this there is still a close connection in some instances between the tribunal and its sponsoring department. The Leggatt Report pointed out that some appointments are 'vulnerable to challenge under the Human Rights Act'. This is because there could be a breach of Art 6 of the European Convention on Human Rights on the right to a fair hearing if the chairman is too closely linked to the department against which the case is being brought.

Other problems

Another problem is that few tribunals follow a system of precedent, which makes it difficult to predict the outcome of cases. The criticisms do not apply to Employment Tribunals where precedent is followed. In addition, there is a problem as some tribunals still do not have to give reasons for their decisions. However, in the case of the vast majority of tribunals, the reasons for the decision must be given if requested (s 10 of the Tribunals and Inquiries Act 1992). Finally, there is no right of appeal from some tribunals (although an application for judicial review may be made). However this problem has lessened as a final appeal on a point of law has been brought in for both social security cases and immigration cases.

4.6.4 The Leggatt Report

In March 2001, Sir Andrew Leggatt's Report on tribunals, *Tribunals for Users: One System, One Service*, was published. This was the first review of tribunals since the Franks Inquiry in 1957.

The four main objects identified by the Leggatt Report were:

- the 70 or so tribunals should be made into one tribunals system
- the tribunals should be made independent of the relevant government department
- the training of chairmen and other members of tribunals should be improved
- the system should be such that it will enable users to participate effectively and without apprehension in tribunal proceedings.

A main recommendation was that the administration of tribunals should become the responsibility of the Lord Chancellor. (Note that the report was made before the proposal to abolish the Lord Chancellor's post and, if this happens, presumably the Secretary of State for Constitutional Affairs would be given the responsibility if the recommendations are carried out.) In fact, in March 2003 the then Lord Chancellor, having consulted on the findings of the Leggatt Report, announced that a new Tribunals Service would be created, under the responsibility of the Lord Chancellor. It was proposed that this service would initially consist of the 10 most important tribunals. These were:

- the Appeals Service
- the Immigration Appellate Authority

- the Employment Tribunals Service
- the Criminal Injuries Compensation Appeals Panel
- the Mental Health Review Tribunal
- the Office for Social Security and Child Support Commissioners
- the Tax Tribunals
- the Special Educational Needs and Disability Tribunal
- the Pensions Appeal Tribunal and
- the Lands Tribunal.

The intention was that smaller tribunals would be brought into the Tribunals Service when it was appropriate. All these tribunals would be accountable to the Lord Chancellor (now the Secretary of State for Constitutional Affairs), rather than spread across a number of different government departments. It was intended to produce a White Paper on this change. However, this has not yet happened.

Although the Leggatt Report recommended there should be one 'overarching' Tribunal Service, it added that this should be divided by subject-matter into Divisions. This would prevent the current problem of the isolation of individual tribunals which leads to duplication of effort and each tribunal inventing its own processes and standards. The proposal was for nine subject divisions:

- immigration
- social security and pensions
- land and valuation
- financial including taxation
- transport
- health and social services
- education
- regulatory
- employment.

There should be a single route of appeal with a right of appeal by permission on a point of law or on the basis that the decision of the tribunal was unlawful; the appeal route should be from first-tier tribunals to an appellate tribunal for the particular division and from there to the Court of Appeal.

It also recommended that there should be a Tribunals Board directing the system whose functions should include advising the Lord Chancellor's Department (now the Department for Constitutional Affairs) on qualifications for chairmen, overseeing the appointment of members, co-ordinating their training and investigating complaints against them. It would also be responsible for recommending changes to the rules of procedure governing all Divisions. The Council on

Tribunals (see section 4.6.5) should be given an increased role with their primary duty being the championing of users' causes and its members should include some with the experience and perspective of users.

4.6.5 Control of tribunals

Since tribunals work outside the court system and are so varied in their procedures, it is important that there is a supervisory body. This was emphasised following what is called the Crichel Down Affair in the 1950s in which civil servants did not follow the correct procedure for offering land requisitioned during the Second World War for military purposes back to the family of the former owner. This matter was investigated by the Franks Committee which reported in 1957 and made several recommendations about decisions by civil servants and tribunals. One recommendation was that there should be an 'ombudsman' appointed to deal with complaints of maladministration and eventually the post of Parliamentary Ombudsman was set up in 1967. The Franks Committee also recommended that a Council on Tribunals should be set up to oversee the whole vast array of tribunals.

Following this, the Tribunals and Inquiries Act 1958 set up the Council on Tribunals to supervise and keep under review the working of tribunals. The Tribunals and Inquiries Act 1992 now governs the Council. Its members are appointed by the Lord Chancellor. The Council has up to 15 members who visit tribunals and observe their work at first hand. It also receives complaints about tribunals and issues an annual report. In its 44th Annual Report published in November 2003 it summarised its statement of purpose as follows:

> **Q** 'The purpose of the Council is to keep under review, and report on, the constitution and working of the tribunals under its supervision, and where necessary to consider and report on the administrative procedures of statutory inquiries.'

The Council seeks to ensure that tribunals and inquiries:

- are independent
- are open, fair and impartial
- are accessible to users
- have the needs of users as their primary focus
- offer cost-effective procedures
- are properly resourced and organised
- are responsive to the needs of all sections of society.

The main problem is that the Council has very little power; it can only make recommendations. The Council's website is at www.council-on-tribunals.gov.uk.

142

Control by the courts

This can occur in two ways. Firstly, there is an appeal system against the decisions of some tribunals. In particular there is a right of appeal from Employment Tribunals to the Employment Appeals Tribunal, which is headed by a High Court judge, and from there to the Court of Appeal. Similarly, in immigration cases, there is the Immigration Appeal Tribunal which hears appeals from decisions of Immigration Adjudicators and since 1993 there has been the right to appeal from the Immigration Appeal Tribunal to the Court of Appeal on a point of law. There is also a Social Security Appeals Tribunal to hear appeals in this area, with the possibility of a further appeal to the Social Security Commissioners and again an appeal can go from here to the Court of Appeal if there is a point of law at issue.

A formal route of appeal is in itself a safeguard and it also allows the Court of Appeal to develop the law on the basis of judicial precedent so that the law becomes more stable and predictable.

Secondly, the Queen's Bench Divisional Court has the power to hear applications for judicial review against tribunal decisions and can use its prerogative powers to quash a decision. This route should not normally be used where there is an appeal route available. However, it is the method to be used where there has been a breach of natural justice.

■ Key facts chart on administrative tribunals

KEY FACTS

Function	To resolve disputes between private individuals and government departments over decisions made by the department To allow private individuals to enforce their rights, eg under employment law
Types of tribunal	The Leggatt Report classified them into nine categories: immigration; social security and pensions; land and valuation; financial including taxation; transport; health and social services; education; regulatory; and employment
Panel	Panel of three: chairman and two lay members with expertise in the area OR One adjudicator

CONTINUED ▸

KEY FACTS

Procedure	Varies but must conform to the rules of natural justice Usually informal and in private Employment Tribunals use more formal procedure and are open to the public
Availability of publicly funded legal representation	Only available for a limited number of tribunals where the applicant's human rights are in issue, eg: • mental health review tribunals • Immigration Adjudicators
Appeals	Available for most tribunals. From Employment Tribunals; Social Security Tribunals; and Immigration Adjudicators there is an appeal to the appropriate Appeals Tribunal and from there to the Court of Appeal
Leggatt Review	Published March 2003 Recommended • one Tribunal System under the Lord Chancellor's responsibility • the Service to be divided into nine divisions and an appeal tribunal to be set up for each division
Control of tribunals	(1) The Council on Tribunals which reports and makes recommendations but has little power (2) The courts through the appeal system and judicial review

4.6.6 Domestic tribunals

These are effectively 'in-house' tribunals set up by private bodies, usually for their own internal disciplinary control. There are disciplinary tribunals to decide whether there has been a breach of professional conduct for professions and occupations including doctors, dentists, opticians, veterinary surgeons, osteopaths, accountants, solicitors, barristers and even footballers. There are also disciplinary committees for a wide range of other organisations including trade unions and universities. Each domestic tribunal must keep to the rules of natural justice and their decisions are subject to judicial review. In addition, for many professional disciplinary tribunals where the tribunal has decided to strike off a member from the professional register, there is an appeal route to the Judicial Committee of the Privy Council. For example, this applies to decisions of the disciplinary committee of the General Medical Council and also to other medical disciplinary tribunals.

4.7 ADR

Using the courts to resolve disputes can be costly, in terms of both money and time. It can also be traumatic for the individuals involved and it may not lead to the most satisfactory outcome for the case. An additional problem is that court proceedings are usually open to the public and the press, so there is nothing to stop the details of the case being published in local or national newspapers. It is not surprising, therefore, that more and more people and businesses are seeking other methods of resolving their disputes. Alternative methods are referred to as ADR which stands for 'Alternative Dispute Resolution'. This includes any method of resolving a dispute without resorting to using the courts. There are many different methods which can be used, ranging from very informal negotiations between the parties to a comparatively formal commercial arbitration hearing. The four main methods are:

- negotiation
- mediation
- conciliation and
- arbitration.

4.7.1 Negotiation

Negotiation is the quickest and cheapest method of settling a dispute. It also has the advantage of being completely private. Anyone who has a dispute with another person can always try to resolve it by negotiating directly with them. If the parties cannot come to an agreement, they may decide to take the step of instructing trained negotiators. Even where the parties have referred the matter to their solicitors, it is usual for the solicitors to try to negotiate a settlement. In fact, even when court proceedings have been commenced the lawyers for the parties will often continue to negotiate on behalf of their clients. This is reflected in the high number of claims which are issued but are then settled out of court. Once lawyers are involved then there will be a cost element and, clearly, the longer negotiations go on, the higher the costs will be. One of the worrying aspects is the number of cases that drag on for years only to end in an agreed settlement literally 'at the door of the court' on the morning that the trial is due to start. It is this situation that alternative dispute resolution methods are aimed at preventing. This is reinforced by the Civil Procedure Rules (CPR) (see section 4.4.5).

4.7.2 Mediation

In mediation a neutral mediator helps the parties to reach a compromise solution. The role of a mediator is to act as a 'go-between'. He will consult with each party and see how much common ground there is between them. He will explore the position with each party, looking at their needs and will carry offers to and fro, while keeping confidentiality. This usually takes place at a neutral venue. The parties are given separate private rooms. The mediator will see each of the parties in their private rooms to explain the format of the day. Then there is usually a joint opening session

in a larger room. After this the parties return to their private rooms (also known as caucuses) and the mediator will discuss each parties case with them privately and explore possible areas for compromise until either a solution is reached or it is obvious that an amicable resolution cannot be reached. Even if the mediation does not resolve the dispute, it is likely to narrow the issues and so make a court case shorter. Mediation can also take different forms and the parties can choose the exact method they want. The important point in mediation is that the parties are in control; they make the decisions.

A mediator will not usually tell the parties his own views of the merits of the dispute; it is his job to act as a 'facilitator', so that an agreement is reached by the parties. However, a mediator can be asked for his opinion of the merits and in this case the mediation becomes more of an evaluation exercise, which again aims at ending the dispute. Mediation is only suitable if there is some hope that the parties can co-operate. Companies who are used to negotiating contracts with each other are likely to benefit from this approach. Mediation is also often successful in divorce cases where there are disputes over the children or property.

4.7.3 Conciliation

This has similarities to mediation in that a neutral third party helps to resolve the dispute, but the main difference is that the conciliator takes a more active role. He will be expected to suggest grounds for compromise and the possible basis for a settlement. This is sometimes referred to as 'evaluative' mediation. As with mediation, conciliation does not necessarily lead to a resolution and it may be necessary to continue with a court action, though the conciliation process, even where unsuccessful, may well narrow the issues and avoid lengthy court cases. It is also similar to mediation in that the parties make the agreement. They remain in control throughout the proceedings; they do not have to accept the conciliator's suggestions.

Formalised settlement conference

This is a more formal method of approaching conciliation. It involves a 'mini-trial' where each side presents its case to a panel composed of a decision-making executive from each party and a neutral third party. Once all the submissions have been made, the executives, with the help of the neutral adviser, will evaluate the two sides' positions and try to come to an agreement. If the executives cannot agree, the neutral adviser will act as a conciliator between them.

An advantage of mediation and conciliation is that the decision need not be a strictly legal one sticking to the letter of the law. It is more likely to be based on commercial common sense and compromise. These methods will also make it more possible for companies to continue doing business with each other in the future. Some settlements may even include agreements about the conduct of future business between the parties, which is something that cannot happen when a court gives judgment. All forms of mediation and conciliation avoid the adversarial conflict of the court room and the winner/loser result of court proceedings as well as minimising the large-scale costs associated with a court case.

Dispute resolution services

There are a growing number of dispute resolution services. One of the main ones is the Centre for Dispute Resolution (CEDR) which was set up in London in 1991. The centre has many important companies as members, including almost all of the big London law firms. Businesses say that using the Centre to resolve disputes has saved several thousands of pounds in court costs. The typical cost of a mediator is about £1,000 to £1,500 for a case. This compares with potential litigation costs which are usually well over £100,000 and in major commercial cases likely to be over £1 million. The Centre has a high success rate, with over 80 per cent of cases in which it is asked to act being settled.

There are also mediation services aimed at resolving smaller disputes, for example those between neighbours. Most areas have local mediation schemes offering a free service that will try to help resolve disagreements between neighbours arising from such matters as noise or boundary fence disputes. Such services are run by trained volunteers who will not take sides or make judgments on the rights and wrongs of an issue. There are even online services offering dispute settlement via the Internet.

In 2004 the Civil Mediation Council was set up to promote mediation in civil and commercial cases. It is working with the Government on the expansion of court-based mediation schemes.

4.7.4 Arbitration

Arbitration is where the parties agree to submit their claims to the judgment of an independent person instead of taking a court case. In fact arbitration was described by Sir John Donaldson as 'usually no more and no less than litigation in the private sector' (*Northern Regional Health Authority v Derek Crouch Construction Co Ltd* [1984] 1 QB 644 at 670). Arbitration is governed by the Arbitration Act 1996 and s 1 of that Act sets out the principles behind it. This says:

's 1 (a) the object of arbitration is to obtain the fair resolution of disputes by an impartial tribunal without unnecessary delay or expense;

(b) the parties should be free to agree how their disputes are resolved, subject only to such safeguards as are necessary in the public interest.'

So arbitration is the voluntary submission by the parties of their dispute to the judgment of some person other than a judge. The agreement to arbitrate will usually be in writing and indeed the Arbitration Act 1996 applies only to written arbitration agreements. The precise way in which the arbitration is carried out is left almost entirely to the parties' agreement. Under s 33 of the Act the parties are free to adopt whatever procedures they think appropriate, but the arbitrator(s) must act fairly and impartially under the rules of natural justice. The procedures adopted must be suitable to the circumstances and avoid unnecessary delay and expense.

The agreement to go to arbitration can be made by the parties at any time. It can be before a dispute arises or when the dispute becomes apparent. Many commercial contracts include what is

called a *Scott v Avery* clause, which is a clause where the parties in their original contract agree that in the event of a dispute arising between them, they will have that dispute settled by arbitration. Alternatively, the agreement to go to arbitration can be made after the dispute arises. Arbitration is often used in commercial cases.

Staying court proceedings

Where there is an arbitration agreement in a contract, the Arbitration Act 1996 states that the court will normally refuse to deal with any dispute. If court proceedings are brought, the court will stay the proceedings and the matter must go to arbitration as agreed by the parties. In *Cable & Wireless plc v IBM United Kingdom Ltd* (2002) EWHC 303 the court extended this principle by holding that proceedings could be stayed not only where there was an arbitration clause but also where there was a contractual term providing for mandatory ADR in the event of a dispute.

The arbitrator

The Arbitration Act 1996 (s 15) states that the parties are free to agree on the number of arbitrators, so that a panel of two or three may be used or there may be a sole arbitrator. If the parties cannot agree on a number then the Act provides that only one arbitrator should be appointed. The Act also says that the parties are free to agree on the procedure for appointing an arbitrator. In fact, most agreements to go to arbitration will either name an arbitrator or provide a method of choosing one and it is often provided in commercial contracts that the president of the appropriate trade organisation will appoint the arbitrator. There is also the Institute of Arbitrators which provides trained arbitrators for major disputes. In many cases the arbitrator will be someone who has expertise in the particular field involved in the dispute, but if the dispute involves a point of law the parties may decide to appoint a lawyer. If there is no agreement on whom or how to appoint, then, in the last resort, the court can be asked to appoint an appropriate arbitrator.

The arbitration hearing

The actual procedure is also left to the agreement of the parties in each case, so that there are many forms of hearing. In some cases the parties may opt for a 'paper' arbitration, where the two sides put all the points they wish to raise into writing and submit this together with any relevant documents to the arbitrator. He will then read all the documents and make his decision. Alternatively, the parties may send all these documents to the arbitrator, but before he makes his decision both parties will attend a hearing at which they make oral submissions to the arbitrator to support their case. If the parties wish, it is possible for witnesses to be called to give evidence. Where witnesses are asked to give evidence orally then this will not normally be given on oath. However, if the parties want, the witness can be asked to give evidence on oath and the whole procedure will be very formal. If witnesses are called to give evidence the Arbitration Act 1996 allows for the use of court procedures to ensure the attendance of those witnesses.

The date, time and place of the arbitration hearing are all matters for the parties to decide in consultation with the arbitrator. This gives a great degree of flexibility to the proceedings; the parties can chose what is most convenient for all the people concerned.

The award

The decision made by the arbitrator is called an award and is binding on the parties. It can even be enforced through the courts if necessary. The decision is usually final, though s 68 of the Arbitration Act 1996 allows it to be challenged in the courts on the ground of serious irregularity in the proceedings or on a point of law.

Advantages and disadvantages of arbitration

There are several advantages which largely arise from the fact that the parties have the freedom to make their own arbitration agreement and decide exactly how formal or informal they wish it to be. The main advantages are:

- the parties may choose their own arbitrator and can therefore decide whether the matter is best dealt with by a technical expert or by a lawyer or by a professional arbitrator
- if there is a question of quality this can be decided by an expert in the particular field, saving the expense of calling expert witnesses and the time that would be used in explaining all the technicalities to a judge
- the hearing time and place can be arranged to suit the parties
- the actual procedure used is flexible and the parties can choose that which is most suited to the situation; this will usually result in a more informal and relaxed hearing than in court
- the matter is dealt with in private and there will be no publicity
- the dispute will be resolved more quickly than through a court hearing
- arbitration proceedings are usually much cheaper than going to court
- the award is normally final and can be enforced through the courts.

However, there are some disadvantages of arbitration, especially where the parties are not on an equal footing as regards the ability to present their case. This is because legal aid is not available for arbitration and this may disadvantage an individual in a case against a business; if the case had gone to court a person on a low income may have qualified for legal aid and so had the benefit of a lawyer to present their case. The other main disadvantages are that:

- an unexpected legal point may arise in the case which is not suitable for decision by a non-lawyer arbitrator
- if a professional arbitrator is used, his fees may be expensive
- it will also be expensive if the parties opt for a formal hearing with witnesses giving evidence and lawyers representing both sides

- the rights of appeal are limited
- the delays for commercial and international arbitration may be nearly as great as those in the courts if a professional arbitrator and lawyers are used.

This problem of delay and expense has meant that arbitration has to some extent lost its popularity with companies as a method of dispute resolution. More and more businesses are turning to the alternatives offered by centres such as the Centre for Dispute Resolution or, in the case of international disputes, are choosing to have the matter resolved in another country. One of the problems was that the law on arbitration had become complex and the Arbitration Act 1996 is an attempt to improve the process. In general it can be said that certain types of dispute are suitable for arbitration. This especially includes commercial disagreements between two businesses where the parties have little hope of finding sufficient common ground to make mediation a realistic prospect and provided there is no major point of law involved.

Key facts chart comparing different methods of dispute resolution

KEY FACTS

Method of dispute resolution and decision-maker	Procedure	Advantages	Disadvantages
Negotiation The parties themselves or through negotiators	Informal Usually through letters or e-mail	Quick No cost Parties in control and agree to outcome	None
Mediation/ The parties with the help of a mediator	Mediator discusses case with each side in turn trying to find a solution which is acceptable to both parties	Cheaper than courts Parties in control and parties agree to outcome Private	Not binding May not lead to settlement

CONTINUED ▶

KEY FACTS

Method of dispute resolution and decision-maker	Procedure	Advantages	Disadvantages
Conciliation The parties with the help of a conciliator	Mediator evaluates the case and gives opinion to parties	Cheaper than courts Parties in control and parties agree to outcome Private	Not binding May not lead to settlement
Arbitration The arbitrator	Use of arbitration may be agreed in advance with a *Scott v Avery* clause Can be paper proceedings or more formal like a court	Cheaper than courts BUT more expensive than mediation Binding	Can be formal Arbitrator's fee may be high Not suitable if dispute is on a point of law
Litigation in the courts A judge	Regarded as last resort Must follow CPR and timetables set by the court	Decision is final and binding	Expensive Lengthy Formal Adversarial Public hearing

4.7.5 Encouraging the use of ADR

There have been many moves to encourage the use of ADR over the past 10 years. In particular this can be seen in the Woolf Report which included more use of ADR as one of its recommendations. This led to the provision in r 1.4(2)(e) of the CPR which states that case management includes encouraging the parties to use an ADR procedure if the court considers that appropriate and facilitating the use of such procedure.

5.2.1 Code for Crown Prosecutors

The decision whether to proceed with a charge involves a Crown Prosecutor using two tests:

1. The evidential test

The evidential test under paragraph 5 – that is, whether there is a realistic prospect of conviction.

'5.3 A realistic prospect of conviction is an objective test. It means that a jury or bench of magistrates or judge hearing a case alone, properly directed in accordance with the law, is more likely than not to convict the defendant of the charge alleged. This is a separate test from the one that the criminal courts themselves must apply. A court should only convict if satisfied so that it is sure of a defendant's guilt.

5.4 When deciding whether there is enough evidence to prosecute, Crown Prosecutors must consider whether the evidence can be used and is reliable. There will be many cases in which the evidence does not give any cause for concern. But there will also be cases in which the evidence may not be as strong as it first appears. Crown Prosecutors must ask themselves the following questions:

Can the evidence be used in court?

a Is it likely that the evidence will be excluded by the court? There are certain legal rules which might mean that evidence which seems relevant cannot be given at a trial. For example, is it likely that the evidence will be excluded because of the way in which it was gathered? If so, is there enough other evidence for a realistic prospect of conviction?

Is the evidence reliable?

b Is there evidence which might support or detract from the reliability of a confession? Is the reliability affected by factors such as the defendant's age, intelligence or level of understanding?'

If the case does not pass the evidential test, it must not go ahead, no matter how important or serious it may be. If the case does meet the evidential test, Crown Prosecutors must decide if a prosecution is needed in the public interest.

2. The public interest test

'5.9 The more serious the offence, the more likely it is that a prosecution will be needed in the public interest. A prosecution is likely to be needed if:

a a conviction is likely to result in a significant sentence;

b a conviction is likely to result in a confiscation or any other order;

c a weapon was used or violence was threatened during the commission of the offence;

d the offence was committed against a person serving the public (for example, a police or prison officer, or a nurse); . . .'

Other factors indicating that a prosecution should be brought in the public interest are where the defendant was in a position of authority or trust (such as theft by an employee from a employer); the offence was premeditated; where the victim was vulnerable (a robbery from an elderly person); or where the offence was motivated by any form of discrimination against the victim's ethnic or national origin, sex, religious beliefs, political views or sexual orientation. On the other hand, there are some common public interest factors against prosecution in the Code. For example, a prosecution is less likely to be needed if the loss or harm can be described as minor and was the result of a single incident, or if the court would be likely to impose only a nominal penalty or the offence was committed as a result of a genuine mistake or misunderstanding, but note that:

 '**5.11** Deciding on the public interest is not simply a matter of adding up the number of factors on each side. Crown Prosecutors must decide how important each factor is in the circumstances of each case and go on to make an overall assessment.'

When the CPS took over prosecutions in 1986, the practice of discontinuing cases in line with the Code, which before 1986 had been very rare, became more common. This is one of the reasons that the CPS did not enjoy particular popularity, especially within the police force. You should note that the Code does not require an examination of the **guilt** of the accused, but the **likelihood of conviction**: a factor which may influence the CPS to drop cases where the evidence is perceived as being weak. But because the police had previously not discontinued cases or downgraded offences in this way, tension between the police and the CPS grew.

Until 1999, it was the role of the police to compile the files for each investigated case and to arrange the date for the first appearance in court. The police **then** sent the file to the CPS. The CPS would review the evidence in the file and decide whether it justified the charge being laid by the police **after** the court date had been fixed. The CPS might discontinue the case, continue as per the charge, or could downgrade the charge which involves substituting it with a lesser offence.

5.2.2 The Glidewell Report

In 1998, the Glidewell Report into the CPS (*The Review of the Crown Prosecution Service*, Cm 3690 (1998)) had found that approximately 12 per cent of cases were discontinued. It identified serious tension between the police and the CPS, with a tendency for each party to blame the other if a case failed. Since 1986, Glidewell found, the CPS had become increasingly isolationist, and a rift in communication and co-operation had resulted. The main recommendation of the Glidewell Report was to place CPS representatives into police stations to form a single integrated unit in charge of assembling and managing the case files, able to call on the police to obtain more evidence where necessary. These changes seem to have succeeded. In the preface to the CPS Annual Report 2002–03, the DPP's letter to the Attorney General (to whom the DPP is answerable) indicated:

> **Q** 'In magistrates' courts, the CPS secured a conviction in 98% of its prosecutions – around 978,000 defendants either pleaded or were found guilty. This is an increase of 45,000 on 2001–2002, and includes a 70% conviction rate in those cases where the defendant pleaded not guilty.
>
> In the Crown Court, almost 90% of cases proceeding to hearing resulted in a conviction – around 72,000 defendants – an increase of almost 9,000 and 14% more than in 2001–2002. Almost 62% of defendants who pleaded not guilty in the Crown Court were convicted.'

The changes do not stop with Glidewell. Now, under Pt 4 (ss 28–31) of and Schedule 2 to the Criminal Justice Act 2003, the CPS is to become responsible for determining the charge. Pilot schemes have been established and will become national, in which CPS lawyers are placed into police stations or are available to provide telephone advice, and in all but the most straightforward cases, it is the CPS lawyer rather than the police who decide the charge. The rationale for the change is to reduce further the number of judge-directed or ordered acquittals by charging the offender with the correct charge from the start.

One of the consequences of this change is that opportunities to reduce the charge through the system of plea bargaining will be limited in all but exceptional circumstances, for example where events have changed since the original decision was made. This is because, in theory, the correct charge will have been brought in the first place.

A change of name?

In the CPS press release of March 2004 (109/04), the DPP indicated that the CPS may change its name from the **Crown** to the **Public** Prosecution Service. He said:

> **Q** 'We are a public prosecution service and for some time I have favoured a change of name to make that clearer. This would reflect the major transformation that we are making in the role of prosecutors within the criminal justice system. I have discussed this with the Attorney General who takes the same view and I am discussing it with my staff. No final conclusion has yet been reached.
>
> When this process is complete the Attorney General and I will announce our decision.'

5.3 Plea bargaining

What is plea bargaining? It is where the defendant pleads guilty in exchange for a lesser sentence for the offence or pleads guilty to a lesser offence on the same facts. For example, a defendant might plead guilty to a common assault charge and receive a fine rather than risking a prison sentence after conviction on a charge of assault occasioning actual bodily harm. The reduction in sentence and/or charge rewards the defendant's show of remorse and contrition by entering the plea of guilty. Statutory provisions provide a sentence discount of up to a third of the full sentence (if the guilty plea is made early in the proceedings: see Chapter 12 below). The reduction in sentence will not be affected by the new charging system (where the CPS decides the charge), but there will be difficulties reducing the charge to a lesser offence in exchange for a guilty plea, because the victim and society in general will not be able to see justice has been done in that case. Plea bargaining does provide benefits to the prosecution. Guilty pleas help the CPS to meet its targets for convictions and they save court time and the expense of a trial.

However, plea bargaining is highly controversial. The victim of the crime (or their family) may feel that justice has not been done because the offender has not pleaded guilty to the offence the victim feels he has been subject to, or has not received the full sentence for the crime. On the other side of the coin, the system might be seen to encourage defendants (especially those with previous convictions) to plead guilty to crimes they did not commit. A further issue is the limited role of the judge in the plea bargaining process. This is according to the guidelines laid down in *R v Turner* (1970) 53 Cr App R 352, by Lord Parker CJ. The guidelines state that the prosecution and defence lawyers are free to consult with each other about pleas in the presence of the judge and;

J '. . . counsel on both sides may wish to discuss with the judge whether it would be proper, in a particular case, for the prosecution to accept a plea to a lesser offence. It is of course imperative that so far as possible justice must be administered in open court. Counsel should, therefore, only ask to see the judge when it is felt to be really necessary and the judge must be careful only to treat such communications as private where, in fairness to the accused person, this is necessary. [However] [T]he Judge should, subject to the one exception referred to hereafter, *never indicate the sentence which he is minded to impose.* A statement that on a plea of Guilty he would impose one sentence but that on a conviction following a plea of Not Guilty he would impose a severer sentence is one which should never be made.'

The rationale for the statement in italics above is that such an indication could be regarded as putting undue pressure on the defendant but, of course, in practice, everyone involved in the criminal courts system knows that an early guilty plea will be reflected in a less severe sentence than following conviction on a not guilty plea. A defendant in this situation might lose the freedom of choice that he deserves. The Lord Chief Justice continued:

> **J** 'The only exception to this rule is that it should be permissible for a judge to say, if it be the case, that whatever happens, whether the accused pleads Guilty or Not Guilty, the sentence will or will not take a particular form, *eg* a probation order or a fine, or a custodial sentence.'

The guidelines in *Turner* (1970) are not supported in all legal circles, and there are advocates for a far more open and judicially involved process. It is true that the current system of plea bargaining certainly leads to a suspicion of overcharging. That is, the CPS would bring a more serious charge in the hope that the offender will plead to a lesser offence, knowing the offender would probably not be convicted of the more serious offence if the matter went to trial. A judge-monitored plea bargaining system would prevent the appearance of overcharging.

However, there is a very strong argument against any increase in the use of plea bargaining. The term 'due process' is generally associated with the American legal system, but it is the principle that a defendant has certain unassailable legal rights; one of which is the right to hear the case against him in full and be heard in response if he so chooses. This is regarded as part of the rules of natural law in the English Legal System; but the term 'due process' neatly summarises the point being made. A defendant under the due process principle is:

* innocent until proven guilty, and therefore
* entitled to insist that the prosecution prove his guilt.

This latter point is often called 'putting the prosecution to proof', and you might like to consider whether **any** legal system that in effect allows a defendant to be pressurised into pleading guilty can meet the demands of due process and natural law. Research carried out for the Runciman Report (Zander and Henderson, *The Crown Court Study*, Royal Commission on Criminal Justice Study 19, 1993, p 145) suggested that 11 per cent of defendants who pleaded guilty as a result of a plea bargain in fact insisted later they were innocent but pleaded guilty to secure a lesser sentence.

5.4 Courts exercising criminal jurisdiction

The courts mentioned below exercise criminal jurisdiction. Some of the courts are also capable of exercising civil jurisdiction and have therefore already been mentioned in Chapter 4 above. Where this is the case, the relevant information has not been repeated.

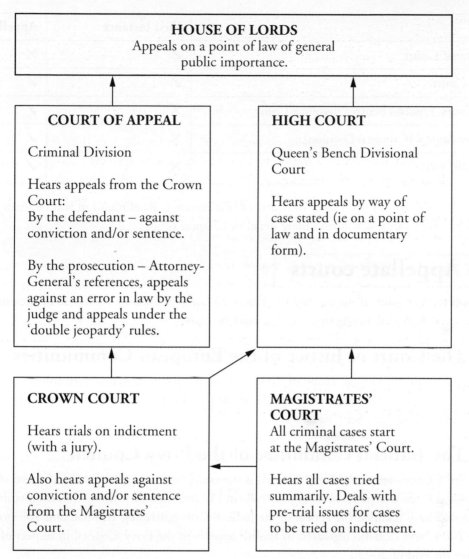

HOUSE OF LORDS
Appeals on a point of law of general
public importance.

COURT OF APPEAL

Criminal Division

Hears appeals from the Crown
Court:
By the defendant – against
conviction and/or sentence.

By the prosecution – Attorney-
General's references, appeals
against an error in law by the
judge and appeals under the
'double jeopardy' rules.

HIGH COURT

Queen's Bench Divisional
Court

Hears appeals by way of
case stated (ie on a point of
law and in documentary
form).

CROWN COURT

Hears trials on indictment
(with a jury).

Also hears appeals against
conviction and/or sentence
from the Magistrates'
Court.

**MAGISTRATES'
COURT**
All criminal cases start
at the Magistrates' Court.

Hears all cases tried
summarily. Deals with
pre-trial issues for cases
to be tried on indictment.

Figure 5.1 Criminal court hierarchy

The courts in the English Legal System can be classified as courts of **first instance** or **original jurisdiction** and courts of **appellate jurisdiction**. Simply, this means:

First instance or original	Hears trials
Appellate	Hears appeals

However, there is no single trial court and no single appellate court. In fact, the Crown Court has both original and appellate jurisdiction, as the following table shows:

	First instance	Appellate
Magistrates' Court	✓	✗
Crown Court	✓	✓
High Court, Queen's Bench Divisional Court	✗	✓
Court of Appeal (Criminal Division)	✗	✓
House of Lords	✗	✓

Our focus in this chapter is on the two courts of first instance. Brief mention will be made of the appeal courts here but you will find more detail in Chapter 6.

5.5 Appellate courts

In addition to the Court of Appeal and the House of Lords, which we will come to presently, there are two courts of special jurisdiction worth a brief mention:

5.5.1 The Court of Justice of the European Communities

Under Art 234 (ex 177) of the Treaty of Rome, this court may be asked to give rulings concerning European Community law. References may be made to it for the interpretation of EC law, where this involves criminal law. See Chapter 1.

5.2.2 The Judicial Committee of the Privy Council

The Judicial Committee of the Privy Council is the court of final appeal for the UK overseas territories and Crown dependencies (eg the Falkland Islands), and for those Commonwealth countries that have retained the appeal to the Judicial Committee (eg Trinidad and Tobago). In October 2003 New Zealand legislated to abolish appeals to the Privy Council in respect of all cases heard after the end of 2003.

In dealing with these appeals from courts outside the United Kingdom the business of this committee is mainly civil. The Committee will not grant special leave for an appeal to be heard in criminal cases, unless there are exceptional circumstances. Leave to appeal will be granted only if there has been a substantial injustice and the accused has been denied a fair trial. It was reported in *The Times* ('Death Under the Sun', 18th January 2000) that Trinidad, Tobago, Barbados, Guyana and Jamaica have all signed up in principle to a new Court of Appeal to curtail the power of the Privy Council in criminal cases. The opinion of the Privy Council expressed in *Pratt* [1993] 4 All ER 769 may have made the Privy Council master of its own destruction. Death row inmates who have been in prison for more than five years had, in the Council's opinion, suffered 'inhuman or degrading treatment' and accordingly their sentences would be commuted to life. *Pratt* (1993) is a very unpopular judgment in these countries where the death penalty is widely supported.

5.5.3 The House of Lords

The House of Lords may hear appeals on matters of criminal law. These appeals may come either from the Court of Appeal (Criminal Division) or from the Divisional Court of the Queen's Bench Division. Certain conditions must be satisfied before the House of Lords can hear appeals in criminal cases, and the details of this will be described in Chapter 6, which deals with the appeals system in greater depth.

5.5.4 The Court of Appeal (Criminal Division)

Originally, the Court of Appeal was created to hear civil cases only, but the Court of Criminal Appeal, as it was then known, was created in 1907, to hear appeals in criminal cases only. This court was replaced in 1966 by the Court of Appeal (Criminal Division) the name by which it is now known. The head of this court is the Lord Chief Justice. It has jurisdiction to hear appeals against sentence or conviction by persons convicted of offences at the Crown Court, but it does not deal with cases which have been heard by the Divisional Court of the Queen's Bench Division; these cases go direct to the House of Lords. Again, you will understand this point more thoroughly when you have read Chapter 6 on the appeal procedures in the court system.

5.5.5 The High Court of Justice
The Divisional Court of the Queen's Bench Division

You may find it odd to see the High Court mentioned here, as it was dealt with in Chapter 4 as a court which deals primarily with civil cases. However, as mentioned there, this court has jurisdiction in respect of offences which have been tried in the magistrates' courts and an appeal may be made on a point of law by way of case stated. Such an appeal may be made by the defendant or the prosecution.

5.5.6 The Crown Court – appellate jurisdiction

There is a right of appeal by a defendant convicted at the magistrates' court against conviction and/or sentence and leave is (uniquely) not required. The prosecution has no right to appeal on a point of law or against an acquittal to this court.

5.6 Criminal courts of first instance

5.6.1 The Crown Court

Students often confuse the names and functions of the Crown Court and the County Courts. Try to memorise now the fact that the Crown Court is a court which exercises criminal jurisdiction, whereas the County Courts exercise civil jurisdiction.

The Crown Court sits in court centres throughout England and Wales. The Crown Court in London is referred to as the Central Criminal Court (known popularly as the Old Bailey). The

Crown Court is regarded as one single court which sits in various parts of the country. It was created to replace the previous system of Assizes and Quarter Sessions.

The personnel of the court consists of all the judges of the High Court, Circuit Judges, Recorders, and Justices of the Peace (who will sit with a judge drawn from one of the other categories). Under the Courts Act 2003, District Judges (Magistrates' Court) can also carry out functions as a judge of the Crown Court, such as interlocutory (pre-trial) matters.

A distinctive feature of the Crown Court is the use of the jury as part of the trial process. See further Chapter 8 on the jury system.

The Crown Court is the only court which has jurisdiction to hear all trials on indictment for offences wherever committed. It also has the power to sentence persons convicted by the magistrates.

5.6.2 The Magistrates' Court

In addition to their work in civil cases (described in Chapter 9), the magistrates' courts deal with a vast quantity of criminal cases: 98 per cent of all criminal matters are dealt with by these courts. Magistrates have jurisdiction in respect of trials of **summary offences**, **either way offences**, and they also have the task of carrying out preliminary matters (bail, remand and related matters) in every case in which a person is accused of an **indictable** offence.

The terms in bold are explained in full at section 5.7 below, but before we examine these terms, we will briefly identify the personnel involved and the new system operating in this court.

Not surprisingly, the personnel of the magistrates' court consists of magistrates. There are two types:

1. Lay magistrates, or Justices of the Peace (JP). These are generally lay (not legally qualified, although a legal qualification is not a bar to becoming a JP), unpaid (expenses only), volunteers who live within the local justice area and have been nominated or have applied to be on the Bench. Some training is provided, but a qualified Bench Legal Adviser (court clerk) advises them on legal matters.

2. Stipendiary Magistrates, now referred to as District Judges (Magistrates' Court) (DJ(MC)) who have been solicitors or barristers for at least seven years (Courts and Legal Services Act 1990 and Access to Justice Act 1999: see Chapters 10 and 11). The title of 'Justice of the Peace' is generally used when referring to lay judges but technically it may refer equally to a lay justice and to a District Judge (Magistrates' Court).

There are approximately 29,000 lay magistrates, compared with approximately 100 District Judges (Magistrates' Court), plus Deputy DJ(MC)s. Lay magistrates work part-time, sitting for 26 half-days per annum. DJ(MC)s are full-time and salaried.

5.7 Classification of criminal offences

Criminal offences are divided into three categories:

(a) Offences triable only on indictment. These are tried only in the Crown Court. These are the offences which are considered too serious to be dealt with by the magistrates' courts and must be heard by a judge and jury. Examples of indictable offences include murder, manslaughter and rape, serious offences against the person, eg causing grievous bodily harm with intent, and aggravated burglary. In the main, these are offences which were developed by the common law, rather than by statute. Indictable offences are themselves divided into four classes according to the gravity of the offence, and then matched to a judge of the appropriate status. Thus, cases in Classes 1 and 2 which include murder, treason and rape, are usually heard by a High Court judge with a jury. Cases in the other classes may be heard by a High Court Judge, a Circuit Judge or a Recorder, with a jury in every case where the defendant pleads not guilty.

(b) Summary offences. These are dealt with summarily (literally briefly, without a jury) in the magistrates' courts. These are less serious offences, including many motoring offences under the Road Traffic Acts, taking a motor vehicle without consent and many other offences created by statute.

(c) Offences triable either way. These are crimes which can be tried **either** summarily by the magistrates, **or** on indictment, ie before a judge and jury in the Crown Court. They are often referred to as **hybrid offences**. They include less serious assaults, criminal damage in excess of £5,000, and many of the offences contained in the Theft Act 1968 but excluding, among other things, blackmail and certain burglaries.

5.7.1 Indictable offences

It is worth noting that **all** criminal offences start at the magistrates' court. The majority (98 per cent) also finish there and will not 'move up' to the Crown Court. The remaining 2 per cent therefore do go up to the Crown Court. This 2 per cent is made up of indictable offences and either way offences to be tried on indictment. The term 'indictment' (pronounced 'inditement') merely means the document containing the charge. The term used in the magistrates' court is 'written charge'.

Traditionally, when faced with an indictable offence, the magistrates undertook a preliminary hearing. These proceedings were known as committal proceedings in which the magistrates acted as examining justices. The aim of committal proceedings was for the magistrates to be satisfied on a preliminary examination of the evidence that there was a case for the accused to answer. Originally, committal proceedings involved the witnesses giving evidence in person before the court, ie an 'old-style committal'. This proved costly, time consuming and traumatic for the witnesses as they had to give evidence twice. A new procedure (the 'paper committal') was therefore developed as an alternative. This simply involved the magistrates making the decision to commit the case to the Crown Court or discharge it, on the basis of written witness statements. The Criminal Procedure

and Investigations Act 1996 effectively abolished 'old-style' committals and more recently s 51(1) Crime and Disorder Act 1998 abolished all committals in indictable offences.

Accordingly, although indictable offences commence at the magistrates' court, as there are no committals, the role of the magistrates in such cases is to deal with legal aid (the Criminal Defence Service Fund: see Chapter 7), bail and remand. Note that a defendant charged with an indictable offence does not enter his plea until the plea and directions hearing at the Crown Court.

5.7.2 Summary offences

Summary offences are dealt with only by the magistrates' courts. Offenders are not entitled to trial by jury in respect of these offences. There are literally hundreds of offences which are triable summarily only, many of them being motoring offences under the Road Traffic Acts. To avoid the court system being totally overwhelmed by minor traffic violations (most of which are non-recordable offences which means a defendant cannot be imprisoned upon conviction), it is possible for defendants in these cases to choose not to appear at court but to plead guilty by post.

Because of the less serious nature of these offences, the magistrates are restricted in the type of sentence which they can impose. Thus, an offender can be given only a maximum of 12 months' imprisonment in respect of a summary offence. Similarly, the magistrates can impose a fine of only £1,000 in respect of summary offences, or such amount as is specified in the statute creating the offence, whichever is higher, up to an overall limit of £5,000 (about to be increased to £15,000).

The magistrates also have power to compensate victims of crime, by ordering a convicted person to pay an amount (again, up to £5,000) to the victim of the crime.

5.7.3 Offences triable either way

The third category of offences with which magistrates may deal is the group of offences known as 'either way' offences. In very basic terms, summary offences 'live' at the magistrates' court, indictable offences 'visit' the magistrates' court but 'live' at the Crown; but either way offences are 'of no fixed abode'. The first thing that has to be done with an either way offence, therefore, is to find it a 'home'. The process starts with the plea.

Plea before venue

Remember that all criminal offences start at the magistrates' court. Under s 17A Magistrates' Courts Act 1980 (as amended, most recently by the Criminal Justice Act 2003) a defendant charged with an either way offence will be first asked at the Magistrates' Court to indicate his plea.

If the defendant pleads guilty, the magistrates' court passes sentence or may commit the defendant for sentence at the Crown Court if the magistrates' sentencing powers are inadequate. A guilty plea obviously means there is no need for a trial, as a trial is a hearing to determine guilt. This provides the defendant with the earliest opportunity to plead guilty.

Mode of trial

If a defendant charged with an either way offence pleads not guilty, the magistrates proceed to a mode of trial hearing or, under the Criminal Justice Act 2003, an 'allocation' hearing. This is a pre-trial hearing to decide which court will hear the trial; it is **not** a hearing to decide guilt or innocence.

Section 19 of the Magistrates' Courts Act 1980 governs the procedure to be followed by a Magistrates' Court in deciding whether a case involving an either way offence (to which the defendant has pleaded not guilty) should be tried summarily or on indictment. Under the new procedure ('allocation') the court is to be informed about, and must take account of, any previous convictions of the defendant in assessing whether the sentencing powers available to it are adequate. Certain cases involving children and serious or complex fraud cases are generally sent to the Crown Court immediately (ss 51B and 51C Crime and Disorder Act 1998).

Under s 20 Magistrates' Courts Act 1980, if the magistrates decide that the case is suitable for summary trial, defendants must be told that they can either consent to be tried summarily or, if they wish, they can choose to be tried on indictment. Before the Criminal Justice Act 2003, a defendant making this choice was informed that if he consented to be tried summarily, if convicted, he could have been committed for sentencing to the Crown Court for **any** either way offence. Now, it is generally no longer possible to be committed for sentence to the Crown Court once the magistrates have accepted jurisdiction. Defendants who elect summary trial can therefore not receive a sentence beyond the magistrates' powers.

The exception to this rule is where committal for sentence under s 3A of the Powers of Criminal Courts (Sentencing) Act 2000 is available for specified violent or sexual offences carrying a sentence of imprisonment of 10 years or more where the court is of the opinion that there is a significant risk to members of the public of serious harm occasioned by the commission by the defendant of further specified offences. The writer cannot foresee many situations in which the magistrates would have decided that such offences would be suitable for summary trial in any event.

Indication of sentence

Defendants also now have the opportunity of requesting an indication from the magistrates whether, if they pleaded guilty at that point, the sentence would be custodial or not. The Magistrates' Court will have a discretion whether or not to give an indication to a defendant who has sought one. Where an indication is given, defendants will be given the opportunity to reconsider their original indication as to plea. Where a defendant then decides to plead guilty, the magistrates' court will proceed to sentence. A custodial sentence will be available only if such a sentence was indicated. Where an indication of sentence is given and the defendant does not choose to plead guilty on the basis of it, the sentence indication is not binding on the magistrates who later try the case summarily, or on the Crown Court if the defendant elects trial on indictment.

Otherwise (ie where the defendant declines to reconsider his plea indication, or where no sentence indication is given) the defendant will be given the choice between accepting summary trial and electing trial on indictment.

Paragraph 7 of the Criminal Justice Act 2003 amends s 21 of the Magistrates' Courts Act 1980 so that, where the court decides that trial on indictment appears more suitable, it will proceed to send the case to the Crown Court in accordance with s 51(1) of the Crime and Disorder Act 1998. There are no committals for either way offences to be tried on indictment.

Allocation guidelines

Under s 170 of the 2003 Act, new allocation guidelines will be issued to assist the magistrates to decide whether summary or trial on indictment is suitable. These are not yet published, but are likely to be based on the Mode of Trial Guidelines found in the Consolidated Criminal Practice Direction, Part V, Further Directions Applying in the Magistrates' Court, para 51 issued by the Lord Chief Justice in 2004:

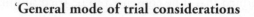

Q	**'General mode of trial considerations** **V.51.2** Section 19 of the Magistrates' Courts Act 1980 requires magistrates to have regard to the following matters in deciding whether an offence is more suitable for summary trial or trial on indictment: (a) the nature of the case; (b) whether the circumstances make the offence one of a serious character; (c) whether the punishment which a magistrates' court would have power to inflict for it would be adequate; (d) any other circumstances which appear to the court to make it more suitable for the offence to be tried in one way rather than the other; (e) any representations made by the prosecution or the defence. **V.51.3** Certain general observations can be made: (f) the court should never make its decision on the grounds of convenience or expedition; (g) the court should assume for the purpose of deciding mode of trial that the prosecution version of the facts is correct; . . .'

The starting point for the magistrates is to consider dealing with the case summarily, but this is far from the end of the matter. Each either way offence is listed in the Practice Direction detailing common aggravating and mitigating features which might make the considered offence more suitable for trial at the Crown or magistrates' court respectively.

It is important for you to grasp the significance of the mode of trial (allocation) procedure because, as you will see below, the right to elect trial by jury has been regarded as a cornerstone of our constitutional rights. It is a right not exercised as frequently as we may imagine, however, as Slapper and Kelly point out:

> 'Most defendants charged with either way offences are tried by magistrates: 9% of cases go to the Crown Court because the magistrates consider their current sentencing powers to be inadequate [note that this was limited at the time of writing to 6 months maximum; now it is increased to 12 months, this percentage may in future be even lower]; 4% of cases go to the Crown Court because the defendants elect trial by jury.'

Slapper and Kelly, *The English Legal System* (7th edn, Cavendish, 2004), p 140

ACTIVITY

> Using the classification of criminal offences given in this chapter, identify the types of offences set out below, and state which of them will be tried by the Crown Court, and which by the magistrates' court:
>
> **(a)** manslaughter
>
> **(b)** taking a motor vehicle without consent
>
> **(c)** taking goods from a supermarket without paying for them
>
> **(d)** deliberately causing damage to another person's property valued at £2,000.

5.7.4 The choice: Magistrates' Court or Crown Court?

A defendant charged with an either way offence where the magistrates have decided in the allocation hearing that the case is suitable for summary trial may consent to trial by the magistrates or may elect trial by jury. What factors influence his decision?

Stay at the magistrates' court	Elect the Crown Court
The sentence maximum is lower and post-trial committals for sentence have (on the whole) been abolished	There may be considerable delay; time served on remand is taken off final sentence (if convicted) and remand prisoners have more rights than prisoners following conviction
Conviction rate is higher on a not guilty plea (see the letter to the Attorney General above)	Conviction rate is lower on a not guilty plea
There is less publicity (journalists are not barred from the magistrates' court but are generally more interested in jury trials)	The CPS will review the files and may decide to drop the charge during the delay between allocation and the plea and directions hearing
If convicted, the right to appeal to the Crown Court does not require leave (permission) and, as the magistrates' court has to give reasons for decisions, it is easier to discover errors in fact or law	If convicted, D will need leave to appeal and it is difficult to persuade the Court of Appeal to overturn a jury verdict. On the other hand, no reasons are given by the jury so the Court of Appeal may be able to find the conviction unsafe where there is a trial judge error in directing the jury (even if it had no effect on jury deliberations)

Criminal court procedure, and in particular allocation of either way offences, can be rather tricky for students to grasp; especially students with no experience of the court system. Figure 5.2 should help, but we also strongly advise you to make the time to visit your local courts.

5.8 The 'right' to trial by jury?

On 18th November 1999, the Criminal Justice (Mode of Trial) Bill was introduced in the House of Lords. This exceptionally controversial Bill would have given effect to the unanimous recommendations of the Royal Commission on Criminal Justice (Runciman) 1993, the Review of Delay in the Criminal Justice System (Narey) 1997 and a Government consultation paper. Both reports stated that the decision on mode of trial should be entirely for the magistrates to make. The defendant should not, said the reports, have the final decision on a not guilty plea to an either way charge to elect jury trial where the magistrates were of the view that the case was suitable for summary trial. One of the reasons behind the proposal was to remove the practice of the 'cracked trial'. This is where a defendant pleads not guilty at the mode of trial hearing and elects trial at the Crown Court but then enters a guilty plea at the Crown Court on the day of the trial. Why might he do this? Have a look at the table in section 5.7.4 to see some of the factors that may influence a defendant to enter a late guilty plea (for example, he may have hoped the CPS might drop the charges). In addition, the delay between mode of trial and plea and directions might be as much as six months. As Slapper and Kelly point out:

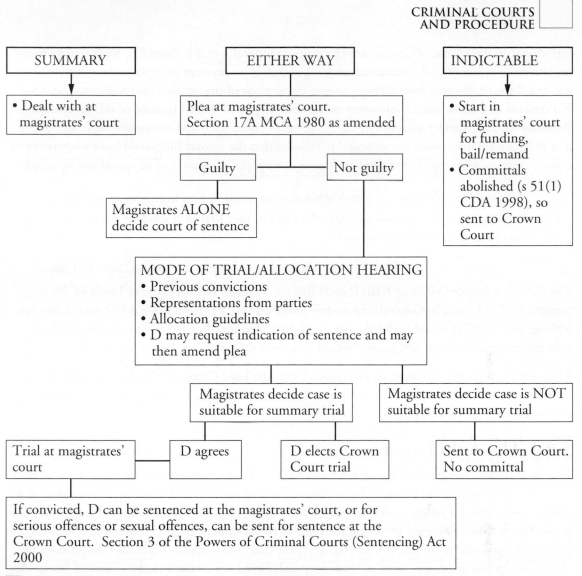

Figure 5.2 Criminal procedure

'The accuracy of testimony becomes less reliable the longer the gap between the original reception of the data [for example, the first time the witness makes his police statement] and his account of it in court'

Slapper and Kelly, *The English Legal System* (7th edn Cavendish, 2004) p 159

Many commentators, such as the human rights organisation Liberty, attacked the proposal for removing a defendant's perceived 'right' to jury trial. Under the Bill, the Magistrates' Court would have been allowed to have regard to previous convictions when deciding venue for trial.

On 20th January 2000, the Criminal Justice (Mode of Trial) Bill was defeated in the House of Lords by a massive majority. On 22nd February 2000, the Criminal Justice (Mode of Trial) (No 2) Bill was introduced in the House of Commons. The central proposal – that it should be for the magistrates to determine venue of trial – remained unchanged but, in an attempt to appease the critics, it prevented the magistrates from taking previous convictions of the accused into account. The No 2 Bill courted at least as much controversy as the first, despite or indeed because of this latter change. Professor Michael Zander, member of the Runciman Commission and outspoken supporter of the first Bill, quickly denounced the second. He believed that the second Bill would leave magistrates to make a decision as to mode of trial where 'the most important question of all' could not be asked:

> 'A case that could ruin someone's reputation or result in him losing his livelihood is serious and the court should have the right to take that into account when deciding where he should be tried.'

> M Zander, 'Why Jack Straw's jury reform has lost the plot' [2000] NLJ 366

The Criminal Justice (Mode of Trial) (No 2) Bill was rejected by the House of Lords on 28th September 2000, and the Government swiftly promised that a third Bill would be passed into law without the Lords' approval under the power of the Parliament Act 1911. This promise did not materialise, however, and the Queen's Speech in June 2001 was silent on this matter.

That was not a great surprise as, in December 1999, the Lord Chancellor had asked Auld LJ to conduct a review into the practices and procedures of, and the rules of evidence applied by, the criminal courts at every level.

5.8.1 The Auld Report

The Auld Report was published on 8th October 2001. Among other things, it recommended that allocation of all either way offences should be for the magistrates' court alone or, in the event of a dispute, for a District Judge, to decide, with a right of appeal to a Circuit Judge. This was the third major report which proposed removing the right of the defendant to elect trial by jury. However, to balance the procedure, committals for trial and post-trial committals for sentence would both be abolished. As you are aware, some of these proposals have been enacted in the Criminal Justice Act 2003.

Accepted in the CJA 2003	Rejected in the CJA 2003
Committals for trial for all either way offences to be tried on indictment have been abolished	The proposal to abolish the defendant's right to elect jury trial (not guilty plea; either way offence)
Post-trial committals for sentence have been abolished (on the whole)	
Magistrates are aware of the defendant's previous convictions in making the allocation decision	

5.8.2 The Criminal Justice Act 2003

Sections 43 and 44 of the Criminal Justice Act 2003 provide for certain trials on indictment without a jury, but these require a statutory instrument to implement the changes which would be subject to an affirmative resolution of both Houses of Parliament.

Serious or complex fraud cases

Under s 43 of the 2003 Act the prosecution may apply for a trial in a serious or complex fraud case to proceed in the absence of a jury. The judge may order the case to be conducted without a jury if he is satisfied that the length or complexity of the case (having regard to steps which might reasonably be taken to reduce it) is likely to make the trial so burdensome upon the jury that the interests of justice require serious consideration to be given to conducting the trial without a jury.

Risk of jury tampering

Section 44 of the 2003 Act also provides for a trial to be conducted without a jury where there is a 'real and present danger' of jury tampering, or to be continued without a jury where the jury has been discharged because of jury tampering. The court must be satisfied that the risk of jury tampering would be so substantial (notwithstanding any steps, including police protection, that could reasonably be taken to prevent it) as to make it necessary in the interests of justice for the trial to be conducted without a jury. In trials already under way where the jury has been discharged because of jury tampering, the trial will continue without a jury unless the judge considers it necessary in the interests of justice to terminate the trial. In that event, he may order a re-trial, and if he does he will have the option of ordering that the re-trial should take place without a jury. It is considered that it is far harder to intimidate a judge than to threaten a jury member. You may wish to note that this is the reason behind the abolition of juries in certain trials in Northern Ireland in 1973. Lord Diplock had chaired a Royal Commission in 1972 (*Report of the Commission to Consider Legal Procedures to Deal with Terrorist Activities in Northern Ireland*, Cmnd 5185) and thus we call single-judge courts in that jurisdiction 'Diplock' courts.

There is a right of appeal to the Court of Appeal for both prosecution and defence against a decision under ss 43 and 44 of the 2003 Act. Where a trial is conducted or continued without a jury and a defendant is convicted, the court will be required to give its reasons for the conviction.

5.8.3 Why have these changes occurred?

There is no specific statutory or recognised legal 'right' to trial by jury, but trial by one's peers has been a tradition for so long that the public and some Members of Parliament strongly oppose any invasion into that perceived right. The Government's two Mode of Trial Bills were defeated and despite three Royal Commission reports supporting its view, the Government conceded in the Criminal Justice Act 2003 that allowing magistrates to have the only and final say in court of trial was not worth the political cost. After much wrangling between the Houses of Common and

Lords, the Criminal Justice Act 2003 did, however, remove this right in serious or complex frauds, and where there is jury tampering. The latter is a logical response to the problem and the former is a matter of expediency; juries may be unable to find time to hear long trials and may be incapable of understanding the complex facts involved in fraud trials.

However, this is not the end of the matter. The Domestic Violence, Crime and Victims Act 2004 contains the following provisions:

- the defendant will be tried before a jury on a sample count [a sample or specimen count is a single offence in circumstances where the alleged conduct has been repeated on several occasions but there are thought to be too many charges to be heard in one trial. For example, a defendant may be charged with one or two sample counts of fraud or downloading indecent images of children from the Internet; but the prosecution alleges there are many more offences committed in the same way]
- if the defendant is convicted by the jury of the sample count
- the defendant is then tried by the judge without a jury for the other offences and is sentenced accordingly.

The background to the proposed changes are neatly summarised by the legal correspondent for *The Telegraph*, Joshua Rosenberg:

> 'The story began in 1996, when Philip Richard Kidd, 49, the headmaster of a primary school in Derbyshire, was convicted of indecently touching girls while they were in the classroom. He was sentenced to 15 months' imprisonment for four offences, three against one girl and one against another.
>
> These were just specimen charges. In all, Kidd had been accused of 17 offences involving eight girls, a factor that the judge took into account when deciding the length of his sentence. But that meant Kidd was being sentenced on offences for which he had not been convicted.
>
> Ruling subsequently on Kidd's appeal, the Lord Chief Justice, Lord Bingham, said that defendants should no longer be sentenced on charges that were neither admitted nor proved – convenient and economical though it might be to try a defendant for specimen offences.
>
> Kidd's sentence was upheld – 15 months was not excessive even for four offences – but, from now on, said the Court of Appeal, defendants would have to be tried on all the charges the prosecution wanted to bring. Some defendants would now face more counts, but the Lord Chief Justice said that this need not be "unduly burdensome or render the trial unmanageable".'

Daily Telegraph, 1st April 2004, Media section, p 18

The decision of the Court of Appeal presented the Government with a problem: time and resources could not always be expended in proving each of hundreds of counts of indecent assault or minor fraud; but unless the defendant was convicted on each and every one, he would not receive a sentence which reflected the totality of his criminal conduct. This is why the new two-stage trial process explained above was recommended. However, the proposal is not uniformly supported:

> 'The definition [of the term "sample"] provided in the Bill simply leaves it up to the court to decide, saying that a count, or charge, is to be regarded as a sample if the judge "considers that the sample count is a sample of the other counts" . . .

> And what . . . if the defendant is acquitted on the sample counts? In principle, the remaining charges should be dropped. But the Bill does not say this. It would be up to the judge to decide.

> There is nothing in the Bill to stop the prosecution having another go . . . courts should be required to direct an acquittal on all remaining counts: to do otherwise would leave more defendants effectively facing double jeopardy.

> [Vera Baird, QC, a Labour backbencher] sees no difficulty in having the second trial heard by a jury, whose members would be told that the defendant had already been found guilty on similar charges. Again, a guilty plea would seem likely.

> But her main concern is the law of unintended consequences. If the two-tier system becomes law, people will soon be singing the praises of trial by judge alone.

> There is no doubt that a judge is speedier and cheaper than a full-blown jury trial; judges will also have to give reasons.

> "The question will then be asked: why do we need 10 of these counts to be tried by a jury if the other 190 are being tried by a judge? Let's do them all by judge," the MP says. "It will be the beginning of the end for juries – again".'

The Daily Telegraph, 1st April 2004, Media section, p 18

Summary

Figure 5.3 was taken from the Home Office Criminal Justice website and is a useful summary of the prosecution process in English courts.

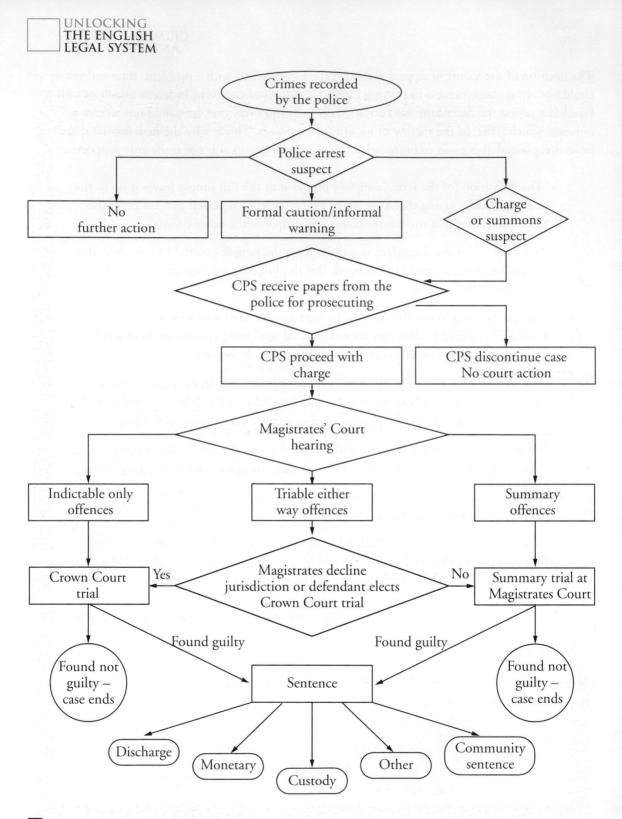

Figure 5.3 The prosecution process

Key facts chart on criminal courts

KEY FACTS

The Crown Prosecution Service	Governed by . . .	Prosecution of Offences Act 1985
	Code for Crown Prosecutors	Stage One – the evidential test Stage Two – the public interest test
	Changes	Glidewell Criminal Justice Act 2003
Plea bargaining	Definition	D pleads guilty in exchange for a lesser sentence and/or to a lesser offence
	Guidelines	*R v Turner* (1970)
	Advantages	D shows remorse Saves time and cost of a trial
	Disadvantages	Due process Putting the prosecution to proof
Courts of criminal first instance	Magistrates' Court	98% of all criminal matters including crimes triable summarily, either way offences tried summarily and allocation hearings. No committals (Crime and Disorder Act 1998 and Criminal Justice Act 2003)
	Crown Court	Trials on indictment
Appellate courts	Crown Court	See Chapter 6
	Queen's Bench Divisional Court of the High Court	
	Court of Appeal (Criminal Division)	
	House of Lords	
	European Court of Justice	
	Privy Council	

ACTIVITY

Consider the following story, and the questions based on it.

Mrs Smith claims that one day last year, she saw Dan point a gun in the direction of his girlfriend, and pull the trigger. The gun failed to fire because the mechanism was faulty, but Dan had not been aware of that until after he had pulled the trigger. Dan is now being tried for the attempted murder of his girlfriend, under the provisions of the Criminal Attempts Act 1981. He claims that he did not point the gun in his girlfriend's direction as alleged and that Mrs Smith was mistaken or is lying. Secondly, he claims that the act of pointing a gun in this way is not legally capable of falling within the relevant section of the 1981 Act.

(a) Who has decided whether Dan should be tried for this offence and by what procedure?

(b) In which court would this case be tried and by whom?

(c) Who will decide whether either Dan or Mrs Smith is lying about what happened?

(d) Who will decide whether Dan's alleged actions are capable as a matter of law of being within the ambit of the Criminal Attempts Act 1981?

Further reading

Herbert, A, 'Mode of Trial and Magistrates' Sentencing Powers: Will Increased Powers Inevitably lead to a Reduction in the Committal Rate?' [2003] Crim LR (May) 314.

Rivlin, G, *Understanding the Law* (3rd edn, Oxford University Press, 2004), Chapters 15 and 17.

Wilcock, P and Bennathan, J, 'Overhauling criminal procedures – part 1' [2004] 154 NLJ 778–779.

APPEALS ▪

Before we examine the court hierarchy and the appeal system in detail, you need to consider: what is the purpose of an appeal? You cannot evaluate the effectiveness of the appeals' system without considering whether it meets its aims.

- What is the aim of an appeal?
- Is that aim the same for criminal and civil cases?
- Should there be any restriction on which party can appeal?
- Should there be any restrictions on how many times either party may appeal?

Lord Woolf wrote in his Report *Access to Justice* (see Chapter 4) that there are two main purposes of an appeals system. The first is the private one of doing justice in individual cases by correcting wrong decisions. The second is the public one of engendering public confidence in the administration of justice by making those corrections and in clarifying and developing the law. Of course, the report focused on the civil justice system, but you might reflect that a similar purpose could be stated to apply in relation to criminal cases. Bear these aims in mind as you progress through this chapter as well as any you considered in response to the think point above.

6.1 Appeals in civil proceedings

6.1.1 The Access to Justice Act 1999

The Access to Justice Act 1999 (AJA 1999) made it clear that being able to bring an appeal in civil cases is not an automatic right for the losing party. This may strike you as rather restrictive, but it must be borne in mind that the rules have to achieve a balance between the rights of the individual wishing to prove his case, and the pressure on the time and resources of the court system.

The AJA 1999 and Pt 52 of the Civil Procedure Rules provide a common and harmonised set of rules for civil appeals. Section 54 of the AJA 1999 provides that before an appeal can be heard, permission to appeal must be granted. Section 55 provides that there should generally be only one appeal in any case, rather than cases progressing, almost automatically, through the court hierarchy, as occurred in the past. The 1999 Act also provides for a great deal of flexibility in deploying judges to hear appeals.

| PRIVY COUNCIL
Devolution issues (esp Wales and Scotland)

Appeals from the Commonwealth in civil cases | HOUSE OF LORDS
Appeals in civil cases from English courts, Northern Ireland and Scotland | ECJ
References from any court on a question of EC law |

COURT OF APPEAL

CIVIL DIVISION
Appeals in civil cases from the multi-track

THE HIGH COURT

Appeals heard in the DIVISIONAL courts

Hearings (trials) heard in the DIVISIONS (Queen's Bench, Family and Chancery)

| MAGISTRATES' COURT
Family cases
Non-payments of bills | COUNTY COURT
Hearings in civil cases |

Figure 6.1 Appeals in civil proceedings

The appeal regime in civil cases was subjected to detailed analysis in *Tanfern Ltd v Gregor Cameron-Macdonald* [2000] 2 All ER 801. This case stated that, unlike appeals in criminal cases (see section 6.2 below), where an appeal lies to the next **court** in the hierarchy, appeals in civil cases generally lie to the next **judge** in the hierarchy.

Appeals from	Heard by	Appeal to
The County Court, fast track	District Judge	Circuit Judge
The County Court, fast track	Circuit Judge	High Court Judge
County or High Court, Multi-track	District, Circuit or High Court Judge	Court of Appeal

Permission to appeal is generally always required, which will be granted only where there is a 'real prospect of success or some other compelling reason'. The appeal court's role is to review the decision of the lower court; it will not conduct a full re-hearing of the case. It will allow an appeal where:

- the decision of the lower court was wrong or

- it was unjust because of a serious procedural or other irregularity in the proceedings of the lower court.

The appeal court also has all the power of the lower court; it may also affirm, set aside or vary any order or judgment made or given by the lower court, may refer any claim or issue for determination by a lower court, may order a new trial or hearing and may make a costs order.

There are also new rules governing subsequent (called 'second-tier') appeals. The relevant point of principle or practice must be an important one and the Court of Appeal must consider that the appeal would raise an important point of principle or practice, or that there is some other compelling reason for it to hear this second appeal. These rules concerning second appeals may also be seen as being harsh, but as Brooke LJ pointed out in *Tanfern v Gregor Cameron-Macdonald*:

> **J** 'All courts are familiar with the litigant, often an unrepresented litigant, who will never take "no" for an answer, however unpromising his/her cause.'

and accordingly:

> **J** 'The decision of the first appeal court is now to be given primacy.'

ACTIVITY

Self-assessment questions

1. Under the rule explained above, where will the following appeals be heard?
   - An appeal from a District Judge in a County Court?
   - An appeal from a Circuit Judge in a County Court?
   - An appeal from a High Court Judge in the High Court?
   - An appeal from a District Judge hearing a multi-track case at the County Court?

2. When is permission to appeal required?

3. Under what circumstances will the appeal court allow an appeal?

4. What are the general rules concerning second appeals?

6.1.2 The Court of Appeal (Civil Division)

The Court of Appeal was established by the Judicature Act 1873 and, with the High Court, makes the Supreme Court of Judicature. You may think it is odd that these courts are called 'supreme' when the House of Lords is superior to them, but this is because the 1873 Act intended for the House of Lords' appellate capacity to be abolished and for the Court of Appeal to be the final appeal court. A change of government saw the reintroduction of the House of Lords as the final appeal court by the Judicature Act 1875, however.

The Court of Appeal consists of 37 Lords Justices of Appeal, the Lord Chancellor (but see below on the role of the Lord Chancellor), the President of the Family Division of the High Court, the Vice-Chancellor of the Chancery Division of the High Court and the Master of the Rolls. In addition, High Court judges may be invited to sit at the Court of Appeal. Judges sit in threes, but for very important cases, they may sit in fives. The Civil Division generally sits in four or five courts each day; so you can see it is a very busy court. In 2003, the Civil Division disposed of more than 3,000 cases, including hearings applying for permission to appeal.

The new appeal rules introduced under the AJA 1999 above in May 2000 did not affect civil appeals to the House of Lords.

6.1.3 The House of Lords

The Appellate Committee of the House of Lords hears appeals in civil cases from:

- the High Court (explained further below)
- the Court of Appeal Civil Division (explained further below)
- courts in Northern Ireland and Scotland.

The Appellate Committee of the House of Lords consists of Lords of Appeal in Ordinary (of which there are 12; two from Scotland and one from Northern Ireland) commonly called the Law Lords (although one is a lady). The judges sit in fives, or in very important cases, sevens. Cases are heard in a committee room in the Palace of Westminster (the Houses of Parliament building on the River Thames in London). Note that the Law Lords deliver **opinions** rather than **judgments**, in **speeches** delivered to the full House.

The Constitutional Reform Bill 2004 contains proposals to replace the Appellate Committee of the House of Lords with a new Supreme Court of the United Kingdom. House of Lords' reform has been on the political agenda for years, but most changes have related to the legislative chamber. As you are aware, Parliament consists of the House of Commons (the directly elected chamber), the House of Lords (the appointed chamber) and the Queen. The House of Lords is itself split into two committees – the legislative and the judicial. Non-judicial Lords have no function in relation to the Appellate Committee, but the judges of the Appellate Committee are Lords of the House, and as such they are entitled to sit and vote in the legislative chamber. Because of this situation, the perception exists that the highest court is also part of the Legislature; and this has led to the criticism of the appearance of the lack of judicial independence from the Legislature and thus also the Executive. The establishment of a completely separate Supreme Court in a new building would ensure that the highest court's judges are separate in all ways from Parliament and mean Parliament has no judicial function related to it.

On 13th July 2004, however, the House of Lords voted by 240 to 208 to reject the Bill during its Committee Stage on the separate matter of the abolition of the post of Lord Chancellor (see more in Chapter 11). The Government quickly vowed to use its majority to reinstate the measure when the legislation reached the Commons later that year, but the reforms may be delayed and may therefore not be in place for the time of publication of this book, so you must keep up to date (broadsheet newspapers as well as legal journals) on this matter.

Appeals to the House of Lords

Generally, appeals from the High Court are heard by the Court of Appeal (Civil Division) unless under ss 12–15 of the Administration of Justice Act 1969, the case is able to 'leap-frog' the Court of Appeal and go straight to the House of Lords. The conditions to be satisfied in order for the 'leap-frog' procedure to be used are:

1. The trial judge must be satisfied that:
    (i) a point of law of general public importance is involved and that it relates to the construction of an Act or statutory instrument or
    (ii) the point of law is one in which the judge is bound by a previous fully considered decision of the Court of Appeal or House of Lords and in both (i) and (ii)
    (iii) all the parties consent to this procedure.
2. The House of Lords gives leave to appeal.

Appeals from decisions of the Court of Appeal lie to the House of Lords, but in order to limit the workload of the Law Lords, permission to appeal must be given by one of these courts. There are also certain classes of cases in which any further appeal from the Court of Appeal is prohibited by statute, eg an appeal from a County Court in probate proceedings. In all other cases, an appellant may seek permission to appeal from the Court of Appeal and if this is refused, he is free to apply to the Appeal Committee of the House of Lords for permission.

Appeals to the House of Lords in civil matters usually concern questions of law, although appeals on questions of fact are possible. Generally speaking, the House of Lords will only hear appeals involving matters of general public importance, although this is not a statutory requirement, in contrast to criminal cases. Where a case does involve an issue which is of general public importance, this will increase the likelihood of permission to appeal being granted.

6.1.4 Other appeals in civil cases
The Privy Council

In dealing with appeals from courts outside the United Kingdom, the business of this committee is mainly civil. It is also the final appeal court for the Channel Islands and the Isle of Man. It also has

jurisdiction to hear appeals from prize courts (ie the Queen's Bench Division, which has considered the ownership of a ship or aircraft captured by an enemy); ecclesiastical courts; and medical tribunals. The Committee may also have special cases referred to it by the Crown.

If the new Supreme Court of the UK becomes a reality, it will take over the Privy Council's current domestic jurisdiction within the United Kingdom, including the function of being the court of final appeal for determining 'devolution issues' under the United Kingdom devolution statutes of 1998 (Northern Ireland, Scotland and Wales).

The Court of Justice of the European Communities

References may be made to the court for the interpretation of European Community law, where this involves civil law. You will find three examples of references made in civil cases under Art 234 of the Treaty of Rome in Chapter 1.

6.2 Appeals in criminal proceedings

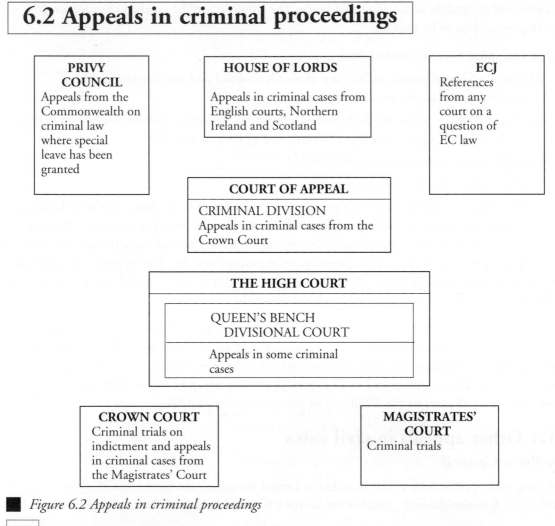

Figure 6.2 Appeals in criminal proceedings

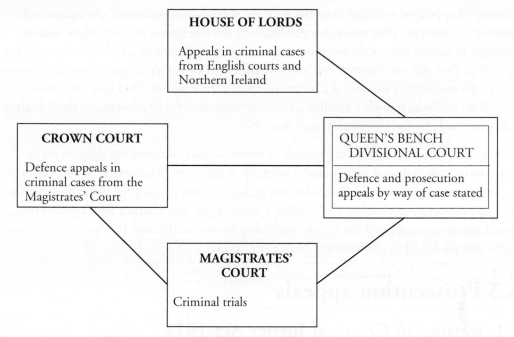

Figure 6.3 Appeals following summary trial

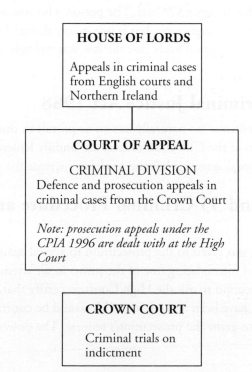

Figure 6.4 Appeals following trial on indictment

The system of appeals in criminal cases has been the subject of considerable discussion and criticism in recent years. One reason for this has been the emergence of cases where serious miscarriages of justice have occurred, resulting in the imprisonment of a number of people for crimes which they did not commit. Partly as a result of the discovery of such cases, the criminal justice system was subject to a Royal Commission which reported in 1993 (the Runciman Commission) and which made a number of recommendations for improvement; those dealing with appeals were made by the Criminal Appeal Act 1995.

More recent controversy surrounding appeals in criminal cases concerns the right of the prosecution to appeal against an acquittal. Generally, if the court (Magistrates' Court or the jury in the Crown Court) has found the defendant not guilty, it is not possible for the prosecution to 'have another go'. However, in October 1999 and as a result of the Macpherson Report concerning the Stephen Lawrence murder and the Law Commission recommendations, this 'rule against double jeopardy' was abolished in the Criminal Justice Act 2003.

6.3 Prosecution appeals

6.3.1 Section 36 Criminal Justice Act 1972

The prosecution can refer a point of law to the Court of Appeal for clarification following an acquittal, but this will not affect the validity of the acquittal in any way. It is not the prosecution who makes the referral, but the Attorney General. The person who was acquitted, the previous 'defendant', has the right to present argument, but is not in any danger by doing so as the acquittal is unaffected even if the Court of Appeal finds that the law was wrongly applied and the defendant should have been convicted.

6.3.2 Section 36 Criminal Justice Act 1988

Following a conviction and sentence (so naturally not an acquittal) in the Crown Court, the Attorney General can use s 36 of the CJA 1988 to refer an 'unduly lenient sentence' to the Court of Appeal. If the Court of Appeal agrees, it has the power to increase the sentence.

6.3.3 Sections 54 and 55 Criminal Procedure and Investigations Act 1996

This was the first time power was given to the prosecution to appeal against a jury acquittal, where a person has been convicted of intimidating one of the jurors in an attempt to secure that acquittal. The power requires the prosecution to ask the High Court to certify that, but for the other's interference, there would not have been an acquittal. If it would be contrary to the interests of justice, the court may refuse to grant the prosecution's request. The power has never been exercised.

6.3.4 Appeals against a judge's erroneous decision – Criminal Justice Act 2003

As a result of the Auld Report (*A Review of the Criminal Courts of England and Wales* (2001)), the prosecution may appeal against a judicial ruling which effectively terminates the prosecution's case (and therefore the case as a whole collapses) before the jury delivers its verdict. For example, the trial judge may agree with a defence submission at the close of the prosecution case that there is not enough evidence against the defendant and the judge makes a finding of 'no case to answer'. The rationale of this new power under s 58 CJA 2003 is to balance the defendant's rights to appeal in similar circumstances.

For example, say a trial judge rules that the defence that the defendant is relying on is not automatism, which would lead to a full acquittal if successful, but is instead the defence of insanity. Rather than risk the chance of being detained in a secure mental institute (which sometimes follows the finding of insanity) the defendant changes his plea to guilty. The defendant could then appeal against his conviction (even though he pleaded guilty) on the ground that the trial judge's decision erred in law. A prosecution appeal in parallel circumstances is felt necessary to ensure that justice for the victims is done despite a trial judge's error of law, which is unfortunately not a rare occurrence.

6.3.5 Abolition of the rule against double jeopardy – Criminal Justice Act 2003

There is a well-established common law doctrine of *autrefois acquit*. This is a special plea, available to a defendant, that he has been previously acquitted of the same or a very similar offence. It is designed to prevent the defendant from being prosecuted for a second time after having been acquitted (so-called 'cherry picking' by the prosecution). It is not an absolute rule and in-roads were made on the principle even before the Criminal Justice Act 2003. For example, there could be a re-trial in a magistrates' court following a successful prosecution appeal by way of case stated to the Queen's Bench Divisional Court. The House of Lords also has the power to restore a conviction that (usually) the Court of Appeal has set aside following the defendant's appeal from the Crown Court against his conviction. The plea of *autrefois acquit* is more commonly referred to as the rule against double jeopardy.

The Law Commission's report, *Double Jeopardy and Prosecution Appeals* (Law Com No 267 (2001), recommendation 1, p 122) proposed a partial abolition of the rule, recommending limiting prosecution appeals against acquittals to murder cases only. The Auld Report (2001) also made a series of recommendations concerning appeals in criminal cases including allowing a prosecutor to request a fresh trial after an acquittal where there was significant new evidence in all grave offences carrying life or a 'long term of imprisonment as Parliament might specify' (Chapter 12, para 63).

This was endorsed by the Government in the White Paper *Justice For All*, Cm 5563 (2002), as summarised below:

'. . . one reform that might certainly produce a few more convictions of guilty people is the proposed change to the double jeopardy rules. As expected, the White Paper accepts the argument for a "new evidence" exception to the old rule that a person may not be tried again for an offence of which he or she has been acquitted. In relation to the offences to which the exception would be applicable, the White Paper prefers the approach advocated by Auld and in this Review to the more cautious proposal of the Law Commission; the exception would accordingly extend beyond murder and related offences to include rape, manslaughter and armed robbery. The power of the Court of Appeal to quash an acquittal and order a re-trial will be retrospective, but re-investigation of the offence will require the personal consent of the DPP, and the power will be exercisable only where there is compelling new evidence of guilt that could not reasonably have been available for the first trial. Only one re-trial will be possible under this procedure.'

Professor L Lustgarten, 'The Future of Stop and Search' [2002] Crim LR 601

Sections 75 and 76 of the Criminal Justice Act 2003 enact these changes. They make it possible in certain cases for a re-trial to take place despite an earlier acquittal. This may occur if there is:

- new (not adduced in the proceedings in which the person was acquitted) **and**
- compelling (reliable, substantial and highly probative) evidence of the acquitted person's guilt **and**
- it is in the public interest (including the defendant's fair trial rights) (s 78).

Examples of new evidence might include DNA or fingerprint tests, or new witnesses to the offence coming forward. Probative means 'of value in proving the case'.

The measures also amend the law to permit the police to re-investigate a person acquitted of serious offences in these circumstances, to enable the prosecuting authorities to apply to the Court of Appeal (s 77) for an acquittal to be quashed, and for a re-trial to take place where the Court of Appeal is satisfied that the new evidence is highly probative of the case against the acquitted person. There are some safeguards aimed at preventing the possible harassment of acquitted persons in cases where there is not a genuine question of new and compelling evidence, by requiring the personal consent of the Director of Public Prosecutions (DPP) both to the taking of significant steps in the re-opening of investigations – except in urgent cases – and to the making of an application to the Court of Appeal (s 76(3)). The DPP will take into account both the strength of the evidence and the public interest in determining whether a re-investigation or application to the court is appropriate.

Possibly the most controversial, but least surprising, aspect is the retrospective application of the rules under s 75(6). This means that the prosecution may apply for a re-trial after an acquittal even where the acquittal occurred before the CJA 2003 came into force. There are 30 offences which are 'qualifying offences' for the purposes of the abolition of the rule, including: murder, attempted murder, soliciting murder, manslaughter, kidnapping, rape, attempted rape, various sexual offences under the Sexual Offences Act 2003, offences concerning Class A drugs, serious criminal damage and arson offences, war crimes and terrorism offences.

ACTIVITY

Self-assessment question

Explain whether, and if so, how, the prosecution can appeal from the Crown Court:

- against an unduly lenient sentence
- on a point of law following an acquittal
- to request a re-trial following an acquittal
- against a jury-tampered acquittal
- against a trial judge's ruling that terminated the prosecution's case.

6.4 Defence appeals

We now turn to the system of appeals for defendants in criminal cases. What must be borne in mind is that the **mode of appeal is always governed by the place of original trial**. This means that if a case was originally tried in the magistrates' court, then the route which an appeal will take will differ from that taken by a case which has been tried before a judge and jury at the Crown Court.

6.4.1 Appeal following summary trial

The route for an appeal against a decision of the magistrates in a criminal case is initially **either** to the Crown Court **or** to the Divisional Court of the Queen's Bench Division of the High Court.

To the Crown Court

The defendant may appeal to the Crown Court concerning a question of fact or law, ie he may dispute either the evidence or a decision on a point of law or both. The prosecution does not have a right of appeal from the magistrates' court to the Crown Court.

If the defendant pleaded not guilty before the magistrates, then there is a right of appeal against conviction or sentence or both. However, if the defendant originally pleaded guilty, then there is no appeal against conviction, only against sentence.

The appeal will take the form of a complete re-hearing (called a 'trial *de novo*') with witnesses but without a jury, and the Crown Court may vary the original decision, or confirm it, and has the

(ii) a safe conviction is a lawful conviction

(iii) 'unsafe' bears a broad meaning.

Therefore the answer to the question above is (b). The Court of Appeal decided that it would be wrong to uphold Mullen's appeal even though he had not directly appealed on the basis of his innocence. It appears from the judgment that it is worse to uphold the conviction if the evidence was obtained unfairly, and therefore it is better to allow the appeal of guilty person where the evidence obtained against him was obtained unfairly. Do you agree?

Since the enactment of the Human Rights Act 1998, the relationship between 'unsafe' under s 2 of the Criminal Appeal Act 1995 and 'unfair' under Art 6(1) ECHR has not been clarified. Would proceedings that fall foul of Art 6 automatically render a conviction unsafe? In *R v Togher* [2001] 3 All ER 463; [2001] 1 Cr App R 33, the Court of Appeal stated that if a defendant had been denied a fair trial, it was almost inevitable that his conviction would be regarded as unsafe. This was the first consideration of this question after the ECHR became part of domestic law under the Human Rights Act 1998. However, in *R v Davies, Rowe and Johnson* [2001] 1 Cr App R 115, and later in *R v Williams, The Times,* 30th March 2001, the Court of Appeal asserted that Art 6 required an examination of the fairness of the trial, and that would **not** necessarily lead to a finding that the conviction was unsafe.

ACTIVITY

Self-assessment questions

1. What is the single ground for allowing an appeal against conviction in the Court of Appeal?

2. What does the term 'leave to appeal' mean?

3. Explain when a defendant requires leave to appeal to the Court of Appeal.

4. Under what circumstances will the House of Lords hear an appeal from the Court of Appeal in a criminal case?

5. What does the word 'unsafe' in s 2 of the Criminal Appeal Act 1995 mean?

6.5 The House of Lords

The Appellate Committee of the House of Lords hears appeals in criminal cases from

• the High Court (Queen's Bench Divisional Court)

- the Court of Appeal Criminal Division (explained above)
- Northern Ireland.

Appeals from the Divisional Court go direct to the House of Lords

Before the House of Lords will hear such an appeal, the Divisional Court must certify that a point of law of general public importance is involved, and leave to appeal must be obtained from either court, as required by s 1 of the Administration of Justice Act 1960.

From the Court of Appeal to the House of Lords

Section 33 of the Criminal Appeal Act 1968 stipulates that an appeal will lie to the House of Lords only if the Court of Appeal certifies that the case involves a point of law of general public importance and it appears that the point is one which ought to be considered by the House of Lords and either the Court of Appeal or House of Lords gives leave for the appeal to proceed.

6.6 Other courts

The Privy Council

The Judicial Committee of the Privy Council must grant special leave for an appeal to be heard in criminal cases. This special leave will not be given unless there are exceptional circumstances, a substantial injustice has occurred and the accused has been denied a fair trial.

The Court of Justice of the European Communities

In the same way that this court may be asked to give rulings concerning civil law, so references may be made to it for the interpretation of European Community law, where this involves criminal law.

6.7 The Criminal Cases Review Commission

Appeals have strict time limits. You may have seen how long it took for the defendant in *Mullen* (1999) above to have his conviction quashed. This is because his application to appeal was too late and he had to apply to appeal out of time. In such cases, unless leave to appeal out of time is granted, wrongly convicted offenders may serve years in prison on an unsafe conviction. This is a miscarriage of justice. How can the Court of Appeal get to reconsider miscarriages of justice where the appeal is time-barred? Or what if the defendant has already appealed and his appeal was dismissed, but doubts remain about the safety of the conviction? And what if the medical or forensic evidence used to convict the defendant has subsequently been discredited?

Under the old law (s 17 of the Criminal Appeal Act 1968), only the Home Secretary was empowered to request the Court of Appeal to review such a miscarriage of justice. He was able to refer any case tried on indictment to the Court of Appeal 'if he thinks fit'. In 1993, the Royal Commission on Criminal Justice, the Runciman Commission, recommended:

> **Q** 'the responsibility for reopening cases [should be] removed from the Home Secretary and transferred to a body independent of the Government'.

The Home Secretary had rarely exercised his power. At Chapter 11, para 5, the Runciman Commission stated:

> **Q** 'The available figures for the number of cases referred by the Home Secretary to the Court of Appeal under section 17 of the Criminal Appeal Act 1968 show that the power is not often exercised. From 1981 to the end of 1988, 36 cases were referred to the Court of Appeal as a result of the doubts raised about the safety of the convictions concerned. This represents an average of between 4 and 5 cases a year. In the years 1989–1992, 28 cases have been referred, including a number of cases stemming from the terrorist incidents of the early 1970s and inquiries into the activities of the West Midlands serious crimes squad. We were told by the Home Office that it receives between 700 and 800 cases a year which are no longer before the courts and where it is claimed that there has been a wrongful conviction. (The figure for 1992 was 790 of which 634 involved a custodial sentence.) Plainly, therefore, a rigorous sifting process is applied, and only a small percentage of cases end in a reference to the Court of Appeal under section 17:

Year	No of cases referred	No of appellants	Results
1989	3	6	6 convictions quashed
1990	7	20	19 convictions quashed 1 re-trial*
1991	10	12	10 convictions quashed 1 re-trial* 1 appeal pending
1992	8	11	10 appellants pending 1 appeal dismissed

[* – Both the re-trials resulted in the defendant's acquittal.]'

Section 17 of the Criminal Appeal Act 1968 was repealed and under ss 8–12 of the Criminal Appeal Act 1995 the s 17 procedure was replaced with a new statutory body, independent of the Government, called the Criminal Cases Review Commission (CCRC). The Commission is not a court and does not decide the appeal. It refers cases to the appropriate court: cases originally heard at the Crown Court are referred to the Court of Appeal; cases originally heard at the Magistrates' Court are referred to the Crown Court, so the new system includes referring doubtful summary convictions.

The role of the Criminal Cases Review Commission

The role of the CCRC is, *inter alia*:

*   to review and investigate cases of suspected wrongful convictions and/or sentence in England and Wales and

*   to refer cases to the appropriate court whenever it feels that there is a real possibility that the conviction, verdict, finding or sentence will not be upheld.

To establish that there is a real possibility of an appeal succeeding regarding a conviction, there has to be an argument or evidence which has not been raised during the trial, or exceptional circumstances. To establish that there is a real possibility of an appeal succeeding against sentence, there has to be a legal argument or information about the individual or the offence which was not raised in court during the trial or at appeal.

References by the CCRC take effect as if they were appeals by the convicted person and, once the reference has been made, the CCRC has no further involvement. The CCRC may investigate cases of its own accord, or individuals may ask the Commission to investigate but, in either event, normal rights of appeal must ordinarily have been exhausted before the Commission can intervene (although failure to do this is not an absolute bar).

The first case referred to the Court of Appeal by the Commission was *R v Mattan, The Times,* 5th March 1998, where the conviction of a Somali seaman was overturned, over 20 years after the Home Secretary had failed to see any reason to re-open the case under s 17. In *Mattan,* Rose LJ specifically recognised the role of the CCRC as:

> **J** 'a necessary and welcome body without which the injustice in this case might never have been identified'.

On 30th July 1998, the Court of Appeal famously allowed the appeal and quashed the conviction of Derek Bentley who was hanged on 28th January 1953. Bentley had been convicted in 1952 as an accessory to the murder of a policeman by his friend. After an unsuccessful appeal, Bentley was hanged while the murderer was sentenced to detention at Her Majesty's pleasure because he was only 16. The trial judge had summed up in a pro-prosecution manner, failing to point out the

standard (beyond reasonable doubt) and burden (on the prosecution) of proof; he even kept secret from the jury that Bentley had a mental age of 11. The representations made to the Home Secretary to exercise his power under s 17 of the 1968 Act had failed to stir him into action; but the CCRC felt differently and the Court of Appeal, in quashing Bentley's conviction, agreed:

> **J** 'the summing-up in the present case had been such as to deny the appellant that fair trial which was the birthright of every British citizen.'
>
> [1999] Crim LR 330

Despite the heavy workload of the CCRC and the criticism that it prioritises cases rather badly (for example, Derek Bentley had been hanged 46 years before the appeal; while other cases where the defendants were still in prison were in the backlog) the value of the CCRC in referring miscarriages of justice cannot be doubted:

> 'In the six years from when it started work to March 31, 2003, the Commission received a total of 5,762 applications for review. 5115 reviews have been completed, 365 cases were under review and 282 were in the pending trays. The vast majority of applications were deemed ineligible for a referral to a court of appeal. The number of cases referred was 196, of which 133 had been determined. The outcomes of the referrals are interesting. 77 convictions were quashed (i.e. 64 per cent of the total of convictions) and 44 (36 per cent of the total) upheld. Ten sentences were varied and two upheld.'
>
> [2003] Crim LR 663

Over an eight-year period, the Home Secretary referred a total of 36 cases. In six years, the CCRC has referred 196. Clearly, the CCRC is not limited to referring cases which have been tried on indictment, but the difference in the approach to the review of miscarriages of justice in the English Legal System is revealing.

ACTIVITY

Self-assessment questions

1. The CCRC is an appeal court.   True/False

2. The CCRC replaced s 17 of the Criminal Appeal Act 1968.   True/False

3. The Home Secretary made over 150 referrals of suspected miscarriages of justice to an appeal court between 1990 and 1992.   True/False

4. The CCRC made over 150 referrals of suspected miscarriages of justice to an appeal court between 1998 and 2003.   True/False

ACTIVITY

A friend has been convicted of a criminal offence and asks you to which court or courts he will have to appeal in order to challenge the conviction. What is the first question you will have to ask him before you can give your reply to this question?

■ Key facts chart on appeals in criminal cases

KEY FACTS

Prosecution appeals	Following summary trial	1	By way of case stated to the Queen's Bench Divisional Court
	Following trial on indictment	1	Attorney General's reference on a point of law
		2	Attorney General's reference against an unduly lenient sentence
		3	Against a jury-tampered acquittal for which a person has been convicted
		4	Against an erroneous decision by the trial judge which effectively terminates the prosecution
		5	For a re-trial following an acquittal (the abolition of the double jeopardy rule)

CONTINUED ▶

KEY FACTS

Defence appeals	Following summary trial	1 Against conviction and/or sentence to the Crown Court
		2 By way of case stated to the Queen's Bench Divisional Court
	Following trial on indictment	1 Against conviction, to the Court of Appeal
		2 Against sentence, to the Court of Appeal
Appellate courts	Crown Court	Appeal by the defendant from the Magistrates' Court
	High Court	Appeals by the defendant or prosecution to the Queen's Bench Divisional Court by way of case stated
	Court of Appeal	Appeals by the defendant or prosecution following trials on indictment
	House of Lords	Appeals by the defendant or prosecution either from the Queen's Bench Divisional Court or the Court of Appeal
Criminal Cases Review Commission	Not an appeal court	Refers cases tried summarily or on indictment to an appeal court where it feels there is a real possibility that the conviction, verdict, finding or sentence will not be upheld

Further reading

Dennis, I, 'Prosecution Appeals and Retrial for Serious Offences' [2004] Crim LR 619.

Taylor, N and Ormerod, D, 'Mind the Gaps: Safety, Fairness and Moral Legitimacy' [2004] Crim LR 266.

chapter 7 FUNDING ■

7.1 Access to justice

When faced with a legal problem, the average person will usually need expert help from a lawyer or someone else with expertise in the particular type of legal difficulty. Most often the need is just for advice, but some people may need help in starting court proceedings and/or presenting their case in court. For the ordinary person who needs to seek legal assistance there are three main difficulties. These are:

- lack of knowledge
- fear of lawyers and
- cost.

The lack of knowledge is not only of the law and legal system, but also of where the nearest solicitor is located and which solicitor specialises in the law involved in the particular problem. The second problem is that many people have a fear of dealing with lawyers. Clients may feel intimidated through fear of the unknown. The final difficulty of cost arises because solicitors charge from about £80 an hour for routine advice from a legal executive in a small local firm to over £300 an hour for work done by a top city firm of solicitors in a specialist field. If the matter can be resolved with just one hour's advice, then the cost is not too great for most people. However, many matters are complicated and will take several hours of work. The cost can quickly run into two or three thousand pounds or even more.

Where a person cannot get the help they need, it is said that they are being denied access to justice. Access to justice involves both an open system of justice and also being able to fund the costs of a case. There have been various schemes aimed at making the law more accessible to everyone. For example, the national network of Citizens' Advice Bureaux was started in 1938 and now operates in most towns. More recently, the Law Society relaxed rules so that solicitors are allowed to advertise and inform the public of the areas of law in which they specialise. And in the last few years the Government has provided an online information service at www.justask.org.uk (now www.cls.direct.org.uk). This gives information on the solicitors available in different areas of the country.

However, the problem of cost still remains a major hurdle. A judge, Mr Justice Darling, once said:

'Cost capping . . . is unattractive in principle, because legal aid would cease to be a benefit to which a qualifying individual is entitled. It would in practice become a discretionary benefit, available at bureaucratic disposal, a benefit which would have to be disallowed when the money ran out, or when another category of case was given precedence. Legal Aid would cease to be a service available on an equal basis.'

However, despite these views, Lord Irvine, when he became Lord Chancellor in the 1997 Labour Government, took up the proposals to introduce capping and made them even more radical. A White Paper, *Modernising Justice*, Cm 4155, was published in December 1998. It set out the objectives of the new system of public funding in civil matters. These were:

• to direct resources to where they were most needed

• to ensure that disputes were resolved in a manner fair to both sides

• to provide high-quality services that achieved the best possible value for money and

• to have a budget that was affordable to the taxpayer and that was under control.

On this last point, about the cost of funding set against the need for access to justice, the White Paper stated:

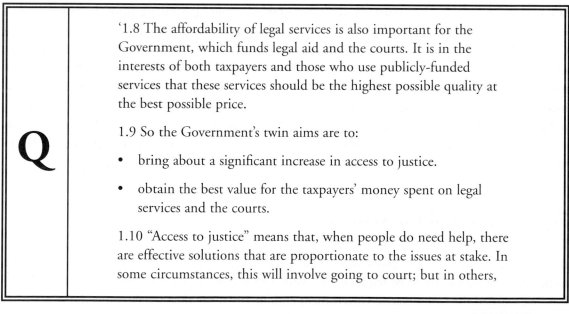

Q

'1.8 The affordability of legal services is also important for the Government, which funds legal aid and the courts. It is in the interests of both taxpayers and those who use publicly-funded services that these services should be the highest possible quality at the best possible price.

1.9 So the Government's twin aims are to:

• bring about a significant increase in access to justice.

• obtain the best value for the taxpayers' money spent on legal services and the courts.

1.10 "Access to justice" means that, when people do need help, there are effective solutions that are proportionate to the issues at stake. In some circumstances, this will involve going to court; but in others,

CONTINUED ▶

> **Q**
>
> that will not be necessary. Someone charged with a criminal offence should have access to proper legal advice and representation, when the interests of justice require it. But in civil matters, for most people, most of the time, going to court is, and should be, the last resort. It is in no-one's interest to create a litigious society. People must make responsible choices about whether a case is worth pursuing; whether to proceed by negotiation, court action, or in some other way; and how far to take a relatively minor issue.'
>
> *Modernising Justice*, Cm 4155 (1998)

In criminal cases the White Paper also wanted to balance the protection of defendants' rights against getting the best value for money from the legal aid system. The White Paper stated:

> **Q**
>
> '6.2 Defence lawyers play a crucial role in our system of criminal justice, which considers an accused person to be innocent until proven guilty. This is because the courts test the evidence by an adversarial process, which depends on the two sides vigorously putting opposing arguments. That is why someone suspected or accused of a crime must have access to criminal defence services, which:
>
> - help ensure that suspects and defendants receive a fair hearing at each stage in the criminal justice process; and in particular that they can state their case on an equal footing with the prosecution.
>
> - protect the interests of the suspect or defendant, for example by making the prosecution prove its case; or advising the defendant to enter an early guilty plea, if that is appropriate. To do this without fear or favour, the defence must be free from influence by the prosecution or the courts.
>
> - maintain the suspect's or defendant's confidence in the system, and ensure his or her effective participation in the process.'
>
> *Modernising Justice*, Cm 4155 (1998)

It was also stated that the importance of criminal defence services was reflected in statutory and international obligations, especially:

- under s 58(1) of the Police and Criminal Evidence Act 1984 which gives people arrested and held in custody the right to consult a solicitor privately
- under Art 6(3) of the European Convention on Human Rights, a defendant has a right 'to defend himself in person, or through legal assistance of his own choosing, or, if he has not sufficient means to pay for legal assistance, to be given it free when the interests of justice so require'.

The White Paper concluded:

Q	'6.5 The Government is determined that the system for funding criminal defences services, for people who cannot afford to pay themselves, should meet the fundamental objectives described in paragraph 6.2. But it should do so at an affordable cost to the taxpayer; and in a way that secures services of the right quality, for the best possible value for money.'
	Modernising Justice, Cm 4155 (1998)

ACTIVITY

Compare the principles of the Rushcliffe Committee with the objectives set out in the paragraphs from the White Paper, *Modernising Justice*.

7.2.3 The Access to Justice Act 1999

The reforms proposed in the White Paper were put into effect by the Access to Justice Act 1999. This Act established the Legal Services Commission. The Commission was to have overall control over public funding of both civil and criminal cases and to establish two services. These were:

- the Community Legal Service for civil matters and
- the Criminal Defence Service for criminal matters.

Funding for the services comes from the Government and a fixed amount is set each year. This reflects the way in which the budget is set for all public services, including health and education. An overall amount is allocated which is intended to cover both civil and criminal matters. This overall amount cannot be exceeded. These funds are then sub-divided into an amount for civil work and an amount for criminal work. The funds for civil matters are held in the Community

Legal Service Fund and there is a fixed cap on this. It is recognised that it is difficult to set a limit on funds for criminal cases for human rights reasons. So, if any more is need for criminal cases, that extra has to be taken from the amount previously intended for civil cases.

This system has led to decreasing amounts being available for civil matters. This is worrying, as the Constitutional Affairs Select Committee, in a report into legal funding published in July 2004, pointed out:

Q	'Provision for civil legal aid has been squeezed by the twin pressures of the Government's reluctance to devote more money to legal aid and the growth in criminal legal aid, as well as the cost of asylum cases . . . The Government should ring fence the civil and criminal legal aid budgets so that funding for civil work is protected and is considered quite separately from criminal defence funding.' *Civil legal aid: adequacy of provision*, Select Committee on Constitutional Affairs, Fourth Report of session 2003–04, para 1

The Access to Justice Act 1999 (s 8) also set down criteria for the production of a funding code on civil cases. These criteria are examined at section 7.4.1. Criteria for the right to representation in criminal cases were set out in Sch 3 to the 1999 Act (see section 7.5). Also, under s 13(2), the 1999 Act paved the way for the Commission to employ lawyers to advise and represent defendants. This was a major new development and has led to the setting up of the Public Defender Service (see section 7.5.4).

7.3 The Legal Services Commission

As already seen, the Commission oversees two services: the Community Legal Service and the Criminal Defence Service. Each of these can make contracts for services with lawyers or with 'not for profit' agencies (NfPs) such as Citizens' Advice Bureaux. In addition, under the Criminal Defence Service, it has set up the Public Defender Service which employs its own lawyers to advise and represent defendants. This structure is shown in Figure 7.1.

(c) boundary disputes

(d) the making of wills

(e) matters of trust law

(f) defamation or malicious falsehood

(g) matters of company or partnership law or

(h) other matters arising form the carrying on of a business.

Any matter not relating to the law of England and Wales is also excluded. Small claims are not specifically excluded but the Funding Code makes it clear funding for any claim for damages of less than £5,000 will be refused unless there is a significant wider public interest point in the case.

Advocacy in the main courts will be funded in appropriate cases, but advocacy is excluded from most tribunals. Of the 70 or so tribunal which exist in our legal system, funding may only be given for cases in the following:

- Employment Appeal Tribunal
- Mental Health Review Tribunal
- Immigration Adjudicator or Appeal Tribunal
- Special Immigration Appeals Commission
- Proscribed Organisations Appeals Commission
- VAT and Duties Tribunal
- s 9 of the Protection of Children Act Tribunal
- General and Special Commissioners of Income Tax.

7.4.3 The merits test

Under the old legal system the applicant had to satisfy the Legal Aid Board that he had reasonable grounds for taking or defending a case. This merits tests operated in two parts: first, was there sufficient prospect of success and, second, would it be reasonable for a client who had the means to spend his own money on the case?

The Access to Justice Act 1999 and the Funding Code have radically altered the merits test. Not only must there be prospect of succeeding in the case, but also that it would be reasonable to fund it out of the Community Legal Service Fund. As result of combining these two criteria, the Funding Code specifically states that Full Representation will be refused unless:

(a) where the prospects of success are very good (80 per cent plus) the likely damages will exceed costs or

(b) where the prospects of success are good (60–80 per cent) the likely damages will exceed costs by a ratio of 2 to 1 or

(c) where the prospects of success are moderate (50–60 per cent) the likely damages will exceed costs by a ratio of 4 to 1.

7.4.4 Means testing

Even, if the matter is one which is included in the public funding scheme, no help will be given unless the applicant can show that they come within strict financial criteria. Their income and capital are considered in deciding this. There is a strict upper limit of gross income and applicants must be below this to qualify for funding. In addition, they must be below specific levels for disposable income and disposable capital. The amounts of these levels may be increased each year.

Disposable income

Disposable income is calculated by starting with the gross income and taking away:

- tax and National Insurance;
- housing costs
- childcare costs or maintenance paid for children
- an allowance for each dependant
- a standard allowance for employment (where the person is employed), currently £45.

People receiving Income Support or Income-Based Jobseeker's Allowance automatically qualify, assuming that their disposable capital is below the set level.

There is a minimum amount of disposable income below which the applicant does not have to pay any contribution towards their funding. For income levels above this minimum level, a monthly contribution has to be paid. The more in excess of the minimum, the greater the amount of the contribution. Monthly disposable income is graded into bands. Those bands are:

Monthly disposable income	Monthly contribution
Band A	$\frac{1}{4}$ of income in excess of the band
Band B	+ $\frac{1}{3}$ of income in excess of the band
Band C	+ $\frac{1}{2}$ of income in excess of the band

This idea of minimum and maximum levels is best explained by a diagram and is shown in Figure 7.2.

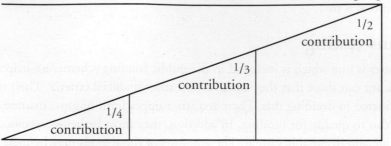

Figure 7.2 Contributions to funding

Disposable capital

Disposable capital is the assets of the person, such as money in a bank or savings account, stocks and shares or expensive jewellery. For Legal Help, Help at Court and representation in immigration matters, the maximum limit for disposable capital is £3,000. Funding is not available if the person has assets worth more than this. For the other publicly funded services there is a minimum limit for disposable capital at £3,000 and a maximum of £8,000. If the assets are below £3,000, then no contribution is payable. If the person has over £3,000 but under £8,000 they will have to pay the extra above £3,000 as a contribution towards their funding. If they have more than £8,000 they must use their own money to fund any legal case, although once they have spent the money in excess of £8,000 they can become eligible for funding. Where a person owns a home the value of that home is taken into account in deciding the disposable capital. This done by deducting the amount of mortgage, but only up to £100,000, from the current value of the property. If the amount left after this exceeds £100,000 then all the excess is counted as disposable capital.

Example

House current market value	£220,000
Mortgage £140,000 – can only deduct £100,000	£100,000
leaves	£120,000
Deduct allowance of £100,000 from the value =	£20,000

So this remaining amount of £20,000 is counted as disposable capital. Clearly, this is over the maximum limit allowed for disposable capital and, therefore, the person would not qualify to receive funding.

7.4.5 Evaluation of civil legal aid

So is this new system being effective? We started the beginning of the chapter by pointing out that people had problems with getting help to deal with a civil matter. The new service for public funding does not appear to have improved this, as shown by a survey by the Legal Services Commission, *Causes of Action: Civil Law and Social Justice*, published in February 2004. This survey was based on interviews with 5,611 adults from 3,348 randomly picked households and showed that many people do not seek help for legal problems. One-third of the adults surveyed had had at least one civil law problem over a three-and-a-half-year period. One-fifth took no action. About 15 per cent of those who sought advice did not succeed in finding any. This tended to be for problems connected with homelessness, rented housing, anti-social neighbours and welfare benefits. About 25 per cent of those who sought advice did so from non-specialist people or organisations.

Eligibility

In section 7.2.1 we saw that, in the 1990s, before the change to the new system under the Access to Justice Act 1999, the percentage of people eligible to receive funding had decreased to about 48 per cent. The new legal funding criteria have caused further decreases. A report by the Legal Services Commission' Research Centre found that in 2001–02 under 43 per cent of the population was eligible. In 2004 the Select Committee on Constitutional Affairs, which investigated the adequacy of the provision of civil legal aid, stated that:

Q	'At present, the legal aid system is increasingly being restricted to those with no means at all. There is a substantial risk that many people of modest means but who are home owners will fall out of the ambit of legal aid. In many cases this may amount to a serious denial of access to justice.' Select Committee on Constitutional Affairs, Fourth Report of session 2003–04, *Civil legal aid: adequacy of provision*, para 105

As well as fewer people being eligible, the Annual Report of the Legal Services Commission for 2003–04 showed that 13 per cent fewer people were given public funding than in the previous year. So funding is being provided for a decreasing number of civil matters.

Advice deserts

In September 2003, at the Citizens' Advice Bureaux annual conference, the Chief Executive gave some specific examples of the non-availability of legal aid. He identified areas where solicitors' firms had pulled out of government-funded work. They also published a report, *Geography of Advice*. This showed that between January 2000 and June 2003 there were large drops in the number of civil contracts offered. For example, contracts in:

- housing law fell from 743 to 489 (a 34 per cent reduction)
- debt law fell from 462 to 206 (a 55 per cent reduction)
- family law fell by 23 per cent
- welfare benefit fell by 50 per cent.

The problems of 'advice deserts' was also considered by the Constitutional Affairs Select Committee in 2004. In the evidence to the Committee, even the Legal Services Commission acknowledged that:

> **Q** 'It is clear that there are parts of England and Wales in which the need for publicly funded legal services is not currently being met. This is likely to be common ground between all the bodies submitting evidence to this enquiry.'
>
> *Civil legal aid: adequacy of provision*, para 50

The Select Committee gave as an illustrative example the position in Northumberland. It found that, in addition to the absence of any housing law advisers in Northumberland (which was admitted by the Legal Services Commission), there was also no contracted provision for health or community care in the North East and no contract for immigration law in Northumberland. Furthermore, there were only two contracts for employment law in the area.

It is clear that certain categories of law suffer from shortage of provision. The Legal Services Commission itself acknowledged in its evidence to the Select Committee that it was worried about this when it reported that it:

> **Q** 'remain[s] concerned about the provision of services in certain categories of law. The number of housing contracts, for example, has fallen from 841 in April 2000 [when the Commission took over responsibility for publicly funded legal help] to 595 in December 2003'.
>
> *Civil legal aid: adequacy of provision*, para 67

Other problems

The Select Committee on Constitutional Affairs also highlighted other problems. For example, on the numbers of contracts offered to solicitors the Committee said:

> **Q** 'If it is the policy of the Legal Services Commission to deal with fewer firms, this creates a number of problems. For example, if fewer solicitors' firms have contracts the problems of supply in rural areas will be exacerbated, especially in family law disputes which require different solicitors' firms for each of the parties. In time, the limited sourcing of legal aid work to fewer firms may result in higher fees being charged, since the bargaining position of the Department will be weaker. Fewer contracts with firms would involve the loss of investment in resources which the current body of experienced, trained and motivated legal aid practitioners represents. Once these valuable practitioners are lost, they will be hard to replace.'
>
> *Civil legal aid: adequacy of provision*, para 67

Another point it raised was the exclusion of Employment Tribunals from the system. In its report the Committee said:

> **Q** 'It is not acceptable that in employment cases employees can be forced to represent themselves in circumstances where private employers are able to employ lawyers to represent them. If proceedings are to be fair, there needs to be equality of arms. Legal aid should not automatically be excluded from such tribunal hearings.'
>
> *Civil legal aid: adequacy of provision*, para 111

Signposting

There has also been research into whether clients are 'signposted' adequately: in other words, that they are referred to solicitors' firms or other agencies with expertise in their particular problem. In research, *Evaluating Entry, Initial Advice and Signposting using Model Clients*, (December 2002), Moorhead and Sherr used clients to test the approach of 294 Specialist Quality Mark holders when approached by clients needing advice in a category of work in which they did not specialise.

Between 35 per cent and 40 per cent of clients were signposted (ie advised to see another supplier) to an appropriate supplier but a similar number were signposted to a less appropriate supplier. About 7 per cent of clients received advice that appeared to be damaging to their interests, while another 5 per cent received advice which was poor. There were also problems in contacting not for profit suppliers by telephone and the researchers found that about 12 per cent of visits resulted in severe access problems.

Human rights

In *Steel and Morris v United Kingdom (Application No 6841/01)*, *The Times*, 16th February 2005, the European Court of Human Rights held that the denial of legal aid to defendants in a defamation case was a breach of Art 6 (the right to a fair trial) of the European Convention on Human Rights.

CASE EXAMPLE

Steel and Morris v United Kingdom (Application No 6841/01), *The Times*, 16th February 2005

The defendants had published a six-page leaflet 'What's wrong with McDonald's? On the basis of what was stated in this leaflet McDonald's had brought a defamation claim against the defendants. The defendants applied for legal aid but were refused as legal aid is not available for defamation actions.

The defendants had to represent themselves, while McDonald's had leading counsel and junior counsel and at least one solicitor present in court throughout the case. The case was very complex, both factually and legally. It lasted 313 days and involved 40,000 pages of documentary evidence and 130 witnesses giving oral evidence.

The European Court of Human Rights held that the denial of legal aid deprived the defendants of the opportunity to present their case effectively before the court and contributed to an unacceptable inequality of arms with McDonald's. There had therefore been a violation of Art 6.

ACTIVITY

Use the Web to look up current rules on financial eligibility in civil matters. The Legal Services Commission website address is www.legalservices.gov.uk

7.5 The Criminal Defence Service

Legal advice and representation are recognised as basic human rights. This is set out in Art 6 of the European Convention on Human Rights which states:

 'Art 6(3) Everyone charged with a criminal offence has the following minimum rights:
...

(b) to have adequate time and facilities for the preparation of his defence;

(c) to defend himself in person or through legal assistance of his own choosing or, if he has not sufficient means to pay for legal assistance, to be given it free when the interests of justice so require . . .'

In compliance with this, s 12 of the Access to Justice Act 1999 required the Legal Services Commission to establish a Criminal Defence Service. This service is aimed at 'securing that individuals involved in criminal investigation or proceedings have access to such advice, assistance and representation as the interests of justice require'. It came into operation in April 2001. It consists of:

- duty solicitor schemes
- advice and assistance
- representation.

7.5.1 Duty solicitors

Section 13 of the Access to Justice Act 1999 states that the Commission shall fund such advice and assistance as it considers appropriate for individuals who are arrested and held in custody at a police station or other premises. Originally this meant that anyone held was eligible to receive free advice from a duty solicitor. However, since May 2004, the work that can be done by duty solicitors has been reduced. They can no longer normally attend at a police station where the client is detained:

- for a non-imprisonable offence
- on a warrant
- in breach of bail conditions
- for drink/drive offences.

They can still attend for the above in situations where the client is vulnerable, eg a youth, mentally ill, cannot speak English. They can also attend where the client complains of serious maltreatment by the police.

One of the problems found in the 1990s with duty solicitor schemes was that in many cases, the solicitor did not attend at the police station but merely gave advice over the telephone. Although this was viewed as a defect in the scheme, telephone advice has now become the Government's preferred method of action for duty solicitors. The changes made in May 2004 mean that solicitors cannot claim for attending at the police station unless they can show that attendance was expected to 'materially progress the case'.

7.5.2 Advice and Assistance

Advice and Assistance is limited to one hour's work. The assistance can only include advocacy if the solicitor has applied for a representation order which has been refused. In May 2004 Advice and Assistance was withdrawn from cases where:

- the offender is on bail and is charged with a non-imprisonable offence
- trial is in the Magistrates' Court; the solicitor must get a representation order (this will presumably lead to more cases being adjourned).

Normally there is a means test for Advice and assistance and only those on low incomes will qualify. However, a duty solicitor at a Magistrates' Court can still see all defendants in custody under the Advice and Assistance scheme. For this there is no charge.

7.5.3 Representation

This covers the cost of a solicitor to prepare the defence before the case gets to court. It also covers representation at court, including such issues as bail. If the case requires a barrister, then this will also be covered. There is a merits test for representation.

Merits

The test on whether a defendant's case merits public funding being spent is whether it is in the interests of justice to do so. Schedule 3 to the Access to Justice Act 1999 lays down the factors to be considered in deciding this: These are:

1. whether the individual would, if any matter arising in the proceedings is decided against him, be likely to lose his liberty or livelihood or suffer serious damage to his reputation
2. whether the determination of any matter arising in the proceedings may involve consideration of a substantial point of law
3. whether the individual may be unable to understand the proceedings or to state his own case
4. whether the proceedings may involve the tracing, interviewing or expert cross-examination of witnesses on behalf of the individual or
5. whether it is in the interests of another person that the individual is represented.

In point 1 of this list, the stress is on whether the defendant is likely to be given a custodial sentence. For example, theft carries a maximum sentence of seven years' imprisonment. However, first-time offenders charged with a small theft are never given a custodial sentence, so they would not meet the test of being likely to lose their liberty. However, a defendant charged with stealing from work might be at risk of losing his job and so might qualify under the 'likely to lose livelihood' part of these criteria. The more serious the offence charged, the more likely there is a risk of loss of liberty, so defendants charged with offences such as rape or a serious assault will come within this test.

Point 3 makes sure that those who are not capable of understanding the proceedings or being able to ask questions or put their own case are given representation. This covers those who have a disability such as deafness, or mental illness affecting their understanding. It also applies to those who do not speak English sufficiently well to present their own case.

The last point, whether it is in the interests of another person that the individual is represented, is necessary to protect victims in alleged sex abuse cases from being questioned directly by the defendant and other similar situations.

Means

Before the setting up of the Criminal Defence Service, there was a means test for representation. This was abolished in 2001. However, at the end of a case, the judge could order a defendant to pay a contribution towards the costs of his defence, but only if it was reasonable in all the circumstances, including the means of the defendant. By 2003, the cost of criminal legal aid had increased so much that the Government was considering ways of reducing the cost and in May 2004 a draft Criminal Defence Service Bill 2004 was issued.

This Bill is aimed at tightening the granting of criminal legal aid and has two basic policies:

1. It is intended to transfer the responsibility for the granting of criminal legal aid from the courts to the Legal Services Commission.
2. It will re-introduce means testing for criminal legal aid.

The detail of these policies is not contained in the Bill. It is proposed that details should be dealt with by way of secondary legislation.

The Select Committee on Constitutional Affairs reported on the Bill in its Fifth Report of session 2003–04. It stated that it supported the underlying aim of the draft Bill to control the rising cost of criminal legal aid. However, they had two major concerns:

1. Whether the law was human rights compliant. Of the models of means testing proposed, they felt that two were unworkable in practice and other one could lead to successful challenges under the Human Rights Act 1998.
2. That means testing would significantly increase the administrative burden on criminal defence solicitors and the Legal Services Commission. This would threaten the Legal Services Commission's efforts to reduce bureaucracy for legal aid solicitors and could dissuade practitioners from undertaking legally aided work.

This finding was made after hearing evidence from The Law Society, the Bar Council, firms of solicitors and other providers. One firm in Sunderland (where there is now a Public Defender Office) pointed out that it could only afford to offer newly qualified staff a salary of £20,000 yet the Public Defender Office had the funding to offer £32,000. The firm felt that it was 'particularly galling to find that the Legal Services Commission is willing to pay more for what is, on present evidence, a less efficient service'. To help with this problem the Legal Services Commission has announced that firms taking part in their preferred supplier scheme will be given a grant of £30,000 towards student training.

Only about 7 per cent of newly qualified solicitors consider a career in legal aid, although about half would have been interested in doing so if the level of pay had been more realistic. The fact that the vast majority had student debts of over £10,000 was one of the factors in turning away from low-paid work.

The Committee was also critical of the level of fees and the amount of bureaucracy involved. On level of fees it reported:

While, on bureaucracy, the chairman of the Committee said:

Q	'There is a serious risk that if legally aided work is associated with very low fees, this may have a serious impact on the quality of people who undertake legally aided cases. The problems that are faced by clients who require legal aid support are often of the most complex variety . . . It is vitally important that they have access to justice which can only be guaranteed by recourse to fully competent advisers.' (para 75)

Q	'During the enquiry we heard repeatedly about problems of excessive bureaucracy associated with civil legal aid contracts and a cost-compliance system that is arbitrary, inaccurate and ill-conceived. Clearly, there is a need to ensure that professional standards are maintained, but the evidence we received drew attention to the fact that reputable firms and competent and honest solicitors are being punished by an audit system that imposes what can only be described as draconian review methods. For the committee, this is the most serious criticism of the current system for managing legal aid work that we have found.' Alan Beith MP, Chair of the House of Commons Select Committee on Constitutional Affairs Committee, on its report *Civil legal aid: adequacy of provision* 2004 (Legal Action, August 2004)

Key facts chart on public funding of cases

KEY FACTS

Civil cases Community Legal Service	Criminal cases Criminal Defence Service
Legal Services Commission oversees both services	
Different levels of help and representation available: • Legal Help • Help at Court • Legal Representation • Support Funding • special services for family cases.	Different levels of help and representation available: • Duty Solicitor at the police station • Advice and Assistance • Legal Representation.
Merits test for representation Whether the case has a reasonable chance of success and the damages will be worth more than the costs. Other criteria, including: • can the matter be funded in another way? • are there funds available?	Merits test for representation Whether it is in the interests of justice: • defendant at risk of losing liberty, livelihood or reputation • substantial point of law involved • defendant unable to understand proceedings • involves tracing, interview or expert cross-examination of witnesses • is in the interests of another person.
Means test Strict means test on gross income, disposable income and disposable capital.	Means test Duty solicitor free of charge and not means tested. Means testing being re-introduced for representation.
Problems • Capping of fund together with increasing criminal expenditure means that less is available for civil matters. • Number of solicitors is decreasing. • Financial level of eligibility exclude people of modest means. • Not available for Employment Tribunal cases.	Problems • The re-introduction of means testing may cause problems. • Does the Public Defender Service give value for money?

225

7.7 Private funding

As pointed out at the beginning of this chapter, it is possible to pay privately for legal advice and representation. However, the costs are high, particularly where a civil case goes to court. The main problem is that it is not possible to predict exactly how long a case will last, and, therefore, what the costs are likely to be. For example, will the other side admit liability or will they fight the case? If so, will they try to delay the hearing for as long as possible? Another major problem is that if the case is lost, then the claimant may be ordered to pay the other side's costs. In order help people to fund cases privately and to avoid unforeseen expense, the Government introduced conditional fee agreements.

7.7.1 Conditional fee agreements

Conditional fees must not be confused with contingency fees. Contingency fees are the system used in the USA for private funding of civil claims. They operate on the basis that, if the case is won, the lawyer will be paid a percentage of the damages awarded to the claimant. In this country there has always been concern that this system of paying a percentage of the winnings to the lawyer gives the lawyer too great a financial interest in the outcome of the litigation. It is thought that it promotes 'ambulance chasing' in which lawyers almost literally follow an injured person to hospital in order to get the right to take the case. In addition, it may tempt some lawyers to use unethical means to ensure that they win the case. Conditional fees do not give the lawyer a stake in the amount of the damages. Instead, the lawyer and the client agree a success fee which will be paid to the lawyer if the case is won. The amount of the damages is irrelevant.

Conditional fee agreements (CFAs) were first allowed by s 58 of the Courts and Legal Services Act 1990. However, they were limited to a conditional fee arrangement in personal injury cases, insolvency cases and human rights cases. Although the 1990 Act paved the way for conditional fees, it took five years before the Conditional Fee Agreements Regulations 1995 (SI 1995 No 1674) set out the details of how the system was to work. So the first such agreements were not actually used until 1995. In 1998, the Government extended the use of conditional fees to all civil cases where there was a money claim (excluding any family matters). In 1998, the Government also issued a White Paper, *Modernising Justice*, in which it set out proposals for extending CFAs further. This White Paper stated:

> '2.34 A person should not have to be very rich, or poor enough to qualify
> for legal aid, to be able to pursue a strong and worthwhile case. But unless
> the case is also a simple one, it will be necessary to pay for one or more
> lawyers. Many people with good cases are put off because they cannot afford
> lawyers' fees. Others are put off simply by fear of a very large bill, because
> they are not sure how the fees will mount up over time. The Government
> intends to make legal bills more affordable and predictable, by:
>
> • working with the insurance industry to develop less expensive
>   legal insurance.
>
> • ensuring that lawyers provide full and clear information to their
>   clients about the likely cost of taking a case; and, where
>   appropriate, regulating the costs which lawyers can charge their
>   own clients or recover from the other side.
>
> • extending and improving conditional fees.'

The White Paper went on to point out that:

> '2.43 Where they are allowed, conditional fees have already greatly
> extended access to justice. With conditional fees, people can take
> good cases, in the certain knowledge that they will not be left out of
> pocket if they lose (except by the amount of any insurance
> premium). In July 1998, following consultation, the Government
> extended the benefits of conditional fees to all types of civil case,
> except family proceedings . . .'

The Access to Justice Act 1999 amended s 58 of the Courts and Legal Service Act 1990 so that
they could also be used in civil claims where there was no money claim (eg a claim for an
injunction).

Success fees

Conditional fees are often referred to as 'no win, no fee', but this is not a completely accurate
description, since the client may be expected to pay something towards the solicitor's costs. It
depends on the precise agreement made between the client and the solicitor. Often they will agree a
fee at the beginning of a case and also agree that if the solicitor wins the case he can charge an
'uplift' known as a 'success fee'; this can be up to 100 per cent. The great advantage is that the
client knows exactly how much the case will cost and can budget accordingly. One problem used to
be that where the amount won by way of damages was small, the uplift could absorb all the client's

damages, even though The Law Society had recommended a cap of 25 per cent of damages in its model agreement. This problem has been overcome by changes to the rules on CFAs so that the agreement can include a clause that, if the amount of damages awarded is less than the success fee, the solicitor will not be able to recover anything in excess of the amount of damages. Another problem was that under the original rules the success fee could not be reclaimed from the losing side as part of the costs of the case. The Access to Justice Act 1999 brought in new rules so that the success fee can now be claimed as costs of the case, however, there were still disputes as to how much of the success the losing party should pay. This problem was addressed in *Callery v Gray* [2002] UKHL 28 and *Halloran v Delaney* [2002] EWCA Civ 1258 (see below).

After-the-event insurance

Once conditional fee agreements were being used it quickly became apparent that claimants were still at risk of paying the other side's costs if they lost the case. This was overcome by the development of 'after-the-event' insurance. Insurance against legal costs already existed, but only where the incident had already occurred. For example, it is common with most car insurance policies to pay an extra amount for any legal expenses which may arise from driving the vehicle in the future. After-the-event insurance allows claimants to insure against the risk of paying costs been after a claim has already been started. However, the insurance premium has to be paid in advance of the case and this causes problems to those who cannot afford the premium. In addition, under the original rules on CFAs, the amount of the premium could not be claimed back from the losing party. This problem was considered in the White Paper, *Modernising Justice*, where the Government stated that:

> **Q**
>
> '2.44 We also intend to widen the scope of conditional fees in another very important way. In practice, at the moment, only people who expect to win money from their case can benefit from conditional fees. This is the only was that most people can afford to pay the success fee. But it means that a successful litigant will not receive all the money which he or she had been awarded. The Government believes that this is wrong. So, in future, we intend to make it possible for the winning party to recover the success fee, and any insurance premium, from the losing party – the person or organisation that has committed the legal wrong. This will make conditional fees more attractive and fairer, and allow defendants and claimants whose case is not about money to use them. This will be a further radical extension to access to justice.'

These proposals were brought into effect by s 29 of the Access to Justice Act 1999, so that where the case is won, the insurance premium can also be claimed as part of the costs from the losing party. Even so there were several disputes about the amount of success fee which could be claimed. The matter was thoroughly considered in *Callery v Gray* (2002).

ASE EXAMPLE

Callery v Gray [2002] UKHL 28

The claimant was injured in a road traffic accident. He entered into a conditional fee agreement with his solicitor which included a success fee of 60 per cent. He also took out after-the-event insurance (ATE) at a premium of £350, on the same day that his solicitors notified the defendant of the claim. The action was settled without proceedings being issued and the defendant agreed to pay the claimant's reasonable costs. There was a dispute about the amount of the success fee to be paid by the defendant and also whether the premium for the ATE could be recovered from a defendant when no proceedings had been issued. The District Judge allowed a success fee of 40 per cent and permitted recovery of the ATE premium. The case was appealed to a Circuit Judge and then to the Court of Appeal.

The Court of Appeal held that:

- it would normally be reasonable for a CFA and ATE insurance to be taken out at the start of a case (ie before contacting the defendant and so prior to any response by him)
- the ATE premium is recoverable in full even where the case settles pre-proceedings
- a 20 per cent success fee is the maximum that the defendant would normally be ordered to pay in a modest and straightforward personal injury case.

The Court of Appeal found that there was overwhelming evidence that the premium for an ATE policy taken out after the commencement of proceedings was considerably higher than one taken out before proceedings were commenced. Indeed, in some cases it might prove impossible to obtain cover at a late stage in the proceedings. This was the reason for holding that it was reasonable to take out ATE insurance at the same time as entering into the CFA. On this point, when the case went to the House of Lords, Lord Scott dissented on the point of ATE being recoverable. He felt that the purchase of the policy amounted to 'useless expenditure' and could not be justified, having regard to the purposes behind the civil justice reforms

The matter was further appealed to the House of Lords where a majority upheld the Court of Appeal's decision. However, they also held that the responsibility for monitoring and controlling the regime for funding litigation lay with the Court of Appeal. One of the main reasons for this was that the House of Lords could not respond to changes in practice with the 'speed and sensitivity' of the Court of Appeal.

Reconsideration of the success fee

Both the Court of Appeal and the House of Lords gave warning that the amount of the success fee might be re-visited. The Court of Appeal made it plain that it was not purporting to lay down rules applicable for all time, but was giving provisional guidance to be reviewed in the light of increased knowledge and developing experience. Lord Woolf gave a hypothetical example:

> **J** 'It is open to a solicitor and client to agree at the outset a two-stage success fee, which assumes that the case will not settle, at least until after the end of the pre-action protocol period, if at all, but which is subject to a rebate if it does settle before the end of that period. Thus, by way of example, the uplift may be agreed at 100%, subject to a reduction to 5% should the claim settle before the end of the protocol period.'

In the House of Lords Lord Bingham admitted that there was obvious force in the argument that even a 20 per cent success fee was generous, given the miniscule risk of failure. It should also be noted that if the solicitor and claimant agree a greater success fee, the solicitor can still claim the excess above 20 per cent from the claimant. The matter did not rest there. The next case on the point was *Halloran v Delaney* (2002). The case involved a claimant who was injured in a road accident and, like the claimant in *Callery v Gray* (2002), he entered into a CFA. This time the success fee was set at 40 per cent. Again, the dispute was only over the costs. In this case the Court of Appeal stated that 5 per cent was the appropriate uplift in a straightforward and simple road accident case which settles with no disputes and without the issue of proceedings.

This difference from the judgment in *Callery v Gray* (2002) caused some confusion. However, so far as road accident cases are concerned, new rules which came into effect in June 2004 now make clear the amount of success fee that can be claimed. Insurers for the defendant will have to pay the claimant's solicitor a 12.5 per cent success fee if they win cases that settle out of court. However, for cases that go to trial, solicitors can claim a 100 per cent success fee.

7.7.2 The legal profession and CFAs

Although a large number of cases are now funded by CFAs, there are still worries about the system. A survey by The Law Society published in January 2003 found that three-quarters of the 100 solicitors questioned believed that CFAs were not working. There were worries over:

- the number of challenges to the enforceability of the agreements (45 per cent of respondents had been challenged) and

- problems caused by front loading of costs which were then challenged on the basis of proportionality (see Chapter 4 for discussion of post-Woolf problems of front-loading of costs).

The Government is consulting on how to make CFAs simpler so that challenges to their enforceability are less likely to arise.

Courts and Legal Services Act 1990	Client pays own success fee
Access to Justice Act 1999	Allows court to order that losing party pays other sides success fee
Callery v Gray (2002)	Decided that losing party should pay only a 20% success fee If agreement is for more the winning client pays the rest of success fee
Halloran v Delaney (2002)	Decided that losing party should pay only a 5% success fee where a simple case settles before going to court (If agreement is for more the winning client pays the rest of success fee) But the losing party should pay a success fee of 100% where case goes to court
2004 Rules on road accident cases	Losing party to pay: • a 12.5% success fee where a simple case settles before going to court and • a success fee of 100% where case goes to court

■ *Figure 7.3 Changes to who pays the success fee*

7.7.3 Claims firms

One of the effects of the introduction of CFAs was the number of claims management firms which came into existence. Initially these firms were very successful. For example, Claims Direct made a pre-tax profit of £10.1 million in 2000, even though it was spending up to £1.5 million a month on advertising. However, two of the biggest of these firms, Claims Direct and The Accident Group, who between them had the major share of the claims market, went into liquidation in 2002 and 2003 respectively. This suggests that even where a firm has a large turnover of cases, it is impossible to make sufficient profit from CFAs to cover the running expenses of a business.

7.8 Advice agencies

Apart from lawyers there are other bodies which provide legal advice and help. The main ones of these are Citizens' Advice Bureaux and Law Centres, but there others which can offer specialist advice on certain topics, for example the RAC and the AA offer members some help in traffic matters, while trade unions will help members with legal problems in work-related matters. There are also charities such as Shelter which offer advice to people with housing problems. The legal

definition of a 'mentally ill person' for the purposes of the Juries Act 1974 is likely to be amended in answer to these criticisms.

However, certain people are not permitted to sit on a jury even though they are within these basic qualifications; these are people who are disqualified or for various reasons lack the capacity to act effectively as a juror.

8.2.2 Disqualification from jury service

Some criminal convictions will disqualify a person from jury service. The type of sentence and the length of a prison sentence decide whether the person is disqualified and the period for which that disqualification lasts.

Disqualified permanently are those who at any time have been sentenced to:

• imprisonment for life, detention for life or custody for life

• detention during Her Majesty's pleasure or during the pleasure of the Secretary of State

• imprisonment for public protection or detention for public protection

• an extended sentence

• a term of imprisonment of five years or more or a term of detention of five years or more.

Disqualified for ten years are those who have:

• at any time in the last 10 years served a sentence of imprisonment

• had a suspended sentence passed on them

• had a community order or other community sentence passed on them.

In addition, anyone who is currently on bail in criminal proceedings is disqualified from sitting as a juror. If a disqualified person fails to disclose that fact and turns up for jury service, they may be fined up to £5,000.

8.2.3 Excusal from jury service

Until April 2004 there was a category of people who were ineligible for jury service. This included judges and others who had been involved in the administration of justice within the previous 10 years. This category was abolished by the Criminal Justice Act 2003. This means that judges, lawyers, police etc are eligible to serve on juries. Many people feel that this could lead to bias or to a legally well-qualified juror influencing the rest of the jury. When Lord Justice Dyson (from the Court of Appeal) was summoned to attend as a juror in June 2004, the Lord Chief Justice, Lord Woolf, issued observations to judges who are called for jury service. These point out that:

• a judge serves on a jury as part of his duty as a private citizen

• excusal from jury service will be granted only in extreme circumstances

• deferral of jury service to a later date should be sought where a judge has judicial commitments which make it particularly inconvenient for him to do jury service at the time he was called to do so

- at court, if a judge knows the presiding judge or other person in the case, he should raise this with the jury bailiff or a member of the court staff if he considers it could interfere with his responsibilities as a juror

- it is a matter of discretion for an individual judge sitting as a juror as to whether he discloses the fact of his judicial office to the other members of the jury

- judges must follow the directions given to the jury by the trial judge on the law and should avoid the temptation to correct guidance which they believe to be inaccurate as this is outside their role as a juror.

The point about letting the court know when someone involved in the case is personally known to the juror is also relevant to practising lawyers who are called for jury service. It was noticeable that when a Queen's Counsel was summoned for jury service at the Central Criminal Court (the Old Bailey) in the summer of 2004, he was prevented from sitting in each case that he was called for, on the ground that he knew one or more people involved each trial.

Before April 2004 mentally ill people were also in the ineligible category. Now, as already seen above, they are disqualified from jury service under the 2003 Act.

The right to be excused jury service

Also prior to April 2004, people in certain essential occupations, such as doctors, had a right to be excused jury service if they did not want to do it. The Criminal Justice Act 2003 also abolished this category. However, for full-time serving members of the forces there is discretion to excuse from service if the commanding officer certifies that it would be prejudicial to the efficiency of the service. This means that doctors and other medical staff will no longer be able to refuse to do jury service, though they can apply for a discretionary excusal.

The removal of the categories of ineligible and excusable as of right was intended to increase the number of people who were available for jury service and also ensure that all levels of society are represented on juries. Whether this alteration will have the required effect is debatable. It was found in that in 2001 nearly one in three people summoned for jury trial was excused from service. However, of the over half a million people summoned, only 32,321 were excused as of right. (These would no longer have the right to be excused.) Also, in a three-week sample from eight courts it was found that only 1.3 per cent were ineligible because of their profession. These figures suggest that the widening of eligibility will have little effect. This is also borne out by figures from April 2002 to March 2003 when the Jury Central Summoning Bureau summoned about 480,000 jurors. Of these:

- only 44 per cent served as jurors (either on the date originally given or on a deferred date);
- 25 per cent were given a discretionary excusal

were only doing their normal duty of preventing crime. Further, the court said that, if in the course of looking at criminal records convictions were revealed which did not disqualify, there was no reason why these should not be passed on to prosecuting counsel, so that this information could be used in deciding to stand by individual jurors (see section 8.3.3 for information on the right of stand by).

The second type of vetting is where a wider check is made on a juror's background and political affiliations. This practice was brought to light by the 'ABC' trial in 1978 where two journalists and a soldier were charged with collecting secret information. It was discovered that the jury had been vetted for their loyalty. The trial was stopped and a new trial ordered before a fresh jury. Following these cases the Attorney General in 1980 published guidelines on when political vetting of jurors should take place. These guidelines were revised in 1988 in a Practice Note (*Jury: Stand By: Jury Checks*) [1988] 3 All ER 1086 and state that:

a) vetting should be used only in exceptional cases involving:

    (i) national security where part of the evidence is likely to be given *in camera* (in private)

    (ii) terrorist cases

b) vetting can only be carried out with the Attorney General's express permission.

8.3.3 At court

The jurors are usually divided into groups of 15 and allocated to a court. At the start of a trial the court clerk will select 12 out of these 15 at random. If there are not enough jurors to hear all the cases going scheduled for that day at the court, there is a special power to select anyone who is qualified to be a juror from people passing by in the streets or from local offices or businesses. This is called 'praying a talesman'. It is very unusual to use this power but it was used at Middlesex Crown Court in January 1992 when about half the jury panel failed to turn up after the New Year's holiday and there were not sufficient jurors to try the cases.

8.3.4 Challenging

Once the court clerk has selected the panel of 12 jurors, these jurors come into the jury box to be sworn in as jurors. At this point in criminal cases, before the jury is sworn both the prosecution and defence have certain rights to challenge one or more of the jurors. There is no right to challenge in a civil case. There are two challenges which can be made and, in addition the prosecution have a special right of 'stand by'. These are:

1. To the array

This right to challenge is given by s 5 of the Juries Act 1974 and it is a challenge to the whole jury on the basis that it has been chosen in an unrepresentative or biased way. This challenge was used successfully against the 'Romford' jury at the Old Bailey in 1993 when, out of a panel of 12 jurors, nine came from Romford, with two of them living within 20 doors of each other in the same street. In *R v Danvers* [1982] Crim LR 680 this method of challenging a jury was also used. In this case the defendant was of an ethnic minority background but all the jurors were white, so the defence used a challenge to the array on the basis that the jury did not reflect the ethnic composition of the jury. The Court of Appeal held that in law there was no requirement that the jury should be ethnically mixed. Also in *R v Ford* [1989] 3 All ER 445 it was held that if the jury was chosen in a random manner then it could not be challenged simply because it was not multi-racial.

2. For cause

This involves challenging the right of an individual juror to sit on the jury. To be successful the challenge must point out a valid reason why that juror should not serve on the jury. An obvious reason is that the juror is disqualified, but a challenge for cause can also be made if the juror knows or is related to a witness or defendant. If such people are not removed from the jury there is the risk that any subsequent conviction could be quashed. This occurred in *R v Wilson and R v Sprason*, *The Times*, 24th February 1995:

 ASE EXAMPLE

R v Wilson and R v Sprason, *The Times*, 24th February 1995

The wife of a prison officer was summoned for jury service. She asked to be excused attendance on that ground, but this request had not been granted. She served on the jury which convicted the two defendants of robbery. Both defendants had been on remand at Exeter prison where the juror's husband worked. The Court of Appeal said that justice must not only be done but must be seen to be done and the presence of Mrs Roberts on the jury prevented that, so the convictions had to be quashed.

3. Prosecution right to stand by jurors

This a right that only the prosecution can exercise. It allows the juror who has been stood by to be put to the end of the list of potential jurors so that they will not be used on the jury unless there are not enough other jurors. The prosecution does not have to give a reason for 'standing by', but the Attorney General's guidelines issued in 1988 make it clear that this power should be used sparingly.

When the prosecution uses this right, it has to make the decision to use it on the information provided through the vetting procedure. It cannot question the prospective juror in court. The system in the United States allows both prosecution and defence to question jurors to ensure that they are not biased or pre-judging the case, but this is not allowed in our legal system.

8.3.5 Aids for the jury

All potential jurors are sent a leaflet when they are summoned to do jury service. This leaflet gives them information on the selection process, including the right of challenge and the prosecution

right to stand by jurors. The leaflet also tells them to inform the clerk of the court if they find that they know someone in the case to which they are assigned. At the start of their jury service at the court they are shown a video which explains the layout of the court and where the judge and lawyers and other people sit in it. Other essential matters are explained to them, such as the need to elect a foreman. Since 2004 they are also warned in criminal cases that if any one of them is concerned about the attitude and behaviour of another juror, for example because they are showing racial bias against a defendant, they must report this before the verdict is given. See section 8.7 for further information on this.

■ Key facts chart on jury qualification and selection

KEY FACTS

Basic qualifications	18–70	s 1 Juries Act 1974
	Registered as an elector	Jurors are randomly selected from the registers of electors by computer
	Lived in UK for at least five years since 13th birthday	
Those not qualified	Mentally disordered persons include those who through mental illness are: • resident in a hospital or • regularly attend a doctor for treatment • under guardianship under s 7 of the Mental Health Act 1983 or • judged to be incapable of administering his property and affairs	Sch 1, para 1 to the Criminal Justice Act 2003
Disqualified	• A life sentence • Imprisoned for public protection • An extended sentence	All these are disqualified for life
	• A custodial sentence of five or more years • A custodial sentence of less than five years	These are disqualified for 10 years

CONTINUED ▸

KEY FACTS

	• A suspended sentence • A community sentence or order	
Discretionary excusals	Full-time serving members of the forces if prejudicial to the efficiency of the service	Normal expectation is that everyone will do jury service
	Those unable to do jury service for a good reason, eg illness	Deferral of service used rather than excusal
Lack of capacity	Unable to be an effective juror, eg too disabled or blind or unable to understand English	Can be discharged from service by the judge at the court
	Deafness is a lack of capacity if a sign interpreter is required	*McWhinney* (1999) 13th person not allowed in jury room
Can be vetted	Vetting normally limited to checking for disqualifying convictions	Attorney General's guidelines (1988)
	Vetting for background only allowed in case of: • national security • terrorism	
Can be challenged	To the array	s 5 Juries Act 1974
	For cause	
	Prosecution right of stand by	Attorney General's guidelines (1988)

8.4 Juries in civil cases

Although juries in civil cases are very rare, it is still possible to a trial by jury in certain civil cases. Where this occurs a jury in the High Court will have 12 members, while a jury in the County Court will have eight members. Juries in civil cases are now used only in very limited circumstances, but where they are used they have a dual role. They decide whether the claimant has

proved his case or not, then, if they decide that the claimant has won the case, the jury also goes on to decide the amount of damages that the defendant should pay to the claimant.

Until 1854 all common-law actions were tried by jury, but from 1854 the parties could agree not to use a jury and gradually their use declined. Then in 1933 the Administration of Justice (Miscellaneous Provisions) Act limited the right to use a jury, so that juries could not be used in disputes over breach of contract. Juries continued to be used for all defamation cases and could also be used for other actions in tort.

8.4.1 Defamation cases

In 1971 the Faulks Committee was set up to consider the role of the jury in defamation cases. In its report, *The Laws of Defamation*, Cmnd 5709 (1974), it concluded that juries should no longer be allowed as of right in defamation cases. Instead there should be a discretion for a trial by jury to be allowed in certain types of cases.

The reasons it gave for recommending trial by judge alone as the normal method of trial in defamation cases included the following:

- in many cases there were matters to be decided where a judge was more competent: eg technical legal concepts such as fair comment and qualified privilege
- judges gave their reasons for their decision whereas juries did not
- juries were unpredictable
- juries had difficulties with more complex cases
- trial by jury was more expensive.

However, the Faulks Committee did concede that in a small number of cases trial by jury might be preferable. It pointed out:

> **Q**
> 'We recognise it to be undesirable, that a judge sitting alone should be embroiled in a matter of political, religious or moral controversy. The same might be true where any party has been outspokenly critical of the Bench. Broadly, where the issue is whether the words were true or false and the subject is one that raises strong feelings among the general public so that a judge alone might be suspected, however mistakenly, of prejudice conscious or unconscious, we should expect that trial by jury might be awarded – but that in cases which did not involve such controversial questions a judge alone would be more likely to be selected.'
>
> para 503

However, Parliament did not implement the recommendations of the Faulks Committee. Trial by jury in defamation cases continued to be a right where either party wanted it until 1981.

The present rules for when juries may be used in civil cases are set out in s 69 of the Supreme Court Act 1981 for High Court cases and s 66 of the County Courts Act 1984 for cases in that court. Section 69 of the Supreme Court Act 1981 states:

's 69(1) Where, on the application of any party to an action to be tried in the Queen's Bench Division, the court is satisfied that there is in issue –

(a) a charge of fraud against that party; or

(b) a claim in respect of libel, slander, malicious prosecution or false imprisonment; or

(c) any question or issue of a kind prescribed for the purposes of this paragraph

the action shall be tried with a jury, unless the court is of the opinion that the trial requires any prolonged examination of documents or accounts or any scientific or local investigation which cannot be conveniently made with a jury.

. . .

(3) An action to be tried in the Queen's Bench Division which does not by virtue of subsection (1) fall to be tried with a jury shall be tried without a jury unless the court in its discretion orders it to be tried with a jury.'

When the Bill which was to become the Supreme Court Act 1981 was going through Parliament, the Government proposed an amendment which would have made trial by jury unavailable where the probable length of the case meant that it could not be conveniently tried by a jury. The case of *Orme v Associated Newspapers Group Ltd*, 31st March 1981, unreported, had led to the attempt to make this amendment. In *Orme* the case had lasted more than 100 days (the then longest ever libel case). The amendment was voted against. However, in deciding applications for trial without a jury under s 69, the courts have taken the word 'conveniently' to refer to the efficient administration of justice. This has allowed them to consider the probable length of the case as well as the other matters set out in s 69. This was shown in *Goldsmith v Pressdram Ltd* [1987] 3 All ER 485 when Lawton LJ said:

J
'[a] trial by jury inevitably takes much longer than a trial by judge alone. If the trial is made much longer because of the time taken up by the jury examining documents, then an element of inconvenience arises.'

All the cases listed in s 69(1) of the Supreme Court Act 1981 involve character or reputation and it is for this reason that jury trial has been retained. However, even for these cases a jury trial can be refused by the judge if the case is thought to be unsuitable for jury trial because it involves

It is also worth noting that, where the defendant has a choice of being tried in the magistrates' court or by a jury at the Crown Court, only about one out of every 20 defendants chooses to go to the Crown Court.

At the Crown Court the trial is presided over by a judge and the functions are split between the judge and jury. The judge decides points of law and the jury decides the facts. At the end of the prosecution case, the judge has the power to direct the jury to acquit the defendant if he decides that in law the prosecution's evidence has not made out a case against the defendant. This is called a **directed acquittal** and occurs in about 10 per cent of cases.

8.6.1 Verdicts

Where the trial continues then at the end of the case the judge will sum up the case to the jury and direct them on any law involved. The jury retires to a private room and makes the decision on the guilt or innocence of the accused in secret. Initially the members of the jury must try to come to a unanimous verdict, that is one on which they are all agreed. The judge must accept the jury verdict, even if he does not agree with it. This long-established principle goes back to *Bushell's Case* (1670). The jury does not give any reasons for its decision.

Majority verdicts

If after at least two hours (longer where there are several defendants) the jury has not reached a verdict, the judge can call them back into the courtroom and direct them that he can now accept a majority verdict. Majority verdicts have been allowed since 1967. Where there is a full jury of 12, the verdict can be 10–2 or 11–1 either for guilty or for not guilty. If the jury has fallen below 12 for any reason such as the death or illness of a juror during the trial, then only one can disagree with the verdict. That is, if there are 11 jurors the verdict can be 10–1; if there are 10 jurors it can be 9–1. If there are only nine jurors the verdict must be unanimous. A jury cannot go below nine members.

Majority verdicts were introduced because of the fear of jury 'nobbling', that is jurors being bribed or intimidated by associates of the defendant into voting for a not guilty verdict. When a jury had to be unanimous, only one member needed be bribed to cause a 'stalemate' in which the jury were unable to reach a decision. It was also thought that the acquittal rates in jury trials were too high and that majority decisions would result in more convictions.

Where the jury convict a defendant on a majority verdict the foreman of the jury must announce the numbers, both agreeing and disagreeing with the verdict in open court. This provision is contained in s 17(3) of the Juries Act 1974 and is aimed at making sure the jury has come to a legal majority, and not one, for example, of eight to four, which is not allowed. Originally this section was interpreted as meaning that the foreman had to announce both the majority for conviction and the number of those who did not agree with the verdict. In *R v Reynolds* [1981] 3 All ER 849 the foreman announced only the number for the conviction (10), but did not announce that two disagreed. The Court of Appeal quashed the conviction.

However, in *R v Pigg* [1983] 1 All ER 56, the House of Lords held that, provided that the foreman announced the number who had agreed with the verdict, and that number was within the number allowed for a majority verdict, then the conviction was legal. It did not matter that the foreman had not also been asked how many disagreed with the verdict. More than a fifth of convictions by juries each year are by majority verdict.

It is not known how many acquittals are by majority verdict as the fact that it was a majority decision is not announced by the foreman when the verdict is given.

8.7 Secrecy of the jury room

The jury discussion takes place in secret and there can be no inquiry into how the jury reached its verdict. This is because s 8 of the Contempt of Court Act 1981 makes disclosure of anything that happened in the jury room contempt of court which is a criminal offence.

's 8(1) Subject to subsection (2) below, it is a contempt of court to obtain, disclose or solicit any particulars of statements made, opinions expressed, arguments advanced or votes cast by members of a jury in the course of their deliberations in any legal proceedings.

(2) This section does not apply to any disclosure of any particulars –

(a) in the proceedings in question for the purpose of enabling the jury to arrive at their verdict, or in connection with the delivery of that verdict; or

(b) in evidence in any subsequent proceedings for an offence alleged to have been committed in relation to the jury in the first mentioned proceedings,

or to the publication of any particulars so disclosed.

The section was brought in because newspapers were paying jurors large sums of money for 'their story'. This is obviously not desirable. In *Attorney General v Associated Newpapers Ltd* [1994] 1 All ER 556, the House of Lords held that s 8 applies even where the information which is disclosed is obtained from a third party.

CASE EXAMPLE

Attorney General v Associated Newspapers Ltd [1994] 1 All ER 556

The *Mail on Sunday* published details of the jury's deliberations in the Blue Arrow fraud case. The information had been obtained from two members of the jury by an independent researcher who later gave transcripts of the interviews to a journalist. The convictions of the newspaper, its editor and the journalist concerned under s 8 were upheld by the

CONTINUED ▸

House of Lords. It ruled that the word 'disclose' in s 8 applied to both the revelation of deliberations by jurors and any further disclosure by publication. It did not matter that the information of what happened in the jury room had come indirectly through another person.

However, the total ban on finding out what happened in the jury room means that it is difficult to discover whether jurors have understood the evidence in complex cases. The Runciman Commission (1993) recommended that s 8 should be changed to allow research into the workings of juries. It was thought that in particular there should be research into the influence that jurors with criminal convictions may have on jury verdicts. However, Lord Justice Auld, in his review of the criminal justice system (2001), disagreed and thought that s 8 should remain (Chapter 5, paras 82–87).

8.7.1 Common law rule

A further protection of the secrecy of the jury room is the fact that the appeal courts will not look into any alleged irregularities in the jury room once the verdict has been given. This is a long-standing common law rule as dating from the case of *Vaise v Delaval* (1785) 1 TR 11; 99 ER 944, KB in which the court refused to consider affidavits (sworn written statements) from two jurors indicating that they had decided on their verdict by tossing a coin. The reason given by the court for refusing to consider the affidavits was to protect the jurors from self-incrimination for what Lord Mansfield described as 'a very high misdemeanour'. Since that case the courts have refused to admit evidence of what occurred in the jury room. The rule was applied in *R v Thompson* [1962] 1 All ER 65.

 ASE EXAMPLE

R v Thompson [1962] 1 All ER 65

After the defendant had been convicted, but before sentence had been passed, one of the jurors told a member of the public that a majority of members of the jury had been in favour of an acquittal until the foreman of the jury produced a list of the defendant's previous convictions. The defendant appealed against his conviction but the Court of Criminal Appeal refused to accept evidence of what happened in the jury room and upheld the conviction.

The rule also applies in civil cases. The rationale for the rule was explained by Atkin LJ in *Ellis v Deheer* [1922] 2 KB 113:

J 'The reason why that evidence is not admitted is twofold, on the one hand it is in order to secure the finality of decisions arrived at by the jury, and on the other to protect the jurymen themselves and prevent their being exposed to pressure to explain the reasons which actuated them in arriving at their verdict. To my mind it is a principle of highest importance in the interests of justice to maintain, and an infringement of the rule appears to me a very serious interference with the administration of justice.'

However, in *Ellis v Deheer* (1922), the Court of Appeal did allow an application for a new trial of a civil case. This was because the foreman had not given the verdict which the jury had agreed on. The other members of the jury had not raised the matter when the verdict was given because they placed in a position in the courtroom where they could not hear what the foreman said. The Court of Appeal held that their decision did not infringe the rule as the jurors could not see or hear what was taking place when the verdict was announced.

The Court of Appeal has also ruled that it is permissible to investigate any happenings outside the jury room, even though these may affect the jury's deliberations. This occurred in the somewhat unusual case of *R v Young* [1995] 2 WLR 430:

CASE EXAMPLE

R v Young [1995] 2 WLR 430

The defendant was charged with the murder of two people. The jury members had to stay overnight in a hotel as they had not reach a verdict by the end of the first day of discussion. During this stay at the hotel four members of the jury held a seance using a ouija board to try to contact the dead victims and ask who had killed them. The next day the jury returned a verdict of guilty. When the fact that the ouija board had been used became known, the defendant appealed and the Court of Appeal quashed the verdict and ordered a re-trial of the case. The court felt able to inquire into what had happened as it was in a hotel and not part of the jury discussions in the jury room.

8.7.2 Human rights and jury secrecy

In the conjoined appeals of *R v Connor: R v Mirza (Conjoined appeals)* [2004] UKHL 4 the question was raised whether the refusal to admit evidence of any irregularity in the jury room was an infringement of the right to a fair trial under Art 6 of the European Convention on Human Rights (the right to a fair trial). The House of Lords (Lord Steyn dissenting) ruled that it did not. Two separate cases were considered in the appeal. These were:

CASE EXAMPLE

R v Connor and Rollock [2004] UKHL 4

The two defendants were jointly charged with wounding. They were both convicted by a majority verdict of 10–2. Five days after the verdict (but before sentence was passed) one of the jurors wrote to the Crown Court, stating that while many jurors thought it was one or other of the defendants who had committed the stabbing, they would convict both in order to 'teach them a lesson'. The complaining juror said that, when she argued that the jury should have considered which defendant was responsible, her co-jurors had refused to listen and remarked that if they did that it could take a week considering verdicts in the case.

R v Mirza [2004] UKHL 4

The defendant was a Pakistani who settled in the UK in 1988. He had an interpreter to help him in the trial and during the trial the jury sent notes asking why he needed an interpreter. He was convicted on a 10–2 majority. Six days after the jury verdict, one juror wrote to the defendant's counsel, alleging that from the start of the trial there had been a 'theory' that the use of an interpreter was a 'ploy'. The juror also said that she had been shouted down when she objected and reminded her fellow jurors of the judge's directions.

The House of Lords dismissed both appeals. It held that the common law rule which protected jurors' confidentiality and which precluded the court from admitting evidence of what had happened in the jury room after the verdict had been given was still effective. It also held that this rule was compatible with Art 6. On the human rights point Lord Hope pointed out what had been said by the European Court of Human Rights in *Gregory v United Kingdom* (1997) 25 EHRR 577:

> **J** 'The court acknowledges that the rule governing the secrecy of jury deliberations is a crucial and legitimate feature of English trial law which serves to reinforce the jury's role as the ultimate arbiter of fact and to guarantee open and frank deliberations among jurors on the evidence which they have heard.'

Lord Hope accepted that in the later case of *Sander v United Kingdom* (2000) 31 EHRR 1003 the majority decision of the European Court of Human Rights did not repeat this observation. However, it was referred to by Sir Nicholas Bratza in his dissenting opinion in

CONTINUED ▸

Sander v United Kingdom (2000). Lord Hope, in *R v Connor: R v Mirza* (2004), pointed out that, in view of that dissent, the European Court did not depart from the rule in any respect in *Sander* and that nothing was said in the judgment which cast doubt on the validity of the rule.

When deciding that the rule should remain in English law the Lords pointed out that:

* confidentiality was essential to the proper functioning of the jury process
* there was merit in finality
* jurors had to be protected from harassment.

The Lords did accept that there might be exceptional circumstances where it would be right to inquire into what occurred in the jury room. Lord Slynn said:

> **J** 'The admission of evidence as to what happened in the jury room cannot be allowed without seriously detracting from the advantages which flow from the present system and which, in my view, need to be protected. If a case arose when all the jurors agreed that something occurred which in effect meant that the jury abrogated its functions and eg decided on the toss of a coin the case might be, and in my opinion would be, different. In the present case everything that happened is said to have happened in the jury room.'

Lord Steyn dissented. He would have allowed the appeal in *Mirza* (2004). He thought that s 8 of the Contempt of Court Act 1981 did not affect the Court of Appeal's jurisdiction to receive evidence it regarded as relevant to the disposal of an appeal. On the human rights aspect he thought that there was a breach of Art 6 where there was known to have been a real risk of racial bias affecting the decision. In these exceptional circumstances he held that the appeal court should admit evidence of what had occurred in the jury room.

8.7.3 Practice Direction

Following the House of Lords' decision in *Connor and Mirza* (2004) a Practice Direction *(Crown Court: Guidance to Jurors)*, *The Times*, 27th February 2004 has been issued. This sets out that:

> **Q** 'Trial judges should ensure that the jury is alerted to the need to bring any concerns about fellow jurors to the attention of the judge at the time and not wait until the case is concluded. At the same time, it is undesirable to encourage inappropriate criticism of fellow jurors, or to threaten jurors with contempt of court.'

Discuss whether it is right or necessary to protect the secrecy of deliberations in the jury room.

8.8 Research into juries

The rigid rule that jury discussions must be kept secret has meant that research into how juries reach a verdict has been limited. Much of the research into how juries reach a verdict has been done by using a 'shadow' or a 'mock' jury. A shadow jury is one which sits in the courtroom and when the real jury withdraws to consider its verdict so does the shadow jury, but this is not in secret but in front of cameras. A mock jury is where the jury members watch a simulated case (or listen to a tape recording) and then deliberate on the verdict in front of cameras. In each case 12 people are selected in the same way as a real jury would be.

The Oxford Penal Research Unit conducted a study, with shadow juries looking at 30 cases. They found that the shadow juries took their task very seriously. McCabe and Purves wrote in *The Shadow Jury at Work* (1974):

> 'The "shadow" juries showed considerable determination in looking for evidence upon which convictions could be based; when it seemed inadequate, they were not prepared to allow their own "hunch" that the defendant was involved in some way in the offence that was charged to stand in the way of an acquittal . . .
>
> There was little evidence of perversity in the final decisions of these thirty groups. One acquittal only showed that sympathy and impatience with the triviality of the case so influenced the 'shadow' jurors' view of the evidence that they refused to convict. One other unexpected acquittal seemed to be wholly due to dissatisfaction with the evidence.'

(62–63)

Other research on jury verdicts has been carried out by asking the judge and/or lawyers in the case whether they agreed with the jury verdict or not. This method of research was used by Baldwin and McConville in their research *Jury Trials* (Clarendon, 1979). They selected a random sample of 500 defendants who had been tried at Birmingham Crown Court and compared the actual verdict with the views of the judge, prosecuting solicitor, defence solicitor, the police and the defendant. Their findings were that jury decisions seemed to be unsatisfactory in a surprising number of cases. They found that a quarter of acquittals were thought to be doubtful or highly questionable by three or more of the respondents. Even more worrying was the fact that about one in 20 convictions was also thought to be doubtful or highly questionable.

The same method of questioning other participants in the trials was used by researchers carrying out investigations for the Runciman Commission (1993). They looked into about 800 cases across the country over a two-week period in the Crown Court Study (M Zander and P Henderson, *Royal Commission on Criminal Justice*, Research Study No 19, 1993). Questionnaires were given to judges, prosecuting and defence lawyers, the police and jurors. The questions to the jurors were carefully framed to make sure that there was no breach of s 8 of the Contempt of Court Act 1981. Jurors were asked 'How difficult was it for you to understand the evidence?'. Ninety-one per cent thought that it was either 'not at all difficult' or 'not very difficult'. Over 90 per cent of jurors also thought that the jury as a whole had understood the evidence. However just under 10 per cent of jurors admitted that they had had difficulty. When the foremen of juries were questioned on the same point, they thought that a small number of jurors (0.2 per cent) could not understand English sufficiently well to follow a case. The foremen also thought that about 1 per cent of jurors could not understand the details of a case, while another 1 per cent could not understand any case. These may be small numbers, but it is still worrying that in some cases a defendant's future is being decided by some members of the public who do not understand the case.

The other participants in the study were asked whether they thought that the jury's verdict was surprising. The results were not as pessimistic as those revealed by Baldwin and McConville, although there were still thought to be questionable verdicts. Prosecution and defence lawyers and the judges thought that 2–4 per cent of jury decisions were surprising and inexplicable. The police thought that 8 per cent of the verdicts were inexplicable.

8.9 Advantages of trial by jury

8.9.1 Public confidence

On the face of it, asking 12 strangers who have no legal knowledge and without any training to decide what may be complicated and technical points is an absurd idea. Yet the jury is considered as one of the fundamentals of a democratic society. The right to be tried by one's peers is the bastion of liberty against the State and has been supported by eminent judges. For example, Lord Devlin said that juries are 'the lamp that shows that freedom lives'. The tradition of trial by jury is very old and people seem to have confidence in the impartiality and fairness of a jury trial. This can be seen in the objection to proposals to limit the right to trial by jury (see section 5.8).

The use of a jury is viewed as making the legal system more open. Justice is seen to be done as members of the public are involved in such a key role and the whole process is public. It also helps to keep the law clearer as points have to be explained to the jury and it enables the defendant to understand the case more easily. It prevents the criminal justice system from being completely dominated by professional judges. This is considered important as judges are perceived by the public as being remote from everyday life.

8.9.2 Jury equity

Since juries are not legal experts they are not bound to follow the precedents of past cases or even Acts of Parliament. Also, juries do not have to give reasons for their verdict. In view of these two facts it is possible for them to decide cases on their idea of 'fairness'. This is sometimes referred to as 'jury equity'. It is likely to occur where a jury believes the law to be unfair and, as a result, refuses to convict the defendant. In some instances the Government has amended the law following a jury verdict showing disapproval of the existing law. The clearest example is *Ponting's Case*, 1984, unreported:

ASE EXAMPLE

Ponting's Case, 1984, unreported

A civil servant was charged under the old wide-ranging s 2 of the Official Secrets Act 1911. He had leaked information on the sinking of the ship, the *General Belgrano*, in the Falklands war to a member of Parliament. He pleaded not guilty, claiming that his actions had been in the public interest. The jury refused to convict him even though the judge ruled that there was no defence. The case prompted the Government to reconsider the law and amend s 2 of the 1911 Act.

8.9.3 Panel of 12

It is thought that having 12 people making the decision is fairer than having one person deciding the verdict. Twelve people will bring a much wider set of experiences to a case than one person can do. In addition, any biases should be cancelled out. The random selection of 12 people to each jury panel also helps to prevent bias. It is also thought that honesty and reputation are best assessed by 12 ordinary people. For example, in the law of theft the test for dishonesty has to be established according to the standards of ordinary people. In other areas of law the test may involve deciding what is reasonable in the circumstances; for example in the law on self-defence. This is a matter on which a panel of 12 ordinary people can make the decision.

8.10 Disadvantages of trial by jury

8.10.1 Racial composition and bias

Although jurors have no direct interest in a case, and despite the fact that there are 12 of them, they may still have prejudices which can affect the verdict. Some jurors may be biased against the police. This is one of the reasons that those with certain criminal convictions are disqualified from sitting on a jury. In particular there is the worry that some jurors are racially prejudiced. This is worrying as the random selection of jury panels can produce a jury which does not contain anyone from the defendant's ethnic minority group. This was the situation that occurred in *R v Ford*

[1989] 3 All ER 445. The defendant asked the judge to order that a new panel be selected but the judge refused. The defendant appealed and the Court of Appeal ruled that the judge could not interfere with the empanelling of the jury simply because it did not produce a racially mixed panel. Lord Lane LCJ said:

> **J** 'The conclusion is that, however well intentioned the judge's motive might be, the judge has no power to influence the composition of the jury, and that it is wrong for him to attempt to do so. If it should ever become desirable that the principle of random selection should be altered, that will have to be done by way of statute and cannot be done by any judicial decision.'

The point was raised again in *R v Smith* [2003] EWCA Crim 283. In this case the defence submitted that the decision in *Ford* (1989) could not stand in the light of the implementation of the Human Rights Act 1998 which incorporated Art 6 of the European Convention on Human Rights, giving a right to a fair trial. The defence asked the Court of Appeal to declare s 1 of the Juries Act 1974 to be incompatible with the 1998 Act. The Court of Appeal rejected this argument, saying:

> **J** 'We do not accept that it was unfair for the appellant to be tried by an all-white jury or that the fair-minded and informed observer would regard it as unfair. We do not accept that, on the facts of this case, the trial could only be fair if members of the defendant's race were present on the jury. It was not a case where consideration of the evidence required knowledge of the traditions or social circumstances of a particular racial group. The situation was an all too common one, violence late at night outside a club, and a randomly selected jury was entirely capable of trying the issues fairly and impartially.'

The Court of Appeal referred to the decision of the European Court of Human Rights in *Gregory v United Kingdom* (1997) 25 EHRR 577 where evidence of racial bias had come to light during the course of the trial. In that case there was held to have been no breach of Art 6 since the trial judge had dealt with the matter in an adequate way. The Court of Appeal in *Smith* (2003) pointed out that the European Court of Human Rights in *Gregory* (1997) had not impugned the legitimacy of the jury system or the procedure by which juries are selected in this country. The Court of Appeal also pointed out that in *Gregory* (1997) there was reference to 'personal impartiality being assumed until there is evidence to the contrary'.

However, where there is proof of bias then the courts have taken a different view on the fairness of trials. In *Sander v United Kingdom* (2000) 31 EHRR 1003; [2000] Crim LR 767 the European Court of Human Rights ruled that there had been a breach of Art 6 of the European Convention on Human Rights.

CASE EXAMPLE

Sander v United Kingdom (2000) 31 EHRR 1003; [2000] Crim LR 767

During the trial one juror wrote a note to the judge, raising concern over the fact that other jurors had been openly making racist remarks and jokes. The judge asked the jury to 'search their consciences'. The next day the judge received two letters, one signed by all the jurors (including the juror who had made the complaint) in which they denied any racist attitudes and a second from one juror who admitted that he may have been the one making racist jokes. Despite the discrepancy between the two letters, the judge allowed the case to continue. The ECtHR held that in these circumstances the judge should have discharged the jury as there was an obvious risk of racial bias.

The possibility of racial bias was shown by the research into juries by Baldwin and McConville in 1979 in which the legal professionals in the cases had serious doubts about the correctness of convictions in one out of every 20 convictions. It was apparent that black defendants were more likely to fall into this 'doubtful' conviction category than white defendants (see section 8.8).

This risk of racial prejudice was the reason that the Runciman Commission recommended that up to three jurors should be drawn from ethnic minority cases in certain cases where either the defendant or a victim was from an ethic minority and there was some special and unusual feature to the case. Lord Justice Auld also made the same recommendation in his review of the criminal justice system in 2001. However, the Government rejected this proposal. The reasons for the rejection were set out in the White Paper, *Justice for All*, Cm 5563 (2001). Paragraph 7.29 stated that it was thought wrong to interfere with the composition of the jury as this would potentially:

- undermine the fundamental principle of random selection and would not achieve a truly representative jury of peers

- assume bias on the part of excluded jurors when no prejudice has been proved

- place the selected minority ethnic jurors in a difficult position – they might feel that they are expected to represent the interests of the defendant or victim

- generate tensions and divisions in the jury room instead of reaching consensus on the guilt or innocence of the accused based on the evidence put before it

- place undue weight on the views of the especially selected jurors and

- place a new burden on the court to determine which cases should attract an 'ethnic minority quota' and provide a ground for unmeritorious appeals.

Another way of preventing bias and allowing 'justice to be seen to be done' could be to reinstate the defence's right of peremptory challenge (a right which existed up to 1988 under which the defence could challenge a certain numbers of jurors without having to give a reason and remove them from the jury panel). This would allow defendants a limited choice over who sits on a jury and might create a racially mixed jury.

8.10.2 Media influence

Media coverage may influence jurors. This is especially true in high-profile cases, where there has been a lot of publicity about the police investigations into a case. This occurred in the case *R v West* [1996] 2 Cr App R 374 in which Rosemary West was convicted of the murders of 10 young girls and women, including her own daughter. From the time the bodies were first discovered, the media coverage was intense. In addition, some newspapers had paid large sums of money to some of the witnesses in order to secure their story after the trial was completed. One of the grounds on which Rosemary West appealed against her conviction was that the media coverage had made it impossible for her to receive a fair trial. The Court of Appeal rejected the appeal, pointing out that otherwise it would mean that if 'allegations of murder were sufficiently horrendous so as to inevitably shock the nation, the accused could not be tried'. They also said that the trial judge had given adequate warning to the jury to consider only the evidence they heard in court.

In *R v Taylor and Taylor* (1994) 98 Cr App R 361 the defendants successfully appealed against their convictions because of high-profile, misleading and, in some instances, untrue press reports on the case.

CASE EXAMPLE

R v Taylor and Taylor (1994) 98 Cr App R 361

Two sisters were charged with murder of another woman. The prosecution case was that one of the sisters, Michelle, had been having an affair with the victim's husband. The press printed misleading stills from a video of the victim's wedding in which Michelle appeared to be giving the bridegroom a passionate kiss. In fact, the full video showed her coming along the receiving line at the reception and giving him what was described as a 'peck on the cheek'. They also printed inaccurate sensational headlines such as 'Love Crazy Mistress Butchered Rival Wife Court Told' when the court had not been told that. The Court of Appeal quashed the sisters' convictions. The coverage of the trial by the media had created a real risk of prejudice against the defendants. As a result, their convictions were regarded as unsafe and unsatisfactory.

8.10.3 Perverse verdicts

In section 8.9.2 we considered the idea of jury equity where a jury refuses to follow the law and convict a defendant. However, it can be argued that this merely leads to a perverse verdict which does not reflect the evidence and is not justified. An example was the case of *R v Randle and Pottle*, *The Independent*, 26th March 1991.

CASE EXAMPLE

R v Randle and Pottle, *The Independent*, 26th March 1991

Twenty-five years after the spy George Blake escaped from prison, the defendants were charged with helping him to escape. They had published a book, *The Blake Escape: How We Freed George Blake and Why*, in which they admitted that they had helped him to escape. They had also discussed the matter in the media and made admissions of guilt. At the trial the judge told the jury that the defendants had no defence. Despite this the jury acquitted them, possibly as a protest over the lapse of time between the offence and the prosecution.

Another case in which the jury acquitted despite clear evidence was *R v Kronlid and others* (1996). In this case four female defendants were charged with causing over £1 million worth of damage to an aircraft. The women admitted breaking into a hangar and using hammers to damage the £10 million aircraft. However, they denied the charges, claiming that they were using reasonable force to prevent a greater crime. They said that disarming the jet, which had been bought by the Indonesian government, would prevent it from being used against the civilian population in East Timor. The jury found all the defendants not guilty.

To try to prevent perverse verdicts, the Auld Report (2001) on the criminal justice system recommended that where a judge thought it appropriate, the jury should be required to answer questions and declare a verdict in accordance with those answers. The report also recommended that juries should not have the right to acquit defendants in defiance of the law or in disregard of the evidence. These recommendations have not been implemented by the Government. There was severe criticism of the recommendation. Professor Zander, in his comments to the Lord Chancellor's Department on this recommendation, said:

> 'I regard this proposal as wholly unacceptable – a serious misreading of the function of the jury. The right to return a perverse verdict in defiance of the law or the evidence is an important safeguard against unjust laws, oppressive prosecutions or harsh sentences. In former centuries juries notoriously defied the law to save defendants from the gallows. In modern times the power is used, sometimes to general acclaim, sometimes to general annoyance, usually one imagines to some of each.'

ACTIVITY

Discuss whether the prosecution should be able to appeal against an acquittal on the ground that it was a perverse decision.

8.10.4 Fraud trials

Fraud trials in which complex accounts are used in evidence can create special problems for jurors. Even jurors who can easily cope with other evidence may have difficulty understanding a fraud case. These cases are also often very long, so that the jurors have to be able to be away from their own work for months. A long fraud trial can place a great strain on jurors. Such cases also become very expensive, both for the prosecution and for the defendants. The Roskill Committee in 1986 suggested that juries should not be used for complex fraud cases. However, this reform has not been implemented. One of the difficulties would be in deciding which fraud cases are sufficiently complex to withdraw them from the right to jury trial.

In 1998, the Home Office issued a Consultation Document, *Juries in Serious Fraud Trials*, inviting views on whether the system for trying fraud trials should be changed. One of the points in the document was the fact that the Court of Appeal had quashed the decision in the Blue Arrow fraud trial because the case had become unmanageable. The Court of Appeal had held that there was a significant risk of a miscarriage of justice because of the volume of evidence and the complexities of the issues which had to be decided by the jury. No further action was taken on the consultation paper, but at the end of 1999 Lord Justice Auld was asked to review the criminal justice system. This review (2001) recommended that fraud cases should be heard by a judge and two lay people taken from a special panel.

Following the review's recommendations, the Government issued the White Paper *Justice for All*. In this it stated:

> **Q**
>
> '4.28 A small number of serious and complex fraud trials, many lasting six months or more, have served to highlight the difficulties in trying these types of cases with a jury. Such cases place a huge strain on all concerned and the time commitment is a burden on jurors' personal and working lives. As a result it is not always possible to find a representative panel of jurors.
>
> 4.29 As well as this, the complexity and unfamiliarity of sophisticated business processes means prosecutions often pare down cases to try and make then more manageable and comprehensible to a jury. This means the full criminality of such a fraud is not always exposed, and there are risks of a double standard between easy to prosecute "blue-collar" crime and difficult to prosecute "white-collar" crime.

CONTINUED ▸

> **Q** '4.30 We have concluded that there should be a more effective form of trial in such cases of serious fraud. The Auld report recommended that the judge should have the power to direct such fraud trials without a jury, sitting with people experienced in complex financial issues or, where the defendant agrees, on their own. We recognise that the expertise of such people could help the trial proceed. However, identifying and recruiting suitable people raises considerable difficulties, not least because this would represent a substantial commitment over a long period of time.'

Criminal Justice Act 2003

The Government proposed that serious fraud cases should be tried by a judge alone. It estimated that there would be only about 15–20 such trials a year. This proposal was contained in the Criminal Justice Bill 2002–03. The original Bill contained two measures aimed at limiting jury trials. One proposal would have allowed a defendant to apply for a trial to be conducted without a jury. This was defeated by the House of Lords and withdrawn by the Government. The other was a provision allowing the prosecution to apply for trial without a jury where:

* the trial was likely to be lengthy or complex or
* there was a danger of jury tampering.

This was defeated by the House of Lords, but the Government reinstated it. The House of Lords voted against it again. Finally, a compromise was reach whereby there are provisions in the Criminal Justice Act 2003 for the prosecution to apply for trial by a judge alone in:

* complex fraud cases (s 43) or
* cases where there has already been an effort to tamper with a jury in the case (s 44).

However, under s 330(5), the commencement of these two sections is subject to an affirmative resolution. In other words, both Houses of Parliament must vote in favour of commencement. The section cannot be brought into effect in any other way.

Domestic Violence, Crime and Victims Act 2004

The Government then put forward yet another way of restricting jury trial. This was in the Domestic Violence, Crime and Victims Act 2004. The effect of ss 17–20 of that Act is that, where there are a large number of counts on the indictment, there can be a trial of sample counts with a jury. Then, if the defendant was convicted on those, the remainder could be tried by a judge alone. The prosecution has to apply to a judge to make such an order and there are three conditions which must be met:

- the number of counts included in the indictment is likely to mean that a trial by jury of all those counts would be impracticable
- a sample of all counts must be tried by a jury
- it must be in the interests of justice for such an order to be made.

When considering the application a judge must have regard to any steps which might reasonably be taken to facilitate a trial by jury. This is being called a two-tier trial, but the idea behind it is that those who commit multiple offences should be convicted and punished for **all** their offences.

ACTIVITY

Discuss whether trial by jury is a suitable method of trying serious fraud cases.

8.10.5 High acquittal rates

Juries are often criticised on the ground that they acquit too many defendants. The figure usually quoted in support of this is that about two-thirds of those who plead not guilty at the Crown Court are acquitted. However, this figure does not give a true picture of the workings of juries as it includes cases discharged by the judge and those in which the judge directed an acquittal.

The judicial statistics for 2003 show that a total of just over 75,000 defendants were prosecuted at the Crown Court during the year. Almost 50,000 of these defendants pleaded guilty to all the charges against them. Just over 25,000 pleaded not guilty to all charges. Of these 25,000 pleading not guilty, just over 67 per cent were found not guilty. However, the majority of these acquittals were by the judge and not the jury. Fifty-eight per cent of these defendants were discharged by the judge without a jury even being sworn in. These were cases where the prosecution offered no evidence. In another 11 per cent the judge directed the jury to acquit the defendant. So, when these cases are excluded, it can be seen that the jury acquitted in only 31 per cent of the cases. Of the cases in which the jury decide the verdict, they convict in far more cases than they acquit. This statistic has remained similar for a number of years, as shown by Figure 8.1:

Year	Percentage convicted by jury	Percentage acquitted by jury
2000	60.9	39.1
2001	60.8	39.2
2002	62.7	37.3
2003	61.1	38.9

Figures are based on the *Judicial Statistics* published for each year

Figure 8.1 Conviction and acquittal rates of juries

8.10.6 Other disadvantages

The compulsory nature of jury service is unpopular, so that some jurors may be against the whole system, while others may rush their verdict in order to leave as quickly as possible. Jury service can be a strain, especially where jurors have to listen to horrific evidence. Jurors in the Rosemary West case were offered counselling after the trial to help them cope with the evidence they had had to see and hear.

Jury 'nobbling' does occur and in some cases jurors have had to be provided with police protection. In order to try to combat this, the Criminal Procedure and Investigations Act 1996 allows for a re-trial to be ordered if, in any case, someone is subsequently proved to have interfered with the jury, although in actual fact there have not yet been any prosecutions under this Act. Also, as seen in section 8.10.4, the Criminal Justice Act 2003 has a provision for allowing trial to continue by a judge alone where there has been interference with a jury.

The use of juries makes trials slow and expensive. This is because each point has to be explained carefully to the jury and the whole procedure of the case takes longer. However, this has to be balanced against the advantage of the procedure of using a jury making the trial more open and understandable.

8.11 Alternatives to trial by jury

Despite all the problems of using juries in criminal case, there is still a strong feeling that they are the best method available. However, if juries are not thought suitable to try serious criminal cases, what alternative form of trial could be used?

Trial by a single judge

This is the method of trial in the majority of civil cases in which it is generally regarded as producing a fairer and more predictable result. Trial by a single judge is also used for some criminal trials in Northern Ireland; these are called the Diplock courts and were brought in on the recommendation of Lord Diplock to replace jury trial because of the special problems of threats and jury 'nobbling' that existed between the different sectarian parties.

However, there appears to be less public confidence in the use of judges to decide all serious criminal cases. The arguments against this form of trial are that judges become case-hardened and prosecution-minded. They are also from a very elitist group and would have little understanding of the background and problems of defendants. Individual prejudices are more likely than in a jury where the different personalities should go some way to eliminating bias. But, on the other hand, judges are trained to evaluate cases and they are now being given training in racial awareness. This may make them better arbiters of fact than an untrained jury.

A panel of judges

In some continental countries cases are heard by a panel of three or five judges sitting together. This allows for a balance of views, instead of the verdict of a single person. However, it still leaves the problems of judges becoming case-hardened and prosecution-minded and their elitist background. The other difficulty is that there are not sufficient judges and our system of legal training and appointment would need a radical overhaul to implement this proposal. It would also be expensive.

A judge plus lay assessors

Under this system the judge and two lay people would make the decision together. This method is used in the Scandinavian countries. It provides the legal expertise of the judge, together with lay participation in the legal system by ordinary members of the public. The lay people could either be drawn from the general public, using the same method as is used for selecting juries at present, or a special panel of assessors could be drawn up as happens in tribunal cases. This latter suggestion would be particularly suitable for fraud cases.

A mini-jury using six members

Finally, if the jury is to remain, then it might be possible to have a smaller number of jurors. In many continental countries when a jury is used there are nine members. For example, in Spain, which re-introduced the use of juries in certain criminal cases in 1996, there is a jury of nine. Alternatively, a jury of six could be used for less serious criminal cases that at the moment have a full jury trial – this occurs in some American states.

ACTIVITY

Self-assessment questions

1. In which courts can juries be used?

2. What are the basic qualifications for jurors?

3. For what reasons are certain people disqualified from jury service?

4. What is meant by a 'discretionary excusal' and when will one be given?

5. Explain   **a)**   challenging to the array

      b)   challenging for cause

      c)   prosecution's right of stand by.

6. When can a jury be used in civil cases?

7. Why are juries considered unsuitable for deciding personal injury cases?

8. What is a majority verdict and what is the law about announcing such verdicts in court?

9. What two factors ensure the secrecy of the jury room?

10. Explain how research into juries has been carried out.

Further reading

Darbyshire, P, 'The Lamp that Shows that Freedom Lives – Is it Worth the Candle?' [1991] Crim LR 740.

Darbyshire, P, 'What can we learn from Published Jury Research? Findings for the Criminal Courts Review 2001' [2001] Crim LR 970.

Devlin, Lord, 'The Conscience of the Jury' (1991) 107 LQR 398.

Ferguson, P, 'Whistleblowing jurors' [2004] NLJ 370.

chapter 9 LAY MAGISTRATES ∎

chapter 9 LAY MAGISTRATES ∎

9.1 Introduction

In our legal system, there is a tradition of using lay people, that is people who are not legally qualified, in the decision-making process in our courts. Today this applies particularly to the Magistrates' Courts and the Crown Court. However, in the past lay people were also frequently used to decide civil cases in the High Court and the County Court, and today there are still some cases in which a jury can be used in the civil courts. There are also lay people with expertise in a particular field who sit as part of a panel as lay assessors. This occurs in the Patents Court and the Admiralty Court in the High Court as well as in tribunals, especially Employment Tribunals and Social Security Appeals Tribunals. However, the greatest use of lay people in the legal system is lay magistrates.

9.1.1 Lay magistrates

There are over 28,000 lay magistrates sitting as part-time judges in the magistrates' courts. Another name for a lay magistrate is Justice of the Peace (JP). They sit to hear cases as a bench of two or three magistrates. The size of panel has been limited to a maximum of three, whereas before 1996 there could be up to seven magistrates sitting together to hear a case. A single lay magistrate sitting on his own has very limited powers. He can, however, issue search warrants and warrants for arrest. He can also sit to decide mode of trial proceedings for offences triable either way when the decision as to whether the case will be tried in the magistrates' court or the Crown Court is made.

As a bench of two or three magistrates, they play a very large role in the legal system with almost 97 per cent of all criminal cases being dealt with by them. In view of their important role in the community the Lord Chancellor, in October 2004, launched the Supporting Magistrates to Provide Justice programme. This is aimed at

- ensuring that the magistracy is **respected** and valued and its orders obeyed

- improving the perception of what magistrates do – **effective** local justice and

- doing more to **connect** courts with their communities.

During 2005 the programme team on this review will be seeking views from a wide range of people, including the public who use the courts, as to how best to achieve these aims. Information on this programme and also on magistrates generally can be found on www.dca.gov.uk.

9.1.2 District Judges

There are also qualified judges who work in magistrates' courts. These are called District Judges (Magistrates' Court). Prior to 1999, they used to be called stipendiary magistrates. They can sit on their own to hear any of the cases that come before the court. Under s 16(3) of the Justices of the Peace Act 1979 they have the same powers as a bench of lay magistrates. In 2004 there were 106 District Judges.

9.2 History of the magistracy

The office of Justice of the Peace is very old, dating back to the twelfth century at least. In 1195 Richard I appointed 'keepers of the peace'. By the mid-thirteenth century the judicial side of their position had developed and by 1361 the title 'Justice of the Peace', was being used. By this time JPs already had the power to arrest suspects and investigate crime. In 1382 they were given the power to punish offenders. A statute in 1363 provided that the justices should meet at least four times a year in each county. These meetings, which became known as Quarter Sessions, continued to be held until they were abolished in 1971.

Over the years Justices of the Peace were also given many administrative duties, for example being responsible for the poor law, highways and bridges, and weights and measures. In the nineteenth century elected local authorities took over most of these duties, though some remnants remain, especially in the licensing powers of the Magistrates' Courts.

The poor quality of the local Justices of the Peace in London and the absence of an adequate police force became a matter of concern towards the end of the eighteenth century. This led to seven public offices with paid magistrates being set up in 1792. This was the origin of the modern District Judge (Magistrates' Court). Until 1839 these professional magistrates were in charge of the police as well as hearing cases in court. Outside London the first appointment of a paid magistrate was in Manchester in 1813. In 1835 the Municipal Corporations Act gave a general power for boroughs to request the appointment of a stipendiary magistrate. At the beginning a paid magistrate did not have to have any particular qualifications, but from 1839 they could be appointed only from barristers. Solicitors did not become eligible to be appointed as stipendiary magistrates until 1949. Today they have to have a seven-year general qualification.

9.3 Qualifications for lay magistrates

In the foreword to the National Strategy for the Recruitment of Lay Magistrates, the Lord Chancellor wrote:

> **Q** 'Magistrates are recruited from members of the local community. No formal qualifications are required, but applicants are expected to demonstrate common sense, integrity, intelligence and the capacity to act fairly. They perform a valuable service on behalf of their communities and their role is pivotal to the administration, not only of local justice, but to our judicial system as a whole.'

Although no formal qualifications are required, certain qualities are required and there are some limitations on who can be appointed. These are set out in sections 9.3.1 to 9.3.5.

9.3.1 Age

Lay magistrates must be aged between 18 and 65 on appointment. Until 2000 it was unusual for anyone over the age of 60 to be appointed but the Lord Chancellor recognised that there were many people who, having retired at 60, had the time for the commitment to magistrates' duties which they did not have when they were working. He increased the age limit and now will consider a person who is over the age of 60. In such cases an appointment is more likely to be made if the person is especially well qualified or their appointment would improve the overall composition of the Bench. The lower age range was reduced to 18 in 2003, but it is unusual for a person under 27 to be considered as it is felt that they will not have enough experience. However, in 2004 one magistrate aged 21 and another aged 23 were appointed.

Before 1906 there was a property qualification which meant that magistrates had to be home owners or tenants of property above a certain value. Also, before 1919 the Bench was an all-male affair with women becoming eligible for appointment only in 1919. Today there are no property qualifications and women now make up almost half of the magistracy.

9.3.2 Limitations

However, there are some people who are not eligible to be appointed. The important factor is that candidates should be of good standing in the local community. So people with serious criminal convictions are disqualified from becoming a magistrate, though a conviction for a minor motoring offence will not automatically disqualify a candidate. Undischarged bankrupts are also disqualified. Those involved in enforcement of the law, such as police officers, civilians working for the police and traffic wardens are ineligible. This is because their work is incompatible with sitting as a magistrate. Members of the armed forces are also ineligible. Close relatives of those working in the local criminal justice system will not be appointed as magistrates in that area as it would not appear 'just' if, for example, the wife of a local police officer were to sit to decide cases. However, there is no bar on them being appointed as a lay magistrate in another area. Close relatives who are both lay magistrates will not be appointed to the same Bench.

The magistracy does try to be inclusive, so people with disabilities may be appointed provided that those disabilities do not prevent them from carrying out the duties of a magistrate. In 1998 a pilot scheme was started to see if it was feasible for visually impaired people to sit as magistrates. This was successful and since 2001 visually impaired magistrates have been appointed.

9.3.3 Six key personal qualities

The only qualifications that lay magistrates need are the six key personal qualities that the Lord Chancellor set out in 1998. These are:

- good character
- understanding and communication
- social awareness
- maturity and sound temperament
- sound judgment
- commitment and reliability.

Aspiring lay magistrates should have certain 'judicial' qualities. It is particularly important that they are able to assimilate factual information and make a reasoned decision on it. They must also be able to take account of the reasoning of others and work as a team.

9.3.4 Area

Up to 2003 it was necessary for lay magistrates to live within 15 miles of the commission area for the court in which they sat. In 2003 the Courts Act abolished commission areas. Instead there is now one commission area for the whole of England and Wales. However, the country is divided into local justice areas. These areas are specified by the Lord Chancellor and lay magistrates are expected to live or work within or near to the local justice area to which they are allocated.

9.3.5 Commitment

The other requirement is that lay magistrate are prepared to commit themselves to sitting at least 26 half-days each year. This is quite an onerous commitment and in the National Strategy for the Recruitment of Lay Magistrates published by the Lord Chancellor in October 2003 it was suggested that the minimum number of days sitting might be reduced to 24 half-days.

9.3.6 Allowances

Lay justices are not paid for sitting as magistrates but they are entitled to certain payments. These are:

- a travelling allowance
- a subsistence allowance and
- a financial loss allowance.

The magistrate can only claim for actual expenses incurred or actual loss.

9.4 Selection and appointment of lay magistrates

Between 1,500 and 1,800 new lay magistrates are usually appointed each year. The Lord Chancellor appoints all lay magistrates. Until 2004 there was an exception for the area of the Duchy of Lancaster, where lay justices were appointed by the Chancellor for the Duchy. This right was abolished by s 10 of the Courts Act 2003 and the Lord Chancellor now makes all appointments. This is done 'on behalf of and in the name of Her Majesty'. The Lord Chancellor is assisted in this by Advisory Committees who recommend candidates for appointment.

9.4.1 Recruitment

In the past, many applicants for the magistracy had their names put forward by existing magistrates, local political parties, trade unions, charities or other local organisations. This ensured that applicants were well known in the local community. Today, although names can still be put forward by these organisations, there is more emphasis on encouraging applicants to apply directly and making the appointment system more open.

The National Strategy for the Recruitment of Lay Magistrates (2003) included a list of objectives for improving recruitment. The most important of these were:

- to continue to develop ways of recruiting magistrates from a wide spread of people, particularly from groups currently under-represented nationally

- to continue to develop a socially diverse Bench that will be representative of all sectors of society

- to consider ways of building more flexibility into court sittings, so those magistrates with other responsibilities are able to meet at least the minimum number of required sittings

- to target employers and encourage them to release staff who are magistrates to enable them to fulfil their duties

- to revise existing methods of recruitment advertising and consider alternative possibilities.

Proposed actions were listed under each of these objectives and given a high, medium or low priority. There were only two proposed actions which were given a high priority. These were to develop a campaign aimed at employers and to direct recruitment campaigns through various media outlets, including local newspapers and radio, and specific publications – among others, those representing specific target groups.

These two priorities underline the main problems in recruiting. The first is that most people are unaware that they can apply to become a magistrate and that no formal qualifications are required. The second is the fact that many employers will not give paid time off for duties and also that

applicants are worried that they may lose out on promotion. Employers are legally obliged to allow employees time off to act as a magistrate, but this does not prevent the above two problems.

9.4.2 Advisory committees

The procedure used by the Advisory Committees for identifying suitable candidates is that they will encourage applications from people directly or through nomination by local organisations. To get direct applications they may advertise in local papers or on the radio and they may hold 'open' days to explain the work of magistrates to potential applicants.

Each Advisory Committee either has a formal Sub-Committee to interview applicants or will set up an interview panel for this task. Advisory Committees are made up of one-third non-magistrates and two-thirds serving magistrates. There is usually a two-stage interview process. At the first interview the panel tries to find out more about the candidate's personal attributes, in particular looking to see if they have the six key qualities required. The interview panel will also explore the candidate's attitudes on various criminal justice issues such as youth crime or drink-driving. The second interview is aimed at testing candidates' potential judicial aptitude and this is done by a discussion of at least two case studies which are typical of those heard regularly in Magistrates' Courts. The discussion might, for example, focus on the type of sentence which should be imposed on specific case facts.

Once suitable candidates have been identified, the Advisory Committee then has to ensure that the Bench broadly reflects the community which it serves, taking account of:

• gender
• ethnic origin
• geographical spread
• occupation and
• political affiliation.

The intention is to create a panel that is representative of all aspects of society. A candidate who is personally suitable may not be recommended for appointment because their appointment would increase an imbalance which already exists on the Bench. For example, there may already be too many magistrates from a particular occupational background, so that an applicant who is in the same occupation will not be recommended.

9.4.3 Political affiliation

A major discussion point is to what extent, if any, the political views of a candidate should be considered. In 1966 the then Lord Chancellor, Lord Gardiner, issued a directive to Advisory Committees, telling them to bear in mind people's political allegiances in order to achieve a balance. At the time this caused a stir, but the reason behind it was to try to achieve better balanced panels of magistrates. That directive said:

> Q
>
> 'The Lord Chancellor cannot disregard political affiliations in making appointments, not because the politics of an individual are a qualification or a disqualification for appointment, but because it is important that justices should be drawn from all sections of the community and should represent all shades of opinion.
>
> This object would not be attained if appointments were made in too large a degree from supporters of any one political party. It is the aim of the Lord Chancellor to preserve a proper balance by the appointment of suitable parties from the main political parties, and, if they can be found, from persons who are independent of any political party.
>
> For these reasons the Lord Chancellor wishes advisory committees to have regard for the political affiliations of the persons whom they recommend for appointment.'

This requirement for the political views of a candidate to be considered continues. The current direction states:

> Q
>
> 'The political views of a candidate are neither a qualification nor a disqualification for appointment. However, the Lord Chancellor requires, in the interests of balance, that the voting pattern for the area as evidenced by the last two general elections, should broadly be reflected in the composition of the bench.'

In addition, there is also a requirement that Advisory Committees and Sub-Committees should be politically balanced:

> **Q**
> 'New members of Advisory Committees and Sub-Committees should be recommended on the basis of their ability, set against the need that Committees broadly reflect the local community. The Lord Chancellor requires each Committee and Sub-Committee to have at least one supporter of each of the main political parties and at least one member who is politically uncommitted. Beyond that the political balance of each Committee and Sub-Committee should broadly reflect the area which it covers. More generally, so far as is practicable, Committees should also be balanced in terms of gender, ethnic origin, geographical spread and age.'

In 1998 the Lord Chancellor issued a Consultation Paper, *Political Balance in the Lay Magistracy*, considering whether the political views of applicants should be considered at all. After consulting he reluctantly decided that political balance was the most practicable method of ensuring a good social balance on the Bench.

ACTIVITY

Discuss whether the political views of applicants to the magistracy should be considered.

9.5 Training of lay magistrates

The training of lay magistrates is supervised by the Magistrates' Committee of the Judicial Studies Board. This Committee has drawn up a syllabus of the topics which lay magistrates should cover during the course of their training. The Auld Review (2001) recommended that the Judicial Studies Board should be made responsible for 'devising and securing the content and manner of training for all magistrates'. The Government accepted this recommendation.

Under the Courts Act 2003 a unified courts administration came into effect in April 2005. This combines the management of the magistrates' court with the Crown Court, County Court and higher courts. It has had an effect on the training of magistrates as the 2003 Act abolishes the 42 independent Magistrates' Court Committees. In their place there are 42 unified areas (effectively covering the same areas as the current Committees) but with responsibility for all the courts within their area under the direction of a new executive agency within the Department for Constitutional Affairs. This new agency is known as Her Majesty's Courts Service.

In June 2004 the Judicial Studies Board issued a consultation paper, *Proposals for the Organisation and Management of Magistrates' Training in the Unified Courts Administration*. In this it sets out five key goals for the new training system. It should:

- uphold judicial independence
- contribute towards public confidence in the magistracy
- enable the Judicial Studies Board to establish minimum standards for the content, design and delivery of magistrates' training that can be monitored and quality assured
- be efficient and effective and
- support recruitment, retention and succession planning of magistrates and staff.

Since 1998 magistrates' training has been monitored more closely. There were criticisms prior to then that, although magistrates were required to attend a certain number of hours' training, there was no assessment of how much they had understood. In 1998 the Magistrates New Training Initiative was introduced (MNTI 1). In 2004 this was refined by the Magistrates National Training Initiative (MNTI 2). The framework of training is divided into four areas of competence, the first three of which are relevant to all lay magistrates. The fourth competence is for chairmen of the Bench. The four areas of competence are:

1. Managing yourself – this focuses on some of the basic aspects of self-management in relation to preparing for court, conduct in court and ongoing learning.
2. Working as a member of a team – this focuses on the team aspect of decision-making in the Magistrates' Court.
3. Making judicial decisions – this focuses on impartial and structured decision-making.
4. Managing judicial decision-making – this is for the chairman's role and focuses on working with the legal adviser, managing the court and ensuring effective, impartial decision-making.

For delivering training there are Bench Training and Developmental Committees (BTDCs) and s 19(3) of the Courts Act 2003 sets out a statutory obligation on the Lord Chancellor to provide training and training materials.

9.5.1 Training for new magistrates

There is a syllabus for new magistrates which is divided into three parts. These are:

1. Initial introductory training – this covers such matters as understanding the organisation of the Bench and the administration of the court and the roles and responsibilities of those involved in the Magistrates' Court.
2. Core training – this provides the new magistrate with the opportunity to acquire and develop the key skills, knowledge and understanding required of a competent magistrate.
3. Activities – these will involve observations of court sittings and visits to establishments such as a prison or a probation office.

The training programme for new magistrates should normally follow the pattern set out in Figure 9.1.

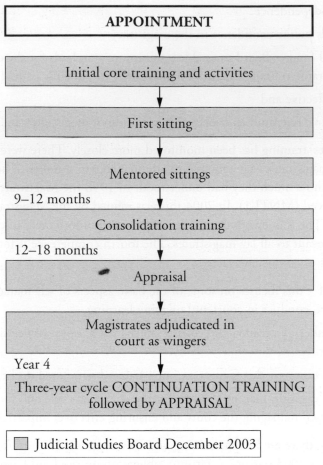

APPOINTMENT
Initial core training and activities
First sitting
Mentored sittings

9–12 months

Consolidation training

12–18 months

Appraisal
Magistrates adjudicated in court as wingers

Year 4

Three-year cycle CONTINUATION TRAINING followed by APPRAISAL

Judicial Studies Board December 2003

MNTI2 Handbook issued by the Judicial Studies Board

Figure 9.1 New magistrates' training and appraisal pathway

Mentors

Each new lay justice keeps a Personal Development Log of their progress. They also have a mentor, who is an experienced magistrate, to assist them. The initial introductory training is covered before the new magistrate starts sitting in court. They will also take part in a structured courtroom observation of cases on at least three occasions. These should be arranged so that they see different aspects of the work and should included preliminary decisions such as bail, a short summary trial and sentencing.

Training sessions

These are organised and carried out at local level within the 42 areas. Much of the training is delivered by Justices' Clerks. The Judicial Studies Board intends that most training should still be delivered locally. However, the new structure will take into account the need to collaborate regionally and nationally where appropriate. In particular, the training of Youth and Family Panel Chairmen will be delivered nationally for areas which do not have enough such Chairmen needing training to run an effective course locally.

Appraisal

After their initial training, magistrates will start by sitting in the ordinary magistrates' court. They will be what are called 'wingers', that is, one of the two magistrates who sit on either side of the chairman of the Bench. During the first two years of sitting in court, the new magistrate is expected to attend about seven or eight training sessions. During the same period between eight and 11 of the sessions in which the new magistrate sits as a member of the Bench will be mentored.

After two years, or whenever it is felt that the magistrate is ready, there will be an appraisal to check whether the competencies have been achieved. Any magistrate who cannot show that they have achieved the competencies will be given extra training. If they still cannot achieve the competencies then the matter is referred to the local BTDC, who may recommend to the Lord Chancellor that the magistrate be removed from sitting on the Bench.

After that, each magistrate should be appraised at least once every three years. When magistrates become more experienced they may be appointed to the Youth Court Bench or the Family Proceedings Court Bench. There is additional training and appraisal for these roles. Finally, a magistrate may be appointed as chairman. Again, there is additional training for this role.

Post-sitting reviews

These were introduced by MNTI2 and are intended to provide an opportunity for the Bench of three to sit down together with the legal adviser to identify what went well and what they would like to do differently in future.

Summary

Overall, the training of lay magistrates has greatly improved. Much of their training is aimed at sentencing and they are also given a sentencing handbook (see Chapter 12 for further information). Despite this there are criticisms that sentences are inconsistent between different lay Benches (see section 9.10.3). Another area in which training is important is on deciding bail applications. Again, there are criticisms that there is a wide variation between Benches on the granting or refusal of bail. The main point of the training is that it is not intended to make the magistrates lawyers. They have a legal adviser who can advise them on the law when a legal point is at issue. As well as being given training on the type of cases they will hear, lay magistrates are also given training on equal treatment. As set out in the training pack provided by the Judicial Studies Board, this covers:

> **Q** 'recognising the effects of discrimination on the basis of race, creed, colour, religion, ethnicity, gender, class, disability, or sexual orientation which can lead to unequal treatment of people in magistrates' courts'.

9.6 Resignation and removal of lay justices

This is governed by s 11 of the Courts Act 2003 which states:

> **S** 's 11(1) A lay justice may resign his office at any time.
>
> (2) The Lord Chancellor may remove a lay justice from his office by an instrument on behalf and in the name of Her Majesty –
>
> (a) on the ground of incapacity or misbehaviour,
>
> (b) on the ground of a persistent failure to meet such standards of competence as are prescribed by a direction given by the Lord Chancellor, or
>
> (c) if he is satisfied that the lay justice is declining or neglecting to take a proper part in the exercise of his functions as a justice of the peace.'

9.6.1 Retirement

Lay magistrates must retire from sitting on the Bench when they reach the age of 70. When a lay magistrate resigns or retires, their name is placed on what is known as the supplemental list. While they are on this list they are still entitled to use the title 'Justice of the Peace'. The explanatory notes to the Courts Act 2003 explain that the supplemental list is now intended to be a recognition of the service given by lay magistrates.

9.6.2 Removal

The Lord Chancellor has powers to remove lay magistrates in the circumstances set out in s 11(2) above. Incapacity will include situations where a magistrate becomes too ill to sit but does not resign. Removal for misbehaviour usually occurs when a magistrate is convicted of an offence. There about 10 such removals each year. However, on occasions in the past there have been removals for such matters as taking part in a CND march or transvestite behaviour. There was considerable criticism of the Lord Chancellor's use of his power of removal in such circumstances and it is unlikely that such behaviour today would lead to removal from the Bench.

The power under s 11(2)(b) of removal for persistent failure to meet the required standards of competence reinforces the training initiative (MNTI2). It overcomes the problems of the old system whereby magistrates could continue to sit on the Bench regardless of whether they had understood their training. This is the first time that this power has been specifically set down by statute.

The power under s 11(2)(c) allows the Lord Chancellor to remove magistrates who refuse to fulfil their obligations to sit a certain number of times. It also allows magistrates to be removed if they refuse to operate a law enacted by the Government.

9.7 Magistrates' duties

They have a very wide workload which is mainly connected to criminal cases, although they also deal with some civil matters, especially family cases.

9.7.1 Criminal cases

Ninety-eight per cent of all criminal cases are tried in the magistrates' court. As well as dealing with all these, magistrates also deal with preliminary hearings in the remaining 3 per cent of criminal cases. This will involve early administrative hearings and bail applications.

The website for the Department for Constitutional Affairs (www.dca.gov.uk) in 2004 listed their role in criminal cases heard in the Adult and Youth Court as encompassing:

- decide on requests for remand in custody

- decide on applications for bail

- decide whether a case should be adjourned

- determine whether a defendant is guilty or not

- pass sentence on a defendant who has been found guilty [or has pleaded guilty]

- commit a defendant to the Crown Court for sentence

- enforce financial penalties and

- may determine the venue at which a case will be heard.

In criminal cases the role of lay magistrates has increased through the statutory downgrading of offences. Over the past 20 years a number of offences which were triable either way have been made summary offences and triable only in the Magistrates' Court; for example, drink-driving and driving while disqualified. It is also thought that the magistrates' workload has also increased through the Crown Prosecution Service charging the lower of two possible charges against the defendant, again making the case triable only in the Magistrates' Court.

An important point to note is that, where a defendant pleads not guilty, the magistrates both decide on guilt or innocence and, if they find the defendant guilty, also pass sentence. This is in contrast to the Crown Court where the two roles of deciding the verdict and passing sentence are kept separate. In the Crown Court the jury decides on guilty or innocence. If it finds the defendant guilty the judge then passes sentence.

Under the Criminal Justice Act 2003 the magistrates' sentencing powers are to be increased from six months' imprisonment to 12 months' imprisonment for one offence and from 12 months' to 15 months' for two or more offences. This increase is aimed at preventing the need for magistrates to send so many cases to the Crown Court for trial or for sentence.

Crown Court appeals

Lay magistrates also sit at the Crown Court to hear appeals from the magistrates' court to hear cases where the defendant is appealing to the Crown Court against their conviction. In these cases the lay justices form a panel with a qualified judge.

9.7.2 Civil cases

Many civil matters are also dealt with in the magistrates' court. These include the enforcing of debts owed to the utilities (gas, electricity and water), non-payment of council tax and non payment of television licences. In addition, they hear appeals from the refusal to grant a licence for the sale of alcohol (Licensing Act 2003) or for a licence to operate a Hackney cab (taxi). Until 2003 magistrates actually had to grant all licences to sell alcohol, including licences for one-off situations, such as extended hours for a bar for a graduation ceremony! This work took up a large amount of their time and it was felt that, as it was mainly administrative in nature, it would be better for local authorities to have the power to grant a licence and magistrates should only deal with appeals where a licence had been refused.

9.7.3 Youth Court

Specially nominated and trained justices form the Youth Court panel to hear criminal charges against young offenders aged 10 to 17 years old. These magistrates must be under 65 and a panel must usually include at least one man and one woman.

Magistrates in the Youth Court have the power to sentence young offenders to a maximum of two years' detention and training.

9.7.4 Family Proceedings Court

There is also a special panel for the Family Proceedings Court. Here, magistrates deal with a wide range of issues affecting family and children. Cases include orders for protection against violence, affiliation cases and adoption orders and proceedings under the Children Act 1989. The magistrates for this court have special training and under the Courts Act 2003 the Lord Chancellor has the power to make rules on:

- the grant and revocation of authorisation of magistrates to sit as a members of the Family Proceedings Court
- the appointment of chairmen of these courts
- the composition of the Bench in the these courts.

These powers are intended to ensure that only trained and suitable magistrates sit in the Family Proceedings Courts.

9.7.5 Immunity from suit

Under the Courts and Legal Services Act 1990 lay magistrates have immunity from being sued for anything they do in their judicial capacity in good faith. So even if an act is in excess of their jurisdiction, they cannot be sued if they believed that they were acting within their powers.

■ Key facts chart on lay magistrates

KEY FACTS

Qualifications	• no formal qualifications required • 18–65 on appointment • no serious convictions: not an undischarged bankrupt • six key personal qualities • live (or work) within or near to the local justice area in which they sit
Selection/ appointment	Can apply or have name put forward by a local organisation such as chamber of commerce or trade union Adverts are used to encourage applications from wide range Local advisory committees interview and make recommendations to Lord Chancellor Lord Chancellor appoints Tries to obtain a balance by taking into account: • gender • ethnic origin • geographical spread • occupation and • political affiliation
Training	Judicial Studies Board has a strengthened role in training (Courts Act 2003) Most training carried out locally by legal advisers (magistrates' clerks) but some training is to be carried out nationally

CONTINUED ▸

KEY FACTS

	Magistrates National Training Initiative (MNI2) • training sessions • mentors • appraisal • post-sitting reviews
Role	Criminal cases • deals with 98% of all criminal cases • also first hearing in other 2% • decide bail applications • decide verdict • pass sentence Civil cases such matters as: • appeals against refusal of a licence to sell alcohol • non-payment of council tax • non-payment of TV licence Youth Court Family Proceedings Court
Retirement/ removal	Retire at 70 Can resign at any time Removal is by the Lord Chancellor for: • incapacity or misbehaviour • persistent failure to meet standards of competence • declining or neglecting to take a proper part in the exercise of his functions as a justice of the peace. (s 11 Courts Act 2003)

9.8 The magistrates' clerk

Every Bench is assisted by a clerk, or as they are now often referred to, a legal adviser. The senior clerk in each court has to be qualified as a barrister or solicitor for at least five years. In 1998 the Government consulted on whether all court clerks (not just senior clerks) should be legally qualified. Following this the Government announced that all clerks appointed after January 1999 would have to be fully qualified and that all existing clerks would have to become qualified within 10 years. However, they subsequently withdrew this latter requirement for existing clerks who were over the age of 40.

The effect is that the court clerks are becoming more professional and this has led to the new name of 'legal adviser'. The Auld Review found that, in March 2001, there were about 1,800 legal advisers, two-thirds of whom were legally qualified. The Judicial Studies Board is hoping to become responsible for training legal advisers, but this is dependent on sufficient government funding being made available.

The clerk's duty is to guide the magistrates on questions of law, practice and procedure. This is set out in s 28(3) of the Justices of the Peace Act 1979 which says:

's 28(3) It is hereby declared that the functions of a justices' clerk include the giving to the justices . . . at the request of [them], of advice about law, practice or procedure on questions arising in connection with the discharge of [their] functions . . . and that the clerk may, at any time when he thinks he should do so, bring to the attention of the justices any point of law, practice or procedure that it or may be involved in any question so arising.'

At the same time as the implementation of the Human Rights Act 1998 in October 2000, a Practice Direction was issued requiring any legal advice given by the legal advisers to the justices to be given in open court.

> **Q**
>
> '8 At any time, justices are entitled to receive advice to assist them in discharging their responsibilities. If they are in any doubt as to the evidence which has been given, they should seek the aid of their legal adviser, referring to his/her notes as appropriate. This should ordinarily be done in open court. Where the justices request their adviser to join them in the retiring room, this request should be made in the presence of the parties in court.
>
> Any legal advice given to the justices other than in open court should be clearly stated to be professional and the adviser should subsequently repeat the substance of the advice in open court and give the parties an opportunity to make any representations they wish on that professional advice. The legal adviser should then state in open court whether the professional advice is confirmed or, if it is varied, the nature of the variation.'
>
> *Practice Direction* [2000] 4 All ER 895

This enforces the decisions in the earlier cases of *R v Sussex Justices, ex p McCarthy* [1924] 1 KB 256 and *R v Eccles Justices, ex p Fitzpatrick* (1989) Cr App R 324.

CASE EXAMPLE

R v Sussex Justices, ex p McCarthy [1924] 1 KB 256

The defendant was being tried in the Magistrates' Courts on a charge of dangerous driving. The clerk to the justices was a member of a firm of solicitors who were representing the claimant in a civil case arising from the collision in the driving incident. When the magistrates retired to decide the case, the clerk retired with them. However, he was not asked for any advice and he did not inform the magistrates about the civil case. Despite the fact that the clerk did not take any part in the decision-making, the Divisional Court quashed the decision. Giving judgment in this case, Lord Hewitt CJ said:

> J 'It is not merely a matter of some importance but it is of fundamental importance that justice should not only be done but manifestly and undoubtedly be seen to be done.'

In *R v Eccles Justices, ex p Fitzpatrick* (1989) the Divisional Court quashed a decision and sent the case back to be dealt with by a new Bench because the clerk had retired with the justices for 25 minutes of the 30 minutes they were absent from court. The court said that any request for the clerk to retire with the justices must be made clearly and in open court.

The role of the legal adviser was substantially increased following the Narey Report, *Review of Delay in the Criminal Justice System* (1997). This had recommended that clerks be given wider role as case manager and with the power to do all the matters that a single justice can do. However, when the Crime and Disorder Act 1998, which implemented these proposals, was going through Parliament, there was some disquiet that the clerks' role was going to be too wide and erode the function of the justices. This point of view was put by Lord Bingham during the Second Reading in the House of Lords when he said:

> **Q**
>
> 'To send a defendant to prison is a judicial act; it is not an order which anyone not exercising judicial authority should make, and it is certainly not a matter of administration.
>
> . . . I object to the possibility that some of these powers might by rule be exercised by the justices' clerk because such a rule would erode the fundamental distinction between the justices and the justices' legal adviser . . . . If the justices' clerk were to be entrusted with these important decisions and judgements, judicial in character, the time would inevitably come when people would reasonably ask whether he or she should not be left to get on and try the whole case.'

As a result, s 49(3) was inserted into the 1998 Act to prevent certain functions being delegated to clerks. The Justices' Clerks Rules 1999 (SI No 2784) sets out what they can do. This includes dealing with routine administrative matters, but also issuing warrants for arrest, extending police bail and adjourning criminal proceedings if the defendant is given bail on the same terms as originally set by the justices.

9.9 Advantages of using lay magistrates

9.9.1 Cross-section of society

The system involves members of the community and provides a wider cross-section on the Bench than would be possible with the use of professional judges. This is particularly true of women, with 49 per cent of magistrates being women against 10 per cent of professional judges. Also, ethnic minorities are reasonably well represented in the magistracy. The National Strategy for the Recruitment of Lay Magistrates (2003) gave the statistics for ethnic minority lay magistrates as being 6 per cent of the total number of lay magistrates as against 7.9 per cent of the population as a whole. This compares very favourably to the professional judiciary where less than 1 per cent are from ethnic minority backgrounds.

The relatively high level of ethnic minority magistrates is largely a result of campaigns to attract a wider range of candidates. A major campaign was launched by the Lord Chancellor's Department in March 1999. Under this, adverts encouraging people to apply were placed in some 36 different newspapers and magazines. Adverts were also placed in national newspapers and also in TV guides and women's magazines. In an effort to encourage those from ethnic minorities to apply, adverts also appeared in such publications as the *Caribbean Times*, the *Asian Times* and the *Muslim News*. This led to an increase in the numbers of ethnic minority appointments, as shown by the following figures. These give the percentage of ethnic minority appointments in the overall appointments:

1994	1999/2000	2000/01	2001/02
5%	8.6%	9.3%	8.5%

The Lord Chancellor, in announcing this campaign in 1999 to attract a wider range of magistrates, pointed out that the magistracy was already very diverse:

> **Q** 'Magistrates come from a wide range of backgrounds and occupations. We have magistrates who are dinner ladies and scientists, bus drivers and teachers, plumbers and housewives. They have different faiths and come from different ethnic backgrounds, some have disabilities. All are serving their communities, ensuring that local justice is dispensed by local people. The magistracy should reflect the diversity of the community it serves.'

However, despite this, lay magistrates are perceived as being 'middle-class, middle-aged and middle minded'. A report, *The Judiciary in the Magistrates' Courts* (2000), which had been commissioned jointly by the Home Office and the Lord Chancellor's Department supported this when it found that lay magistrates:

- were drawn overwhelmingly from professional and managerial ranks and
- 40 per cent of them were retired from full-time employment.

Although they are not a true cross-section of the local community and have little in common with the young working-class defendants who make up the majority of defendants, lay magistrates are more representative than District Judges in the Magistrates' Courts. The same report pointed out that in comparison with lay magistrates District Judges were:

- younger, but
- mostly white and male.

Davies, Croall and Tyrer, in their book *Criminal Justice*, raise the question of what would a more demographically representative panel achieve.

> 'What more would a more representative magistracy achieve and just what, or who, should it represent? A representative magistracy on the grounds of demographic characteristics alone may not make different decisions in relation to either guilt or sentencing from the current magistracy. Women magistrates appear no more sympathetic, for example, to female offenders who often come from very

different socio-economic backgrounds (see for example, Eaton 1986) [*Justice for Women?*, Open University Press], and there is little evidence of any direct bias on the grounds of social status in respect of business offenders (see, for example, Croall 1991) ['Sentencing the Business Offender', *The Howard Journal*, 30(4) 280].'

M Davies, J Tyres and H Croall, *Criminal Justice* (2nd edn, Longman, 1998) p 177

9.9.2 Local knowledge

Lay magistrates used to have to live within 15 miles of the area covered by the commission, so that they should have local knowledge of particular problems in the area. Under the Courts Act 2003 there is no longer a formal requirement that they should live in or near the area in which they sit as a magistrate, although the explanatory notes for the Act say:

Q	'It is envisaged, however, that Advisory Committees (who advise the Lord Chancellor on appointments of lay magistrates) will continue, under guidance from the Lord Chancellor, to recommend that lay magistrates be assigned to the local justice area in which they reside unless there is a good reason to do otherwise (for example, should an applicant find it easier to sit where he or she works rather than where he or she lives).'

However, as most magistrates come from the professional and managerial classes, it is unlikely that they live in or have any real knowledge of the problems in the poorer areas. Their main value is that they will have more awareness of local events, local patterns of crime and local opinions than a professional judge from another area.

In addition, during the last 10 years, some 125 magistrates' court have been closed. This causes problems of access and attendance as in some areas people have long journeys to their 'local' court. It also means that the advantage of lay magistrates having local knowledge is being lost. There also a proposal to centralise family courts in London. This would mean having just three centres: one at the existing Wells Street court, one at Marylebone and one at Waltham Forest, instead of more local courts. Indeed there would be no Family Proceedings Court in South London. Magistrates are very opposed to this as they point out that it would mean very long journeys (and expense) for disadvantaged families.

9.9.3 Cost

The use of unpaid lay magistrates is cheap. The report *The Judiciary in the Magistrates' Courts* (2000) found that at that time the cost of using lay magistrates was £52.10 per hour. As against this, the cost of using District Judges in the Magistrates' Courts was £61.78 an hour. When this is multiplied by the number of hours' work carried out by lay magistrates in the course of the year, it is obvious that the cost of replacing them with professional judges would be several millions of pounds. In addition, there would also be the problem of recruiting sufficient qualified lawyers.

The cost of a trial in the Magistrates' Court is also much less than a trial in the Crown Court. This is partly because cases in the Crown Court are more complex and therefore likely to take longer, but even so it is clear that the cost both to the Government and to defendants who pay for their own lawyer is much higher.

9.9.4 Legal adviser

Since 1999 all newly appointed magistrates' clerks have to be legally qualified. In addition, existing clerks under the age of 40 in 1999 have to qualify within 10 years. This brings a higher level of legal skill to the Magistrates' Court. The availability of a legal adviser gives the magistrates access to any necessary legal advice on points that may arise in any case. This overcomes any criticism of the fact that lay magistrates are not themselves legally qualified. In addition, the training of lay magistrates is improving, with MNTI1 and MNTI2 and the strengthened role of the Judicial Studies Board in their training.

9.9.5 Few appeals

Comparatively few defendants appeal against the magistrates' decisions, and many of the appeals that are made are against sentence, not against the finding of guilt. In 2003 the Judicial Statistics Annual Report showed that only 11,858 appeals were made to the Crown Court from the Magistrates' Courts. Out of these, only 2,811 were allowed and in another 2,179 cases the Crown Court varied the decision/sentence. This was out of a total workload of over 1.9 million criminal cases dealt with in the Magistrates' Courts. There are also very few instances where an error of law is made. This is shown by the fact that there were only 96 appeals by way of case stated to the Queen's Bench Divisional Court. Of these appeals, 43 were allowed. From this it can be argued that despite the amateur status of lay magistrates they do a remarkably good job.

9.10 Disadvantages of lay magistrates

9.10.1 Middle-aged, middle-class

Lay magistrates are often perceived as being middle-aged and middle class. The report *The Judiciary in the Magistrates' Courts* (2000) showed that this was largely true. It found that 40 per cent of lay magistrates were retired and also that they were overwhelmingly from a professional or managerial background. However, as already discussed at section 9.9.1, lay magistrates are from a wider range of backgrounds than professional judges.

9.10.2 Prosecution bias

It is often said that lay magistrates tend to be prosecution biased, believing the police too readily. However, part of the training is aimed at eliminating this type of bias. There is also the fact that the magistrates will see the same Crown Prosecution Service prosecutor or designated case worker frequently and this could affect their judgment. Another point is that there is a lower acquittal rate in magistrates' courts than in the Crown Court.

9.10.3 Inconsistency in sentencing

Magistrates in different areas often pass very different sentences for what appear to be similar offences. The Government's White Paper, *Justice for All*, set out differences found in the Criminal Statistics for 2001 when it gave these following examples:

- for burglary of dwellings, 20 per cent of offenders are sentenced to immediate custody in Teesside, compared with 41 per cent of offenders in Birmingham. Thirty eight per cent of burglars at Cardiff Magistrates' Courts receive community sentences, compared with 66 per cent in Leicester

- for driving while disqualified, the percentage of offenders sentenced to custody ranged from 21 per cent in Neath Port Talbot [South Wales] to 77 per cent in Mid North Essex

- for receiving stolen goods, 3.5 per cent of offenders sentenced at Reading Magistrates' Court received custodial sentences, compared with 48 per cent in Greenwich and Woolwich [South London] and 39 per cent at Camberwell Green [South London].

However, the Chairman of the Magistrates' Association pointed out that only 4 per cent of offenders dealt with by magistrates receive a prison sentence, so that the problem may not be as severe as thought. He also said that in any local sentencing pattern there is always going to be variation. This is partly because there is an enormous variation in crime itself. He felt that variation is desirable provided that it can be justified. Since these figures were compiled these has been a new edition of the Magistrates' Association's Sentencing Guidelines. It is thought that these are helping to promote common standards.

9.10.4 Reliance on the clerk

The lack of legal knowledge of the lay justices should be offset by the fact that a legally qualified clerk is available to give advice. However, this will not prevent inconsistencies in sentencing since the clerk is not allowed to help the magistrates decide on a sentence. In some courts it is felt that the magistrates rely too heavily on their clerk.

■ Key facts chart on advantages and disadvantages of using lay magistrates in the legal system

The points in this table are balanced against each other, so you will see the advantages and disadvantages of the same facts:

KEY FACTS

Advantages	Disadvantages
Cross-section of local people	Not a true cross-section
Good gender balance	40% are retired people
Improving ethnic balance	Majority are from professional or managerial background
Much better cross-section than District Judges	Older than District judges
Live (or work) locally and so know the area and its problems	Unlikely to live in the poorer areas and so do not truly know the area's problems
Cheaper than using professional judges as they are only paid expenses	
Cheaper than sending cases to the Crown Court	
Improved training through MNTI2 and the increased role of Judicial Studies Board	There are inconsistencies in sentencing and decisions on bail
Have legal adviser for points of law	
Very few appeals	

ACTIVITY

Self-assessment questions

1. What powers does a single lay magistrate have?

2. Who is disqualified from being a lay magistrate?

3. What are the six key personal qualities that the Lord Chancellor sets out for lay magistrates?

4. How often do lay magistrates normally sit in court?

5. What initiatives have been taken to encourage applications from a wide range of people?

6. What is the role of (a) the Advisory Committee and (b) the Lord Chancellor in selecting and appointing magistrates?

7. Outline the training of lay magistrates.

8. On what grounds can the Lord Chancellor remove a lay magistrate from the post?

9. What are the roles of magistrates in criminal cases?

10. Apart from criminal cases, what other cases can magistrates deal with?

Further reading

Darbyshire, P, 'An Essay on the Importance and Neglect of the Magistracy' [1997] Crim LR 627.

chapter 10 THE LEGAL PROFESSION ■

Legal work involves a great many different personnel, who perform widely varying roles. Thus in the course of your involvement with the law you may encounter 'paralegal' workers, qualified legal executives, licensed conveyancers, and different types of legal clerks. There are also many non-lawyers who specialise in the law, such as accountants who work in tax and revenue law. However, the terms 'lawyer' and 'legal profession' are generally understood to describe those who belong to either of the two legal professions; that is, solicitors and barristers.

Solicitors traditionally provide a wide range of legal services as the 'front-line' lawyers. They provide general legal advice, prepare cases for court and can also conduct litigation. Barristers are specialist legal advisers and on the whole conduct litigation (advocacy) in the courts. However, as you will see, this overview is rather simplistic and the changes made to the legal profession since the mid-1980s have blurred the distinction between solicitors and barristers. For example, 25 years ago, the demarcation between the role of the barrister and that of the solicitor was clear; solicitors rarely undertook advocacy work outside the magistrates' and County Courts; the code of professional conduct for solicitors prohibited them from advertising, and solicitors enjoyed a monopoly in conveyancing (that is, the legal work associated with the buying and selling of property). All this has changed in the intervening period of time, and as you read this chapter you will discover how many of these aspects of the professions have altered.

10.1 Paralegals and legal executives

The term 'paralegal' is one that is difficult to define precisely. Many of the personnel who work in a law firm may have a job title of this description; but they may or may not have any formal legal qualifications. There is one recognised paralegal qualification which is offered by the Institute of Legal Executives (ILEX) for those candidates who work in the legal field but do not satisfy the entry requirements to take the ILEX diploma courses which are explained below. Otherwise, the term is a rather general one that does not necessarily denote how involved in the practice of law they are; they may or may not attend court or even meet clients. They may not even be a fee earner (a fee earner's work is billed directly to the clients, so they contribute directly to the income of the firm). That is not to say that paralegals lack importance. Many of the more straightforward issues (such as the form-filling required to enter a conditional fee agreement; or the routine searches carried out when a house is being sold and so on) are time consuming but not necessarily complex so are therefore best carried out by a paralegal, rather than a qualified and higher salaried lawyer.

ILEX is the awarding body for fully qualified legal executives (this is also a term often used broadly to describe a non-solicitor working in a law firm, but should strictly be used only of a person who is a Fellow of ILEX; a legal qualification which can be a step towards qualification as a solicitor). ILEX defines itself as the third branch of the legal profession and it has 22,000 members (which as you will see is rather more than the Bar Council). The Institute was established in 1963 to provide education and training for salaried non-solicitors doing paid legal work in law firms while they work.

The entry requirements to start the ILEX qualifications are four GCSE passes in academic subjects including English, or two A levels and one GCSE, or three AS levels or NVQ level 3. However, applicants aged 21 or over can register as mature students. Even without formal qualifications, enrolment can be on the basis of business, commercial, academic or other experience. Full membership of the Institute generally takes four years but, during this time, the student is earning money working in a law firm. After becoming a Fellow, it is possible to go on and qualify as a solicitor (see Figure 10.1).

10.1.1 Training routes

SOLICITOR – LAW DEGREE ROUTE	SOLICITOR – NON-LAW DEGREE ROUTE	FILEX ROUTE – FELLOW OF ILEX
A levels or other access qualification Law degree (usually an LLB (Hons)) provided it is a qualifying law degree, which means that it includes study of the 7 foundation subjects*	A levels or other access qualification Degree in any subject	GCSEs, A levels or other access qualification ILEX Diploma and employment in a firm
	Common Practice Examination (also called the Postgraduate or Graduate Diploma in Law). Study of the 7 foundation subjects* in law plus an extended project	ILEX Higher Diploma and employment in a firm
Join as student member of the Law Society	Join as student member of the Law Society	Membership of the Institute

CONTINUED ▸

SOLICITOR – LAW DEGREE ROUTE	SOLICITOR – NON-LAW DEGREE ROUTE	FILEX ROUTE – FELLOW OF ILEX
		Fellowship of the Institute (Members of ILEX who are at least 25 years of age, and have had 5 years' qualifying employment under the supervision of a solicitor, including a minimum of 2 years after passing all the examinations)
Legal Practice Course	Legal Practice Course	Legal Practice Course
Training contract	Training contract	
Professional Skills Course	Professional Skills Course	Professional Skills Course
Application to be entered on the Roll of Officers of the Supreme Court. This is admission to the profession as a qualified solicitor	Application to be entered on the Roll of Officers of the Supreme Court. This is admission to the profession as a qualified solicitor	Application to be entered on the Roll of Officers of the Supreme Court. This is admission to the profession as a qualified solicitor

* Contract Law, the Law of Torts, Public (also called Constitutional and Administrative) Law, Land Law, Criminal Law, European Union and the Law of Trusts.

Figure 10.1 Solicitors qualification routes: graduates and FILEX

10.2 Solicitors

10.2.1 Organisation

The Law Society of England and Wales is the governing body for solicitors, influencing all aspects of training, professional conduct, complaints and the organisation of the profession. The profession is governed by the Solicitors Act 1974, as amended.

The following information is taken from The Law Society's *Annual Statistical Report 2003*, available at www.lawsociety.org.uk:

- As at 31st July 2003, there were 116,110 solicitors on the Roll, an increase of 2.4 per cent on the year before.

- At the same date, 92,752 solicitors held practising certificates, an increase of 4.2 per cent on the previous year. [Section 1A of the Solicitors Act 1974 requires that any solicitor employed in connection with the provision of legal services in England and Wales will need a practising certificate ('PC'). They cost £790 each in 2004.]

- Since 1973, the total number of solicitors holding practising certificates has grown by 238.8 per cent at an average annual rate of 4.2 per cent.

- 78.2 per cent of solicitors holding practising certificates work in private practice; the remainder work mainly in commerce and industry and the public sector.

- In the year to 31st July 2003, admissions to the Roll, ie newly qualified solicitors and transfers from other legal professions, were 6,924, an increase of 4.2 per cent on admissions in the year before.

- Of these new admissions 56.8 per cent were women, and admissions from the ethnic minorities represented 17.3 per cent of all admissions with known ethnicity.

- In 2003 there were 15,212 separate organisations employing solicitors, of which 13,893 were based in England and Wales.

- In 2003, there were 9,198 solicitors' firms in England and Wales listed in the Society's database, a small decrease of 0.4 per cent on 2002.

- The vast majority of law firms are relatively small, with 84.7 per cent of them having four or fewer partners.

- In 2003, the 1.6 per cent of firms with 26 or more partners employed over one-third (37.3 per cent) of all solicitors in private practice. Sole practices accounted for 44.8 per cent of firms, and employed 8.5 per cent of all solicitors.

ACTIVITY

Self-assessment questions

1. What trends on the composition and size of the profession are indicated by the statistics above?

2. What percentage of firms employs most solicitors?

All in private practice				Partners				Sole practitioners			
Age	Men	Women	Total	Men	Women	Total	Men	Women	Total
Total	45,582	26,963	72,545	22,859	6,182	29,041	3,174	887	4,061
Average age	43.2	36.3	40.6	46.4	41.8	45.4	51.3	46.6	50.3

Law Society's REGIS database: The Law Society, *Annual Statistic Report 2003*

■ *Figure 10.2 The age distribution of sole practitioners and partners as at 31st July 2003*

The Law Society points out in its leaflet *Key facts 2003: the Solicitors' Profession*:

> **Q**
>
> 'The overwhelming majority (78.2%) of solicitors with practising certificates work in private practice. But this is changing. In the decade from 1993 to 2003 the numbers of employed solicitors grew from 10,312 to 20,207 – a 96% increase. The largest category of employment is commerce and industry at 7.1%, followed by local government, which employs 3.5% of practising certificate holders. (It should be noted that the number of solicitors working in the employed sector is likely to be greater than these figures suggest. This is because many, as a consequence of their employed status, are not required to hold a practising certificate.) A further 7.3% of solicitors are not attached to any organisation: the majority of these are in the youngest age group, which suggests that they are the most recently qualified. Women account for a higher proportion of employees in the employed and other sectors than in private practice. In private practice 37.2% of solicitors are women, compared to 48.8% in other sectors.'

Solicitors in private practice are generally regarded as more accessible to the public than barristers, solicitors' firms being found in the high streets of every town. Clients can employ the services of a solicitor directly, which is not necessarily the case with barristers. Solicitors are also able to advertise their services (within the limits of the professional rules), and this enables potential clients to select a practitioner with experience of their particular legal problem.

Region	Population total = 52,943 million (estimated using Office for National Statistics mid-1999 data) %	Firms (9,198) %
London	13.8	27.0
Rest of South-East	15.4	15.1
South-West	9.5	8.2
Wales	5.6	5.2
West Midlands	10.1	7.8
East Midlands	8.0	4.7
Eastern	10.4	10.0
North-West including Merseyside	12.9	12.1
Yorkshire and Humberside	9.5	6.6
North-East	4.8	3.3
Total	**100.0**	**100.0**

The Law Society, *Annual Statistic Report 2003*

■ *Figure 10.3 Location (standard regions) of population and private practice firms and practitioners in 2003*

ACTIVITY

Self-assessment question

Geographically, which areas are best served in terms of numbers of solicitors compared with the percentage of the population, and which areas are worst? Why do you think these areas have such a high/low proportion of solicitors' firms?

10.2.2 Training

First, refer back to Figure 10.1. That chart shows the most common routes for entry to the solicitors' profession, but there are in fact seven routes to qualification as a solicitor:

- law graduate
- non-law graduate
- Fellow of the Institute of Legal Executives (FILEX)

- overseas lawyer (transfer)
- barrister (transfer)
- Scottish/Northern Irish lawyers (transfer)
- justices' clerk (a Magistrates' Court clerk who passes the LPC and has at least five years' experience as a clerk).

Most solicitors (approximately 55 per cent) are law graduates. The remainder are either graduates of another discipline who have undertaken a conversion course in law (the Common Professional Examination or the Graduate Diploma in Law) or have qualified through Fellowship of the Institute of Legal Executives route (FILEX).

The academic stage

In 2002 there were almost 12,000 undergraduates studying for a law degree and more than 9,000 students graduated with one. In the year ending 31st July 2003, 9,195 students enrolled with the Law Society. Of these students 62.4 per cent were women and 22.1 per cent were drawn from the ethnic minorities. The number of law students is increasing, as is the proportion of women and ethnic minorities studying law.

| Year of graduation | University graduates in law* | | |
	Male	Female	Total
1997	4,016	4,876	8,892
2002	3,487	5,717	9,204
% change 2002/1997	−13.2	+17.2	+3.5

* Figures relate to single honours law degrees and do not include modular or joint honours degrees which may also allow graduates to proceed directly to study the Legal Practice Course.

1995 and onwards, Higher Educational Statistical Agency: The Law Society, *Annual Statistic Report 2003*

■ *Figure 10.4 Number of students graduating in law from universities in England and Wales in 1997 and 2002*

The vocational stage

All potential solicitors must complete a professional course, the Legal Practice Course, which prepares them for the practical aspects of the work.

Students on the LPC study conveyancing, business and litigation plus legal ethics, skills, solicitors' accounts and professional conduct, as well as taking options in their chosen fields of specialism (for example family, welfare, legal aid, commercial, property, corporate law).

The training contract – the practical stage

Fellows of ILEX are exempt from the practical stage because they will have been working in a law firm for at least five years. However, all other students must serve a prescribed period of training (usually two years) attached to a practising solicitor. At this stage, the trainee solicitor is in effect serving an apprenticeship. The trainee will be salaried during the term of the training contract (there is a minimum salary of £15,900 in Inner London and £14,200 elsewhere at July 2004). Obtaining training contracts is not easy and competition is fierce, but the best students are rewarded financially:

'Solicitors may all hold the same qualification but there are huge differences in what they earn depending on whether they work for a "magic circle" firm, a regional corporate or a high street practice dealing with legal aid cases. These differences are apparent from the first day.

Herbert Smith, for example, is typical of the big City practices in offering £28,500 to trainees in their first year and £32,000 to those in their second. This is rather more than the average City rate of £25,000. But contrast this with the recommended minimum of about half that figure paid by many suburban and regional firms. According to figures provided by the Trainee Solicitors' Group, the present London average is £15,300, whereas in the rest of England and Wales it is £13,600.'

'The secret is to work hard and fit in', Student Law Supplement,
The Times, 18th May 2004

Q

'The composition of the profession is also changing. Between 1993 and 2003, male admissions rose by 38.5%, whilst female admissions grew much more rapidly, by 74.3%. Women have accounted for the majority of new admissions in each year since 1992–93 and, in 2002–03, 56.8% of those admitted were female. This proportion, which is showing some increase over time and is the highest recorded to date, contrasts with the position 10 years ago when, in 1993, 51.1% of new entrants to the profession were women. Of the new trainees registered, 62.7% were women and 17.9% of trainees with known ethnicity were drawn from the ethnic minorities. Male trainees are much more likely than female trainees to be placed in the very largest firms and this may explain why, on average, male trainees were offered starting salaries which were 7.6% above the average level for females.

The Law Society, *Annual Statistic Report 2003*

ACTIVITY

Discuss what factors may influence the average lower age of women partners and sole practitioners than that of men.

10.2.3 Work

Solicitors are largely occupied in providing legal services to clients on a face-to-face basis, or by telephone or letter. They have direct personal contact with clients and therefore need to employ personnel to assist in proving this service.

Increasingly, solicitors tend to specialise in their work in order to gain expertise in particular areas of the law. Within a firm in private practice, therefore, you may find different departments specialising in, for example, criminal matters, family law, probate (ie dealing with the property of those who have died), land law matters, and civil cases such as personal injuries. Research carried out by The Law Society in July 2004, based on responses from solicitors on their renewal forms for their practising certificate, shows that the categories of work undertaken by solicitors in England and Wales were:

Administrative and public law	1,882	Fraud	1,553
Advocacy	814	Immigration and nationality	2,248
Agricultural law	704	Insolvency and bankruptcy	1,553
Aviation	333	Insurance	3,067
Banking law	2,907	Intellectual property	4,559
Business affairs	18,711	International law (non-EC)	784
Chancery	520	Landlord and tenant – residential	11,000
Charity law	2,040	Libel and defamation	488
Children law	1,773	Liquor licensing/gambling	2,984
Civil liberties/human rights	1,173	Litigation – commercial	13,897
Commercial property	18,393	Litigation – general	19,176
Common law	815	Maritime/shipping/admiralty	800
Computer and IT law	2,598	Media/entertainment law	1,468

Figure 10.5 Categories of work: Practising Certificate Renewal Form Information (July 2004)

CONTINUED ▶

Construction/civil engineering	1,659	Mediation – civil/commercial	1,106
Consumer problems	3,493	Mediation – family	589
Conveyancing residential	17,755	Medical negligence	3,577
Corporate finance	4,839	Mental health	1,466
Crime – general, motor, juvenile	10,081	Mergers and acquisitions	4,716
Debt and money advice	4,198	Neighbour disputes	2,166
Education	641	Personal injury	13,713
Employment	10,509	Taxation	3,570
Energy and natural resources	731	Transport, road and rail	642
Environment law	2,009	Travel and tourism	232
European Community law	1,330	Trusts	5,120
Family	12,955	Welfare benefits	2,160
Financial and investment services	2,209	Wills and probate	13,467

Law Society REGIS database

ACTIVITY

In which areas do most of the solicitors renewing their practising certificates work? Do the statistics surprise you?

The Courts and Legal Services Act 1990

The most significant change in the work of solicitors occurred in the Courts and Legal Services Act 1990 (CLSA 1990). This Act was introduced with the specific aim of developing and improving the way in which legal services were offered to the public. Section 17(1) made it clear that the 1990 Act was an attempt to strike a balance between the desire to ensure that justice was administered properly and the wish to allow people other than members of the two professions to carry out some of the work which had hitherto been reserved for barristers and solicitors alone. This meant, for the first time, the professions were faced with competition for their clients. The hope of those drafting the legislation was that this element of competition would lead to better services being offered to the public, for more realistic fees.

Conveyancing

In the past, solicitors enjoyed a complete monopoly in matters of conveyancing (ie transferring ownership in land from one person to another) but, in 1985, the first significant change in the work of solicitors occurred. Despite the fact that many solicitors were financially dependent on the income produced by conveyancing, there had been criticisms of the low quality of the work and the relatively high charges for it. So the Administration of Justice Act 1985 (Part II) introduced a system of **licensed conveyancers** which allowed non-solicitors to carry out work for members of the public and s 37 of the CLSA 1990 ensured that non-solicitors involved in conveyancing work would be suitably qualified, accountable and insured against the risk of loss to the client. There had been considerable pressure from banks and estate agents to open up the market to enter into competition with solicitors. There is a growing culture in this country and elsewhere for what is often referred to as a 'one-stop shop'. This means one professional service provider who is able to provide all of the relevant services for a particular range or type of transaction(s). Consumers are believed to want access to one professional; for example, an estate agent to show them properties, advise them on finance and mortgages and convey the relevant land, without having to use, unless they wish, three different advisers. This concept is explained further under the discussion of multi-disciplinary partnerships below.

Rights of audience

So solicitors lost their monopoly on conveyancing, but at the same time practice rules of the courts ensured that only barristers had the right of advocacy in the High Court, Court of Appeal and House of Lords. Barristers also had a virtual monopoly in the Crown Court. In 1979, the (Benson) Royal Commission on Legal Services examined the exclusivity of the work of solicitors and barristers and, although it recommended that no change should be made in the rights of audience in the courts, solicitors challenged the position whereby they enjoyed advocacy in the Magistrates' and County Courts and not the higher courts. Solicitors who, for example, had carefully prepared a case for Crown Court trial were frustrated that they had to hand over the case to a barrister (who would be less acquainted with it) for presentation at court. Over time, barristers' monopoly on higher courts advocacy has also been lost.

Section 27 of the CLSA 1990 established a new system for the professional bodies to grant rights of audience before the courts subject to the requirements of those bodies (specifically The Law Society, the Bar Council and the Institute of Legal Executives). Thus, since 1993, The Law Society has been able to grant a Certificate of Advocacy to those solicitors who have met the necessary training requirements. Solicitors with Higher Rights Certificates are called solicitor-advocates.

There are three categories of Higher Rights qualification:

- **Higher Courts All Proceedings** – the solicitor can exercise rights of audience in all proceedings before all the higher courts in England and Wales

- **Higher Courts Civil Proceedings** – the solicitor can exercise rights of audience in all civil proceedings in the higher courts of England and Wales, including judicial review proceedings in any court arising from any criminal cause

- **Higher Courts Criminal Proceedings** – the solicitor can exercise rights of audience in all criminal proceedings in the higher courts and judicial review proceedings in any court arising from any criminal cause in England and Wales.

From 2005, there will be three routes to becoming a solicitor-advocate under the Access to Justice Act 1999:

- **Development Route** (for trainee or newly admitted solicitors, involving additional training and assessment under the supervision of a mentor)

- **Exemption Route** (for more experienced solicitors, where credit is given for advocacy experience gained in the lower courts) or

- **Former Barrister Route** (for any barrister who transferred to the solicitors' profession prior to 31st July 2000. Barristers transferring to the Roll of Solicitors after 31st July 2000 automatically carry over their rights of audience).

However, it was only independent solicitors who could apply for the Higher Rights Certificates: it was not until 1997 that employed solicitors (in particular the solicitors employed by the Crown Prosecution Service) gained any new rights and, even then, they were very limited. About 2,000 solicitors have higher rights, but those who have rarely get the opportunity to exercise them because most cases that progress to the higher courts still use barristers. Whether this is because of the expertise of the latter, or the tradition of instructing counsel and the 'newness' of the solicitor-advocates' system is unclear. Lawyers have the reputation for being rather reactionary – reluctant to change. In 1995 when a Circuit Judge was trying to find a barrister to take on the case of an unrepresented defendant at Sheffield Crown Court, he was told that there was a solicitor-advocate available. He remarked 'We don't need to stoop that low, do we?' Although he later unreservedly withdrew the remark and apologised for any offence caused, this example shows that there is a fear that solicitor-advocates could be subject to bias and prejudice from judges if they were to use their rights of audience in the higher courts. Perhaps this factor contributes to the few numbers of solicitor-advocates and the reluctance of those with the certificate to put their qualifications into practice.

All senior advocates, and this includes solicitor-advocates and barristers, can be appointed as Queen's Counsel (QC). Appointments are made by the Queen on the advice and recommendation of the Lord Chancellor, but despite the implication in the title, QCs do not advise the Queen; rather it is the 'gold star' of advocacy (and a mark of quality) and a very big step on the ladder to high judicial office. The role and current controversy surrounding QCs is examined in more depth in section 10.3.3.

ACTIVITY

Self-assessment questions

1. What is the name of the governing body of solicitors?

2. How many solicitors are there in England and Wales?

3. What percentage are women?

4. What is a practising certificate?

5. How long does a training contract last?

6. Name the seven foundation subjects.

7. Summarise the effect of the CLSA 1990 and the AJA 1999 on (i) conveyancing and (ii) rights of audience.

10.2.4 Complaints

The essence of the operation of both branches of the legal profession is self-regulation. The professions are subject to a degree of statutory control, but on the whole it is the professionals who run the professions, with very little independent oversight of them.

> 'It ha[s] been sometimes seen as worrying that The [Law] Society combined two roles with a possible conflict of interests: maintenance of the professional standards for the protection of the public, and as the main professional association to promote the interests of solicitors. Consider a rather basic example. Acting for its members, The Law Society should perhaps try to ensure that insurance policies against claims for negligence are always available for solicitors even if they have been sued for this several times. For such insurance to be granted to someone with such a questionable professional record is, however, clearly not in the best interests of the public who use solicitors.'

Slapper and Kelly, *The English Legal System* (7th edn, Cavendish, 2004), p 544

Whether or not self-regulation is indeed the best way to operate is at the heart of the Clementi review on Legal Services (see section 10.4) but, at this stage, we will examine the nature of self-regulation as it currently operates where a client has a complaint about his or her solicitor.

In-house schemes

The first port of call for the client is the firm itself. Each solicitors' firm must be able to deal with the complaint in-house first and The Law Society regulates the form and nature of the in-house system by the Solicitors' Practice Rules 1990 (currently in their eighth edition). For example, rule 15 of the Client Care Code provides:

> 'Complaints handling
>
> (b) Every principal in private practice . . . must:
>
> > (i)   ensure the client is told the name of the person in the firm to contact about any problem with the service provided;
> >
> > (ii) have a written complaints procedure and ensure that complaints are handled in accordance with it; and
> >
> > (iii) ensure that the client is given a copy of the complaints procedure on request.'

The Law Society

If the complaint is not resolved using the in-house procedure, the next step is for the client to take the matter to The Law Society itself. Its Consumer Complaints Service deals with complaints about the service offered by a solicitor and the Compliance Directorate deals with conduct issues. (These two bodies jointly used to be the Office for the Supervision of Solicitors until 19th April 2004.)

The Independent Commissioner to The Law Society, Sir Stephen Lander, oversees the complaints system. He advises The Law Society on handling of complaints and makes recommendations where necessary. The Commissioner is appointed by the Master of the Rolls (a very senior judge).

However, this self-regulatory framework does not satisfy the Government and under the powers of the Access to Justice Act 1999, in February 2004, the Secretary of State and Lord Chancellor formally announced that he was activating the role of the Legal Services Complaints Commissioner in respect of The Law Society. He has appointed the current Legal Services Ombudsman (see below) to this role. The primary objective of the LSCC will be to provide additional independent oversight of The Law Society's complaints-handling operations and to intervene effectively to improve standards of complaints handling by The Law Society.

Solicitors Disciplinary Tribunal

The Solicitors Disciplinary Tribunal (SDT) is a statutory tribunal whose function is to adjudicate upon allegations of professional misconduct or breaches of professional rules by solicitors. The SDT's powers arise from the Solicitors Act 1974 (as amended). The rules governing the SDT's procedures are contained in the Solicitors (Disciplinary Proceedings) Rules 1994. The SDT is independent of The Law Society although its administration is funded by The Society. Members of the public or The Law Society itself can bring alleged misconduct to the attention of the SDT. The Tribunal has the power to:

- strike a solicitor off the Roll
- suspend a solicitor for a fixed or indefinite period
- reprimand a solicitor
- fine a solicitor (fines are payable to HM Treasury)
- ban a solicitor's employee from working in a law practice without the consent of The Law Society (under s 43 Solicitors Act 1974).

Year end 30 April	Number of strike-offs	Suspensions	Fines	Reprimands	No order, costs only order or case dismissed
1998	58	32	76	13	3
1999	81	37	105	11	4
2000	73	38	72	14	7
2001	62	29	78	29	5
2002	77	39	75	4	8
2003	78	39	83	14	6

Annual Report available at: www.solicitorstribunal.org.uk

Figure 10.6 An overview of orders made by the SDT since 1998

Office of the Legal Services Ombudsman

If the client still does not feel that the issue is resolved, the final port of call is the Office of the Legal Services Ombudsman (LSO). The term 'Ombudsman' is Swedish in origin and means 'independent judge'. In English usage, the term denotes an official appointed by government to investigate complaints against public authorities.

The current incumbent is Zahida Manzoor CBE. She is not a qualified lawyer and is independent from The Law Society and the other regulatory bodies within her remit. The LSO is appointed by the Lord Chancellor.

The Legal Service Ombudsman's functions are:

- to ensure that individual complaints are handled properly by the appropriate legal professional bodies (it oversees complaints made to The Law Society, the Bar Council, the Institute of Legal

Executives, the Council for Licensed Conveyancers and the Chartered Institute of Patent Agents)

- to act as a public watchdog on the standards of complaints handling across legal services providers and
- to raise standards within legal services complaints systems.

The LSO has the power to:

- recommend that the professional body concerned re-considers a complaint and
- recommend the payment of compensation to complainants for distress or inconvenience.

In early 2003, the Ombudsman was concerned at the number of live cases waiting to be dealt with by The Law Society and she decided to monitor the complaints handling and produce an Interim Report in late 2003. However, her Annual Report 2003–04 continued to be rather critical of the Law Society:

> **Q** 'The Law Society's complaints-handling performance appears to be improving in terms of quantity; it reduced its live caseload by 1,090 cases (8.5%). However, the Ombudsman was only satisfied with the quality of handling in 53.3% of cases, a substantial reduction from 67.2% the previous year, and well below the DCA target of 75%. The Law Society continues to fail all but one of its targets for turnaround times, which have actually deteriorated during 2003/2004. The number of cases older than 12 months has increased by 30.8%, suggesting a focus on closing newer cases at the expense of older ones.'

However, there was a substantial reduction in the number of cases referred to the LSO – from 14.7 per cent to 9.2 per cent.

The LSO does not have the power to review the case files of The Law Society randomly, but the Access to Justice Act 1999 grants such a power to the Legal Services Complaints Commissioner and this is one reason why the LSO was also appointed as LSCC in early 2004.

In comparison with the operation of the LSO, The Law Society has some way to go:

> **Q** 'Regarding casework, [the LSO] completed more cases than it received for the third consecutive year, accepting 1,485 cases and closing 1,731 cases, thereby reducing the live caseload from 451 to 205. The number of new cases received declined by just under 15% during the year, despite the complaints received by the professional bodies rising by 7%. The decrease in numbers has produced substantial improvements in average case turnaround times, which over the year have fallen from 5.6 to 2.5 months. Almost 87% of cases were completed within 3 months and over 95% within 6 months.'

Professional indemnity insurance

All solicitors in private practice must be insured against loss caused to their clients through negligence. This insurance is compulsory and, without it, The Law Society will not issue a practising certificate. Under the Society's *Minimum Terms and Conditions of Professional Indemnity Insurance for Solicitors* (2004):

> **Q** '**2.1 Any one Claim**
>
> The Sum Insured for any one Claim (exclusive of Defence Costs) must be at least £1 million.
>
> **2.2 No limit on Defence Costs**
>
> There must be no monetary limit on the cover for Defence Costs.
>
> This means that if an allegation of negligence is admitted by a firm, or is found against the firm through any of the complaints procedures above, the firm is insured against the loss. This guarantees that the injured party will be able to obtain compensation even if the size of the claim would ordinarily be beyond the financial reach of the firm and would cause bankruptcy.'

Actions against solicitors for negligence

See Actions against barristers for negligence at section 10.3.4.

ACTIVITY

You are working for your university's free legal advice clinic. A member of the public asks you for information about how to make a complaint about his solicitor. It appears that the client feels he was overcharged by his solicitor and the solicitor will not return his calls or respond to his letters. What advice can you give the client about how to proceed?

10.3 Barristers

You have already examined much of the work of barristers indirectly as a result of the discussion about solicitors above. What we have not considered, however, is why there is a divided profession in England and Wales. This division has its roots in history and although critics point out that the system can result in duplication of effort, increased costs and sometimes confusion for the public, suggestions that there should be fusion (ie one single profession of 'lawyer') have never been accepted by either branch of the profession. Perhaps in view of the changes in the work done by each branch, fusion is no longer the issue it once was. The abolition of the traditional monopolies has blurred the line of demarcation between solicitors and barristers.

10.3.1 Organisation

From as early as the fourteenth century, the Bar has been organised around the four Inns of Court. These are the Inner and Middle Temple, Lincoln's Inn and Gray's Inn. Since the seventeenth century, it has been necessary to belong to one of the Inns in order to practise advocacy. The Inns are responsible for the 'call to the Bar', part of the procedure by which students become qualified barristers. The General Council of the Bar of England and Wales, commonly referred to as the Bar Council, is the regulatory and representative body of the profession and is responsible for its Code of Conduct, complaints and disciplinary matters, standards, ethics and education and training. Its regulatory framework is provided for in the Courts and Legal Services Act 1990. The Council in fact operates on the basis of a series of committees, each with clear responsibility for different areas of professional work.

In December 2003 there were 13,985 practising barristers, 11,248 of whom were self-employed. The profession currently comprises 68 per cent men and 32 per cent women and, of those, 10.67 per cent expressed they were a member of an ethnic minority. The low representation of women will change over time because, during 2003, of the 1,502 barristers who entered the profession (this is called being 'called to the Bar') 51 per cent were women.

Fears that the Higher Rights Certificates available to solicitors would dramatically reduce the number of barristers have not materialised; entry to the Bar has **increased** since Higher Rights Certificates were introduced.

Barristers do not form partnerships as solicitors do. Instead, most are self-employed, taking tenancies in 'chambers', most of which (nearly 60 per cent) are in London. Because the professional rules of the Bar prohibit barristers from forming partnerships, from an economic point of view, it makes sense for them to share expensive resources, such as premises, secretarial support, library facilities and, most importantly, a clerk who acts a business manager. When a solicitor sends instructions (known as a 'brief to counsel') to chambers for the attention of a barrister, unless a particular barrister has been named on the brief, the clerk will allocate it to a member of the chambers and will also arrange the fee. The clerk is therefore able to control the amount of work each barrister receives.

10.3.2 Training

Most barristers are graduates but, as you know, it is not necessary to have a degree in law to be called to the Bar. Conversion courses are available for graduates of other disciplines (the CPE or GDL mentioned above). A Bar student must become a member of one of the Inns of Court, eat a certain number of dinners there (known as 'keeping terms') as admission to an Inn is required before registration on the Bar Vocational Course (BVC). Many undergraduates in fact join an Inn before this stage in order to participate in the activities, use the library, or start dining. A student's choice of Inn does not affect the area of law in which they wish to practise or their choice of pupilage or tenancy – it is a matter of personal choice. The professional course equivalent to the Legal Practice Course is the BVC on which students study:

- Case Preparation
- Legal Research
- Written Skills
- Opinion-writing (that is giving written advice)
- Drafting (of various types of documents)
- Conference Skills (interviewing clients)
- Negotiation
- Advocacy (court or tribunal appearances).

The subject-specific knowledge taught on the BVC is:

- Civil Litigation and Remedies
- Criminal Litigation and Sentencing
- Evidence
- Professional Ethics
- Optional subjects, for example commercial law.

Pupillage

Once the examination stage has been successfully completed, the student is called to the Bar and can then undertake the next stage in the process, known as 'pupillage'.

This is the practical stage of training and, without it, a barrister is not able to practise. The newly called barrister has to find an established barrister who will take him as an 'apprentice' for one year. Pupillage is divided into two parts: the non-practising six months during which pupils shadow their pupil master and the second practising six months when pupils, with their pupil master's permission, can undertake to supply legal services and exercise rights of audience. Once pupillage is completed, the barrister can look for a place in chambers from which to work (a tenancy). Competition for such places is extremely fierce.

Because of the need for students to become acquainted with the customs and etiquette of the Bar, the requirement that they keep terms by dining at their chosen Inn for a specified number of times helps them to discover how the Inns work and the type of conduct which is expected. However, this does involve a certain amount of expense in addition to the fees required for attending Bar School. Although a limited number of scholarships and bursaries are available, students generally have to support themselves, usually by means of loans, during their training period. However, in March 2002, the Bar Council approved changes relating to pupillage funding, stating that pupils must be paid not less than £833.33 per month plus reasonable travel expenses where applicable (a figure unchanged at March 2005).

10.3.3 Work

If asked to describe the work a barrister does, most people would think of a man or woman in gown and wig, using their skills of advocacy in the courtroom. However, about 3,000 barristers are employed rather than self-employed; working in commerce, industry, government or for a solicitors' firm and, even for self-employed barristers, advocacy is not their only work, for they also spend a lot of time researching points of law and giving advice to solicitors (known as 'counsel's opinion'). Barristers are not paid directly by the client but by the solicitor who selected and instructed them. All barristers, like solicitors, must have practising certificates. They cost from £53 (junior in years 0–4 of calling) to £678 for Queen's Counsel.

Access to barristers

Another striking feature about the way in which barristers work is that, traditionally, self-employed barristers were only permitted to take instruction from 'professional clients', a term which is carefully defined by the Bar Council's Code of Conduct. In practice this meant that they received instructions through the medium of a solicitor (or perhaps, for example, an accountant) and were not approached directly by the individual who needed their services. However, in June 1998 the Lord Chancellor published a consultation paper which suggested that the public should be allowed direct access to barristers in order to instruct them, without using a solicitor as an intermediary.

confidence and a feeling that barristers were too remote and insufficiently prepared. It was also submitted that it was more expensive. A client was paying for two lawyers rather than one. The logic behind these arguments is not in doubt, but nevertheless The Law Society and the Bar Council strongly oppose a fused profession and thus no changes were made.

Subsequently, in the response to the Consultation Paper *Review Of The Regulatory Framework For Legal Services in England and Wales* in May 2004, the Bar Council insisted:

> **Q**
> 'The existence and structure of the Bar has the following very substantial public advantages:
>
> Barristers develop expertise in advocacy and in specialist areas of the law which enables them to provide expert advice and services to solicitors (and other professional clients). This is of vital importance to the 80% of solicitors' firms with five partners or fewer, which are spread throughout the country and provide the point of access to legal services for the majority of the general public. Such firms cannot have their own expertise in every branch of the law, nor in advocacy . . .'

The response continues that a divided profession is best for the consumer because it generates a free market and competition keeps costs down.

> **Q**
> 'It also promotes competition among solicitors because it gives smaller solicitors' firms access to the full range of expertise and enables them better to compete with the larger firms. It also promotes access to justice because it enables the smaller solicitors' firms based in local communities to provide a much higher quality and range of services to their clients than would otherwise be possible, and thereby goes some way to redressing the advantages enjoyed by the wealthy and experienced in obtaining legal advice and effective representation.'

The cab-rank rule also provides an advantage in a separated profession because it requires barristers to fulfil their:

> **Q** 'public obligation to act for any client in cases within their field of practice on being offered a proper fee, and to do so irrespective of any belief or opinion which the barrister may hold about the client or the nature of the case'.

Changes to the work and organisation of the two professions since the mid-1980s have blurred the lines of demarcation to such an extent that a law student with any oral advocacy skill has a more difficult career choice than one without – each side of the profession offers advocacy and increased client contact. Formal fusion is unlikely – the energy of the debate has diminished and the fight has left many of the antagonists as a result of the changes made, especially by the CLSA 1990. However, discussion continues in the background, especially in light of the OFT report in 2001; but it did not recommend abolition of the dual professions either, rather it called for an examination of the organisation and regulation of the governing bodies.

The Clementi Report

Concerns expressed by the OFT and the Office of the Legal Services Ombudsman since 2001 have motivated calls for a review of the self-regulatory nature of both of the legal professions. In July 2003, the Lord Chancellor and the Secretary of State for Constitutional Affairs, Lord Falconer, invited Sir David Clementi, chairman of a financial services plc and former Deputy Governor of the Bank of England, to review the operation and regulation of the legal services sector. A consultation paper was published in March 2004, proposing two models for the regulation of the professions, including complaints handling. On the one hand, all regulatory functions of the professional bodies could be placed entirely in the hands of an independent regulator; on the other, an approximate *status quo* could be maintained but with a new regulator, similar to the current LSO, but with increased powers.

The Legal Services Ombudsman expressed a preference for the latter:

> **Q** '[The Ombudsman's] view is that a new regulatory regime should allow the professional bodies to retain aspects of regulation necessary to guarantee professional autonomy, while ensuring public accountability through an overarching independent regulator. This regulator and an independent complaints-handling office is the minimum publicly acceptable outcome of the present review. Accordingly, the Ombudsman has proposed a "Legal Services Authority" (LSA) together with an independent complaints-handling organisation, the "Legal Services Complaints Office" (LSCO).'
>
> *LSO Annual Report 2003–04*

327

The Supreme Court would probably operate *stare decisis* as the House currently does. The current Law Lords would be the first Justices of the Supreme Court and thereafter a Supreme Court Appointments Commission would be established, comprising representatives from the JAC and the President of the Supreme Court.

The Law Lords would no longer be able to sit as members of the House of Lords. This would ensure independence from the other two branches of State. However, unlike some other countries which have a Supreme Court, the UK court will not be a constitutional court with the power to strike down legislation. That, it seems, would be pushing judicial independence too far and sacrificing parliamentary sovereignty.

The controversy surrounding the proposal (and the reasons for the House of Lords' rejection of it) appear to be the lack of consultation regarding the abolition of the post of Lord Chancellor and the fact that there is no new building suitable to house the Supreme Court (searches for suitable premises seem to have been limited to London). As reported in *The Times* of 9th June 2004, 'Supreme Court to be housed in refitted building', the Secretary of State is considering taking over the West Wing of Somerset House from the Inland Revenue. The cost of re-fitting the House? £32 million.

'Under the Bill, supreme court judges are to be appointed on the advice of a quango of 15, of whom six (including the chairman) must be lay people. This is a great insult to the judiciary and affects their independence. What do lay people know about the qualities needed in a judge? The Judges' Council, or some similar body entirely composed of senior judges, should advise the Crown on the making of appointments to their number. That would indeed protect judicial independence. To suggest that the senior judges cannot be trusted to do this is to imply that they are incompetent, which, if true, would be worrying . . .'

Francis Bennion, 'The great myth of judicial independence', *The Times*, 13th July 2004

ACTIVITY

Self-assessment questions

1. Explain some of the reasons behind the abolition of the post of Lord Chancellor.

2. Why does the system of judicial appointments have to be changed when the Lord Chancellor's position is abolished?

3. What are the reasons behind the establishment of a UK Supreme Court?

11.2 The judicial hierarchy

We now turn to examine the current system of judicial appointments. Just as the court system is based on a hierarchy, so too is the Judiciary. Judges are grouped into inferior and superior judges. Inferior judges preside, on the whole, in the inferior courts (the magistrates' court, the County Court and the Crown Court). Superior judges preside, on the whole, in the superior courts (the High Court, the Court of Appeal and the House of Lords).

Judicial title	Full-time or part-time?	Main court in which the judge presides	Appointed by the . . .	On advice (A) or recommendation (R) of . . .	Salary 2004	Summary of qualifications (CLSA 1990*)
Inferior judges						
District Judge (Magistrates' Court)	FT	Magistrates' Court	Queen	R – Lord Chancellor	£90,760–£108,850	7 year general qualification
District Judge	FT and PT	County Court	Lord Chancellor	n/a	£90,760–£94,760	7 year general qualification
Recorder	PT	Crown Court and County Court	Queen	R – Lord Chancellor	Pro-rata Circuit Judge	10 year general qualification
Circuit Judge	FT	Crown Court and County Court	Queen	R – Lord Chancellor	£113,121–£122,139	10 year general qualification or 3 years as a District Judge

Figure 11.3 Inferior judges

Judicial Title	Full-time or part-time?	Main court in which the judge presides	Appointed by the . . .	On advice (A) or recommendation (R) of . . .	Salary 2004	Summary of qualifications (CLSA 1990*)
Superior judges						
High Court Judge	FT	High Court and Crown Court (and Court of Appeal if invited)	Queen	R – Lord Chancellor	£150,878	10 year High Court qualification
Lord or Lady Justice of Appeal	FT	Court of Appeal	Queen	R – Prime Minister A – Lord Chancellor	£170,554	In practice only High Court Judges are appointed
Head of Division	FT	Court of Appeal	Queen	R – Prime Minister A – Lord Chancellor	£179,431–£205,242 (Lord Chief Justice)	Appointed from the Lords Justices of Appeal or Lords of Appeal in Ordinary
Lord or Lady of Appeal in Ordinary	FT	House of Lords (and Privy Council)	Queen	R – Prime Minister A – Lord Chancellor	£179,431–£185,705	2 years in high judicial offices: in effect, to be a judge of one of the superior courts in England and Wales, Scotland or Northern Ireland

* Courts and Legal Services Act 1990

■ *Figure 11.4 Superior judges*

11.3 Training

In addition to certain mentoring and appraisal schemes that operate in the inferior courts, and are mentioned in the relevant discussion at section 11.4 below, judicial training is provided by the Judicial Studies Board (JSB). The JSB also has an advisory role in the training of lay magistrates and of chairmen and members of tribunals.

The Judicial Studies Board (JSB) was established in 1979. It is chaired and directed by senior judges but includes lay magistrates, lawyers, administrators and academics. An essential element of the philosophy of the JSB is that the training of judges and magistrates is under judicial control and directions.

The JSB organises 'refresher' seminars to which both full-time and part-time judges are invited, covering changes in the law and topics of current importance or special interest and it issues books and other guidance for use by judges.

11.4 The inferior judges

Eligibility for all judicial posts is subject to the requirements of the Courts and Legal Services Act 1990 but appointments are all made on merit. The *Judicial Appointments in England and Wales; Policies and Procedures* document, which is available at www.dca.gov.uk, provides that:

Q	'The Lord Chancellor appoints those who appear to him to be the best qualified regardless of gender, ethnic origin, marital status, sexual orientation, political affiliation, religion or disability. Decisions on merit are based on assessments of candidates against the specific criteria for appointment. Extraneous matters such as a candidates' chambers or firm are immaterial.'

In summary, the current criteria for appointment are:

- legal knowledge and experience
- sound judgment
- communication and listening skills
- integrity and independence
- understanding of people and society
- courtesy
- intellectual and analytical ability
- decisiveness
- authority and case management skills
- fairness and impartiality
- maturity and sound temperament
- commitment, conscientiousness and diligence.

The Lord Chancellor's 'fundamental principles' for judicial appointment are:

1. appointment is strictly on merit

2. part-time judicial service is normally a prerequisite of appointment to full office

3. significant weight is attached to the independent views of members of the professional community (and others) as to the suitability for appointment. This is a controversial criterion to which we will return below.

11.4.1 District Judge (Magistrates' Court)

The first inferior judges for our consideration are District Judges (Magistrates' Court). These judges are appointed by the Queen on the recommendation of the Lord Chancellor. The statutory qualification is a seven year general qualification. This means that the applicant must have been qualified as a solicitor or barrister for at least seven years. The Lord Chancellor will normally only consider applicants who have served as Deputy (part-time) District Judges (Magistrates' Courts) for a minimum of two years.

11.4.2 District Judge (Civil Court)

There is a larger number of District Judges who do **not** work in the magistrates' court than who do. District Judges, formally known as Registrars, have civil jurisdiction and work in the County Court. They are appointed by the Lord Chancellor. The statutory qualification is a seven year general qualification. The Lord Chancellor will normally consider only applicants who have been serving as Deputy (part-time) District Judges for two years. An appraisal and mentoring scheme has operated for all Deputy District judges since 2002. The scheme provides a structured system to monitor the performance of the Deputy District Judges by District Judges and to assist in the consideration of the suitability of Deputy District Judges for appointment as full-time District Judges.

11.4.3 Recorder

Recorders are part-time judges who have mainly criminal jurisdiction in the Crown Courts, but under s 5(3) of the County Courts Act 1984, may also sit in the County Courts. Recorders are appointed by the Queen on the recommendation of the Lord Chancellor. Appointments are for five years and will normally be automatically extended by the Lord Chancellor for further successive terms of five years, subject to the retirement age of 65. The statutory qualification for appointment as a Recorder is a 10 year Crown Court or 10 year County Court qualification.

Recorders benefit from an induction training run by the JSB. Very intensive residential courses, lasting four to five days, have to be completed before a Recorder can sit in their own Crown Court. Emphasis is placed on practical exercises such as sentencing, directions to the jury and summing up. The newly appointed judges must also sit in for at least a week with an experienced judge and they must also visit local prisons and the Probation Service.

11.4.4 Circuit Judge

Recordership is a step on the ladder to appointment as a Circuit Judge. Circuit Judges are appointed by the Queen on the recommendation of the Lord Chancellor. The statutory qualification is a 10 year Crown Court or 10 year County Court qualification, or to be a Recorder, or to be the holder of one of a number of other judicial offices of at least three years' standing in a full-time capacity. Circuit Judges are permanently assigned to a particular area, or circuit, on appointment. There are six circuits: Midland and Oxford; North Eastern; Northern; South Eastern; Western; and Wales and Chester. Each circuit also has two presiding judges who are High Court Judges.

11.5 The superior judges

11.5.1 High Court Judge

The first superior judge to be considered is a High Court Judge, but this title does not denote the only court in which they preside. Obviously a High Court Judge does work in the High Court and they are assigned to one of the three divisions of the High Court on appointment, but they also have important jurisdiction in the Crown Court and may sit in the Court of Appeal if requested. High Court Judges are appointed by the Queen on the recommendation of the Lord Chancellor. Before making recommendations the Lord Chancellor customarily consults senior members of the Judiciary about the possible appointees. It is this process that is currently so topical. It is referred to as the 'secret soundings system'. To be fair, the Lord Chancellor has repeatedly pointed out that it is neither secret, as it is common knowledge that it takes place, nor a 'sounding', which has negative connotations, as it is more a consultation process. We will examine this process in more detail at section 11.6 below.

The statutory qualification for appointment to the High Court is a 10 year High Court qualification (to have enjoyed rights of audience in the High Court for at least 10 years) or to have been a Circuit Judge for at least two years. Applications for appointment to the High Court are invited on a regular basis by advertisement in the press from suitably qualified practitioners and Circuit Judges, but the Lord Chancellor reserves the right to appoint those who have not made an application. In practice, appointments are made from the ranks of Queen's Counsel, particularly from QCs who have sat as a Deputy High Court Judge and/or Recorder. Queen's Counsel was once the exclusive domain of the Bar, but is no longer (see Chapter 10) because of the progression now available from a solicitor to a solicitor-advocate and then a High Court Judge. Sadly, since this avenue of promotion was opened by the CLSA 1990, only two solicitors have been appointed to the High Court. There are no job interviews to become a High Court Judge. Selection is made based on the consultation process alone.

Above the High Court, all judicial appointments are by invitation only.

11.5.2 Lord Justice of Appeal

There are 37 Lords Justices of Appeal who are appointed by the Queen, acting on the advice of the Prime Minister, who is in turn advised by the Lord Chancellor. Before giving advice the Lord Chancellor customarily consults senior members of the Judiciary. Lords Justices of Appeal, broadly speaking, preside in the Court of Appeal. There is a statutory qualification which can be found in s 10 of the Supreme Court Act 1981, as amended by s 71 of the Courts and Legal Services Act 1990, but appointment is usually on promotion from the ranks of experienced High Court Judges. Section 63 of the Courts Act 2003 repeals s 2(3) of the Supreme Court Act 1981 requiring a judge of the Court of Appeal to be a Lord Justice of Appeal whatever his or her gender. The first woman to be appointed to the Court of Appeal, Elizabeth Butler-Sloss, was called 'Lord' before the law was changed. It had not originally been envisaged that a woman would rise to such high judicial office. Men are knighted on appointment; woman are made Dames.

11.5.3 Head of Division

In addition, with the same statutory qualification requirements as the Lords Justices of Appeal, and also appointed by the Queen on the recommendation of the Prime Minister, who is advised by the Lord Chancellor, there are four Heads of Division. The four are the Lord Chief Justice (currently Lord Woolf CJ), the Master of the Rolls (currently Lord Phillips MR), the President of the Family Division (currently Dame Elizabeth Butler-Sloss P) and the Vice-Chancellor (Sir Andrew Morritt CVO). The Heads of Divisions are appointed from among the Lords of Appeal in Ordinary (below) or Lords Justices of Appeal.

11.5.4 Lord of Appeal in Ordinary

At the top of the judicial hierarchy are the 12 Lords of Appeal in Ordinary, commonly referred to as the Law Lords (in fact there are 11 Law Lords and one Law Lady). They preside over the House of Lords and they also have an important role in the Judicial Committee of the Privy Council. The senior Law Lord is Lord Bingham. The statutory qualification for appointment as a Law Lord is to have been the holder for not less than two years of one or more of the high judicial offices described in the Appellate Jurisdiction Act 1876, as amended. In practice, Lords of Appeal in Ordinary are generally appointed from among the experienced judges of the Court of Appeal in England and Wales, the Court of Session in Scotland and the Court of Appeal in Northern Ireland. There are currently two Law Lords from Scotland (Lords Hope and Rodger) and one from Northern Ireland (Lord Carswell). On appointment, Law Lords are made life peers.

The first woman to be appointed to the House of Lords was Baroness Hale of Richmond, appointed a few weeks before her 59th birthday, in January 2004.

Appointments to the House of Lords are made by the Queen, acting on the advice of the Prime Minister, but the effective voice is, again, that of the Lord Chancellor.

ACTIVITY

Self-assessment questions

1. Name two inferior judges.

2. Name two superior judges.

3. Who appoints:
   - Lords of Appeal in Ordinary?
   - High Court Judges?
   - Recorders?

4. What are the titles for the four Heads of Division? Name the current appointees.

5. How many Law Lords are there?

11.6 Judicial appointments

All judicial appointments are overseen by the Legal and Judicial Services Group which is a division of the Department for Constitutional Affairs

All appointments of inferior judicial post are made on the basis of open competition. Vacancies are advertised in the national press and/or legal journals. Candidates must provide the names of three referees (members of the legal profession or Judiciary) and each referee will be invited to comment on the suitability of the applicant for the post, but other judges and lawyers can also be asked to comment. None of the comments are available to the applicant.

For all senior posts, the senior Judiciary is consulted and the Lord Chancellor personally considers the applications before making his decision.

A senior judge explains this process of 'secret sounding' best (and very critically):

> 'There were sheaves of cuttings from the trials I had done. There were press cuttings from the *Evening Standard* about an actress I had been to a first night with. There was even an advertisement in *The Times* offering the charter of a yacht I had in the Mediterranean. But what really finished me off were getting on for a hundred scrappy notes addressed to the Lord Chancellor, many of them from one particular judge I had crossed swords with. Some of them were downright bloody lies. The most damning one was from this judge saying : "Sleeps with his divorce clients". It was totally untrue.'

The Guardian, 28th June 1986

The consultation process is designed to discover factors that may influence the Lord Chancellor's advice to the Queen on judicial appointment, but it is seen by the Law Society as being objectionable because it is not open and neither can the applicant have a chance to counter any allegations made because he will not know what has been said. Of course, added weight is given to the accusation that the unseen faces of the Bar Council are given more credit than the comments made by the executive of The Law Society as the majority of applicants are barristers (remember also that the same system is used for appointing QCs). The Law Society alleges discrimination against barristers too. This is because more than 50 per cent of the judicial appointments come from seven sets of chambers.

Because of the weight given to the consultation process, especially in the appointment of the senior Judiciary where no interview is held, Karon Monaghan, a barrister with Matrix Chambers, complains that:

> 'Thus appointment to the senior judiciary depends upon:
>
> 1. In the case of the appointment to the appellate courts, experience in the higher courts below – thus appointment to the Court of Appeal depends upon experience in the High Court and appointment to the House of Lords depends upon experience in the Court of Appeal;
>
> 2. Being 'known' by members of the professional community (senior lawyers and judges) who are consulted over such appointments . . .
>
> [but] there is strong evidence that the requirement to be *known* by the consultees (who are largely senior judges) disadvantages Black and ethnic minority lawyers and women who tend to be outside the traditional networks . . . There is real concern that our homogenous judiciary lacks democratic legitimacy and undermines public confidence in the judicial process. Further, and in particular in relation to appointments from the Court of Appeal to the Lords, the practice of recruiting exclusively from the Court of Appeal has only developed over recent decades, this without public explanation.'

> 'Discrimination in the appointment of the senior judiciary and Silk', available at:
> www.womenbarristers.co.uk/doc/k_monaghan.doc

In October 1999, the Association of Personal Injury Lawyers (APIL), the Commission for Racial Equality and the Equal Opportunities Commission all openly expressed support of The Law Society's campaign against the 'secret soundings'. Both APIL and The Law Society informed the Lord Chancellor that they will not be taking part in 'secret soundings' in the future. The EOC and

CRE have also pointed out that the dramatic increase in the number of women and ethnic minority lawyers has not been reflected in the Judiciary.

The controversy surrounding judicial appointments has existed for a number of years. In December 1999, Sir Leonard Peach published his report *Independent Scrutiny of the Appointment Processes of Judges and Queen's Counsel* and as a result the Commission for Judicial Appointments (CJA) was established in March 2001. The CJA's role is to carry out a continuing audit of the judicial and Queen's Counsel appointment procedures and to investigate complaints of discrimination, unfairness or maladministration in the way the procedures have been applied. The Commission also considers comments about the judicial appointments and Queen's Counsel appointment processes from individuals, representative bodies and other organisations and is able to relay them, and/or make recommendations on them, to the Lord Chancellor. The Commission does not deal with complaints about the appointment system in general nor does it respond to complaints from the public about individual appointments. It has no role in making or recommending judicial appointments.

Sir Colin Campbell, the first Commissioner for Judicial Appointments, was appointed in March 2001 and seven further commissioners (none of whom has ever worked as a practising solicitor or barrister) were appointed in December 2001.

In its second Annual Report, the CJA raised the following issues:

- poor record-keeping in relation to the decisions of some appointment panels
- concerns about the reliance on automatic consultation in the competitions in which it was used, including failure of consultees to relate their comments to the appointment criteria, lack of clarity about the weight given to comments by the appointments panels and failure by panels to treat comments in line with guidance
- High Court Judges; without suggesting that the present appointment system results in the appointment of unsuitable judges, concerns were raised about the transparency and fairness of the process. The retention by the Lord Chancellor of the right to invite practitioners who had not applied was not felt to satisfy the requirements of an open and merit-based system.

The Peach Report may be viewed by history as one of the catalysts for change because the Commission for Judicial Appointments is likely to be succeeded soon by a Judicial Appointments Commission. The change of name may seem to be a matter of semantics, but the role of the new body might meet some of the criticisms outlined above. Under the Constitutional Reform Bill 2004, it is clear that the Government foresees a JAC to handle all appointments to judicial positions. For further information, refer back to section 11.1.2 above.

On 9th February 2004, Lord Falconer indicated the Government's thinking behind the proposals:

Note: the information provided below may not be correct as it is supplied by the judiciary on a voluntary basis.

Correct as at 1st July 2004	Asian	Black	Other	Total ethnic minority	Total in post	% Ethnic minority
Lords of Appeal in Ordinary	0	0	0	0	12	0%
Heads of Division	0	0	0	0	5	0%
Lords Justices of Appeal	0	0	0	0	37	0%
High Court Judges	0	0*	0	0	107	0%
Circuit Judges	3	1	5	9	623	1.4%
Recorders	20	18	25	63	1,366	4.6%
District Judges	8	0	9	17	431	3.9%
Deputy District Judges	6	5	13	24	782	3.1%
District Judges (Magistrates' Courts)	3	0	3	6	124	4.8%

* Linda Dobbs QC, appointed to the High Court Bench on 31st August 2004, is a black woman. She is the first black High Court judge.

Figure 11.6 Ethnic minority representation in the Judiciary

The accusations are certainly true. The overwhelming majority of the senior Judiciary is male and all of the senior Judiciary is white, bar one judge: Linda Dobbs QC. Lord Irvine, the previous Lord Chancellor, in a speech to the Association of Women Barristers in February 1998, admitted:

> 'Yes, it is true that many judges today are white, Oxbridge educated men. But, it is also true that they were appointed on merit, from the then available pool, at the time the vacancies arose . . . It does not mean that the social composition of the judiciary is immutably fixed. For too long barristers were drawn from a narrow social background. As this changes over time, I would expect the composition of the Bench to change too. That is inherent in the merit principle.'

Disagreement with this view comes from the Commission for Judicial Appointments' Annual Report 2003:

> 'We reject the notion that the "trickle up" of women and ethnic minority practitioners from the lower ranks of the profession will redress the lack of diversity in the judiciary . . . we have built up a picture of wider systematic bias in the way the judiciary and the legal profession operate that affects the position of women, ethnic minority candidates and solicitors in relation to Silk and judicial appointments . . . Action is needed by the Government, the judiciary and the profession to address obstacles to diversity.'

Smith, Bailey and Gunn take a middle approach:

> 'The social and educational background of the judges has been examined in a number of surveys. These show that the judges are overwhelmingly upper or upper middle class in origin, with over three-quarters having attended public school, and a similar proportion either Oxford or Cambridge University . . . The process of socialisation at the Bar tends to mean that those from other backgrounds do not seem markedly different, if different at all, from the majority. The extent to which judicial attitudes can be related to the social background of the judges is a large and debatable question. Given the continuance for the foreseeable future of the policy of appointing senior judges largely from the Bar, it is unlikely that there will be any significant change in the background of the people appointed. What is more plausible is that the attitudes of successive generations may gradually change.'

Smith, Bailey and Gunn on the English Legal System (4th edn, Sweet & Maxwell, 2002)

Increasing diversity in the judiciary is one of the Secretary of State for Constitutional Affairs' prime concerns. See his Judicial Appointments Annual Report 2003–04 at www.dca.gov.uk/judicial/ja-arep2004.

Research carried out by University College London and the National Centre for Social Research (*The Paths to Justice*) in November 1999 found that two out of every three people think judges are out of touch with ordinary people's lives. They are also seen as anachronistic, inconsistent in the sentences they hand down, and given to inexplicable utterances on rape and other subjects (Clare Dyer, 'A very public wigging', *The Guardian*, 22nd November 1999).

Further:

> 'The intellectual isolation of appellate judges who resolve "hard cases"
> with reference to notions of social justice and public policy which they
> are singularly (and collectively) ill-equipped to understand . . . remains
> a deeply worrying feature of our judicial process.'

G Drewry [1984] 47 MLR 380

Mr Justice Harman, who retired in February 1998, said in three different cases that he had not heard of the footballer Paul Gascoigne, the rock band Oasis or the singer Bruce Springsteen. Make of that what you will.

One of the problems appears not to be failure of the system to appoint women and ethnic minority lawyers to judicial post, but that women and ethnic minority lawyers do not **apply** to become judges. In the findings of the Peach Report:

'The outcome of the 1998–9 judicial appointments round is as follows and these illustrate the relationship between the application rate and the success rate.

	Total	Men	Women
Applicants	3,719 (100%)	2,803 (75.4%)	916 (24.6%)
Interviews	1,423 (100%)	1,048 (73.6%)	375 (26.4%)
Appointments	634 (100%)	485 (76.5%)	149 (23.5%)
	White	**Other ethnic origin**	**Not known**
Applicants	3,426 (92.1%)	190 (5.1%)	103 (2.8%)
Interviews	1,324 (93%)	81 (5.7%)	18 (1.3%)
Appointments	589 (92.9%)	34 (5.4%)	11 (1.7%) '

Figure 11.7 The Peach Report findings

Despite the Lord Chancellor's affirmation that he will recommend for appointment the candidates who appear to him to be best qualified regardless of ethnic origin, gender, marital status, sexual orientation, political affiliation, religion or (subject to the physical requirements of the office) disability, it would appear that the biggest hurdle is getting women and ethnic minority lawyers to apply for judicial appointment. One of the strategies for encouraging applications from all lawyers is a new 'work shadowing' scheme introduced by the DCA in August 2004. The scheme encourages solicitors and barristers to apply to spend up to five days shadowing either a Circuit

Judge or a District Judge (Civil, rather than Magistrates' Court). The DCA leaflet on the scheme openly admits:

> **Q** 'It is designed to encourage a more diverse judiciary, with more applications for judicial appointments from women, minority ethnic and disabled lawyers.'

11.8 Dismissal and judicial independence

Retirement

Under the terms of the Judicial Pensions and Retirement Act 1993 all judges must retire on their 70th birthday.

The rules governing judicial pensions have recently been changed. To qualify for a full pension, a judge has to have served 20 years on the Bench instead of 15. This means that younger lawyers who wish to become judges will be going to the Bench earlier than perhaps they would have done. While this will result in a younger Judiciary, many QCs take a substantial drop in salary (often half) when appointed to the Bench and, under the new rules, would have to make judicial appointment by their 50th birthday. This change may back-fire and suitable potential judges may refuse to apply or be appointed as a result.

Dismissal and judicial independence

One way in which the independence of the Judiciary is protected is through the principle of 'security of tenure during good behaviour'. This means that the Heads of Division, Law Lords, Lords Justices of Appeal and High Court Judges can only be removed by the Queen after a vote to that effect by both Houses of Parliament. This security of tenure derives from the Act of Settlement 1701, but is now governed by the Supreme Court Act 1981. No English judge has ever been removed in this way.

Inferior judges may be dismissed on the grounds of incapacity or misbehaviour by the Lord Chancellor and he does not need approval from Parliament. The only occasion on which that power has been used against a full-time judicial office-holder was in 1983, when a Circuit Judge was removed from office when the judge concerned pleaded guilty to several charges of smuggling.

District Judges (Magistrates' Courts) are subject to removal by the Queen on the recommendation of the Lord Chancellor.

On 12th April 2000 the Lord Chancellor announced new terms of service for those judges appointed on fixed-term contracts, such as Deputy District Judges. To ensure a degree of judicial independence from the Executive, the judges are appointed for terms of five years and the only grounds for non-renewal of such contracts are:

- misbehaviour

- incapacity

- persistent failure to comply with sitting requirements (without good reason)

- failure to comply with training requirements

- sustained failure to observe the standards reasonably expected from a holder of such office

- part of a reduction in numbers because of changes in operational requirements

- and part of a structural change to enable recruitment of new appointees.

For all but the last two grounds, decisions not to renew or to remove an office holder are taken by the Lord Chancellor with the concurrence of the Lord Chief Justice and following an investigation conducted by a judge nominated by him. Decisions not to renew on the final two grounds are on a 'first in, first out' principle and the decision to use such grounds and the extent to which they are used are decided by the Lord Chancellor with the concurrence of the Lord Chief Justice.

The Constitutional Reform Bill 2004 continues to protect the security of tenure of the senior Judiciary. Disciplinary matters may be dealt with by the Secretary of State, with the agreement of the Lord Chief Justice, who is also given powers to advise, warn or formally reprimand judges.

Judicial impartiality

In addition to being as independent as possible from the Legislative and the Executive, a judge must remain independent from the parties to the case he is hearing.

CASE EXAMPLE

R v Bow Street Metropolitan Stipendiary Magistrate and Others, ex parte Pinochet Ugarte (No 2) [1999] 2 WLR 272

Pinochet was the former head of state of Chile who was on a visit to London for medical treatment. He was arrested under extradition warrants issued by a Spanish court alleging various crimes against humanity, including murder, hostage-taking and torture, committed during his period of office in the 1970s and for which he was knowingly responsible.

CONTINUED ▶

Before the main hearing, Amnesty International, a human rights body which had campaigned against Pinochet, obtained leave to intervene and was represented by counsel in the proceedings. Pinochet claimed diplomatic immunity in an attempt to quash the warrants, but his claim was rejected by the House of Lords by a 3:2 majority, including Lord Hoffmann in the majority. However, Pinochet's advisers then discovered that Lord Hoffmann, although not a member of Amnesty International, was an unpaid director and chairman of Amnesty International Charity Ltd; one of the objects of which was to procure the abolition of torture, extra-judicial execution and disappearance. Lord Hoffmann had neither withdrawn from the case nor declared his interest in Amnesty International (he may have thought that the parties knew, or that the opposition to torture was a commonly held belief and as such he was no different from the other judges).

Pinochet applied for the House of Lords to set aside its previous decision on the ground of apparent bias on the part of Lord Hoffmann, and the House did so. Lord Browne-Wilkinson held that, as regards the appearance of judicial bias, the fundamental principle that a man may not be a judge in his own cause was applicable if the judge's decision would lead to the promotion of a cause in which he was involved together with one of the parties. Therefore, in order to maintain the absolute impartiality of the judiciary, there had to be a rule which automatically disqualified a judge who was involved, whether personally or as a director of a company, in promoting the same causes in the same organisation as was a party to the suit; and that, accordingly, the earlier decision of the House would be set aside.

In *Locabail Ltd v Bayfield Properties* [2000] 1 All ER 65, the Court of Appeal heard five conjoined appeals alleging bias in the Judiciary.

In the first two, the application concerned a Deputy High Court Judge, Mr Lawrence Collins QC (interestingly, he is only the second solicitor to have been appointed to the High Court). As a partner in a law firm's litigation and arbitration department and a judge, he became aware that his firm had acted for a company which had claims against one of the defendants (the applicant's husband). On becoming aware of the issue, he had made immediate disclosure and the parties had done nothing to object. No bias was found. Nor was there in *Williams v HM Inspector of Taxes* (2000), where the applicant asserted that the Chair of the Industrial Tribunal, having worked for the Inland Revenue, should not have chaired her unfair dismissal case against the same party (many years later). Nor was there even the appearance of bias in *R v Bristol Betting and Gaming Licensing Committee, ex parte O'Callaghan* (2000), even though the judge was a director of a company which owned property of which one of the businesses in the case was a tenant.

However, in *Timmins v Gormley* (2000) the judge was an author of a number of articles on personal injury claims in which he criticised some defendant insurers. The issue was not that fact that Mr Recorder Braithwaite was the author of the articles, but of their tone. The Court of Appeal

held that there was a real danger that he might have leaned unconsciously towards the claimant. The Court also issued guidance on judicial bias:

> **J** 'There can be no objection to a judge on the grounds of ethnic or national origin, religion, gender, age, class or sexual orientation. Nor can there be objection on the grounds of social, educational or employment background, or that of his family or membership of bodies such as the Freemasons.
>
> A judge should recuse himself if aware he is in a situation like that involved in *Pinochet*, or where he has a financial interest in the outcome of the case, or he should make disclosure as soon as he becomes aware he is in such a situation. If the parties do not object following appropriate disclosure in the latter case, that party cannot later complain of a real danger of bias.'

Key facts chart on the Constitutional Reform Bill 2004

KEY FACTS

The Future?	Why?	Effect
Abolition of the post of Lord Chancellor	Breaches the Separation of Powers doctrine. Affects the independence of the Judiciary	Roles to be split between Secretary of State and President of the Courts of England and Wales (the Lord Chief Justice)
Judicial Appointments Commission	To remove as much political influence from the process as possible. To create a more transparent system	Panel of lay people, judges and legal practitioners; but still requiring approval of Secretary of State
Supreme Court of the UK	To take the senior Judiciary away from the political system (the House of Lords)	In terms of jurisdiction and power, very little. Not to be a constitutional court

■ Key facts chart on the Judiciary

KEY FACTS

Refer to figures 11.3 and 11.4 on pages 341–342.

Inferior judges	District Judge (Magistrates' Court)
	District Judge (Civil Court)
	Recorder
	Circuit Judge
Superior judges	High Court Judge
	Lord Justice of Appeal
	Lord of Appeal in Ordinary

The appointments process

Inferior judges	Vacancies are advertised
	Referees are consulted
	Interviews are held
	Lord Chancellor retains role in appointment
	Overseen by Commission for Judicial Appointments
Superior judges	Vacancies advertised (High Court)
	No applications (except High Court and even here application not a prerequisite)
	Extensive consultation with senior judiciary
	No interviews
	Appointment by invitation

CONTINUED ▸

THE ENGLISH
LEGAL SYSTEM

■ Key facts chart on the composition and independence of the Judiciary

<table>
<tr><td colspan="2">KEY FACTS</td></tr>
<tr><td colspan="2">*Composition and independence*</td></tr>
<tr><td>Women</td><td>Count for less than 20% of the total Judiciary, but less than 9% of the senior Judiciary</td></tr>
<tr><td>Members of an ethnic minority</td><td>Count for less than 4% of the total Judiciary, but less than 1% of the senior Judiciary</td></tr>
<tr><td>Retirement</td><td>Retirement age of 70, but need 20 years on the Bench for a full pension</td></tr>
<tr><td>Dismissal</td><td>Senior judges have security of tenure. Inferior judges on grounds of incapacity or misbehaviour</td></tr>
<tr><td>Impartiality</td><td>*R v Bow Street Metropolitan Stipendiary Magistrate and Others, ex parte Pinochet Ugarte (No 2)* [1999] 2 WLR 272; *Locabail Ltd v Bayfield Properties* [2000] 1 All ER 65</td></tr>
</table>

Further reading

Cornes, R, 'How to create a new Supreme Court: Learning from New Zealand' (2004) 27 PL 59.

Paterson, J, 'A partnership of equals?' [2004] 154 NLJ 442.

Woodhouse, D, 'The office of Lord Chancellor' [1998] UKPL 617.

chapter 12 SENTENCING ▪

12.1 Introduction

Whenever a person pleads guilty, or is found guilty of an offence, the role of the court is to decide what sentence should be imposed on the offender. Judges and magistrates have a fairly wide discretion as to the sentence they select in each case, although they are subject to certain restrictions. Magistrates can only impose a maximum of six months' imprisonment for one offence (will increase to 12 months) and a normal maximum fine of £5,000 (about to be increased to £15,000). However, for some offences committed by companies, such as pollution or breach of health and safety laws, a maximum fine of £20,000 is available to magistrates. Judges in the Crown Court have no such limits; they can impose up to life imprisonment for some crimes and there is no maximum figure for fines. As well as custody and fines, the courts have a wide range of community sentences which they can impose and they can also give an offender an absolute or conditional discharge.

Figure 12.1 shows the different use of sentences in the magistrates' courts and the Crown Court. The Crown Court deals with the more serious offences and this is reflected in the type of sentences imposed.

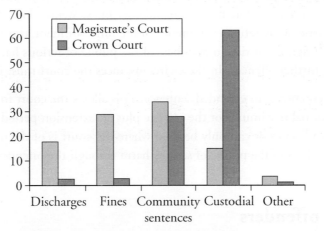

Figure 12.1 Sentences given at Magistrates' Courts and the Crown Court in 2002

12.1.1 Maximum sentences

However, there are other restrictions, both in the magistrates' court and in the Crown Court. Each crime has a maximum penalty for that type of offence set by Parliament. For example, the crime of theft has a fixed maximum of seven years' imprisonment, so that no matter how much has been

stolen, the judge can never send an offender to prison for longer that this. Some offences have a maximum sentence of life imprisonment; these include manslaughter and rape. In such cases the judge has complete discretion when sentencing; the offender may be sent to prison for life or given a shorter prison sentence or a non-custodial sentence may even be thought appropriate. Murder is the exception as it carries a mandatory life sentence; in other words the judge has to pass life imprisonment, there is no other sentence available. The judge does, however, set the minimum period which the offender should serve before he can be considered for release on licence.

12.1.2 Minimum sentences

Although Parliament has set down maximum sentences for all offences, there are only a two offences for which minimum sentences have been set down. Minimum sentences apply only to repeat offenders who have committed a third (or further) offence and are for:

- burglary (minimum of three years' imprisonment)
- Class A drug trafficking offences (minimum of seven years' imprisonment).

For these offences the courts must impose at least the minimum level unless there are particular circumstances relating to the offender which would make it unjust in all the circumstances to do so.

12.1.3 Dangerous offenders

The Criminal Justice Act 2003 makes special sentences available to the Crown Court when the offender is a dangerous offender. The first is a mandatory life sentence. This is imposed where the offence committed carries a discretionary sentence of life imprisonment **and** the court is of the opinion that there is a significant risk to members of the public of serious harm through the offender committing further offences. In these circumstances the court must impose a life sentence.

The second type of sentence is an extended sentence. This allows the court to impose a custodial sentence up to the normal maximum for the offence plus an extension period during which the offender is subject to a licence. It can only be used where the court is of the opinion that there is a significant risk to members of the public of serious harm through the offender committing further specified offences.

12.1.4 Young offenders

In addition, for offenders under the age of 21, both the Magistrates' Courts and the Crown Court have to comply with the current legislative rules on what sentences are available for young offenders. This is an area where there have been frequent changes over the last 10 years or so. It is an area which is constantly under review and it is possible that government policy will bring further changes. The sentences currently available for young offenders are considered briefly at section 12.5.

12.2 Aims of sentencing

When judges or magistrates have to pass a sentence, they will not only look at the sentences available, they will also have to decide what they are trying to achieve by the punishment they give. These aims or purposes of sentencing are now set down by statute in s 142 of the Criminal Justice Act 2003. They apply only to offenders aged 18 and over.

's 142 Any court dealing with an offender in respect of his offence must have regard to the following purposes of sentencing–

(a) the punishment of offenders,

(b) the reduction of crime (including its reduction by deterrence),

(c) the reform and rehabilitation of offenders,

(d) the protection of the public, and

(e) the making of reparation by offenders to persons affected by their offences.'

The Sentencing Guidelines Council pointed out, in draft guidelines, *Overarching Principles: Seriousness and New Sentences: Criminal Justice Act 2003,* published in 2004, that:

Q	'1.2 The Act does not indicate that any one purpose should be more important than any other and on practice they may all be relevant to a greater or lesser degree in any individual case – the sentencer has the task of determining the manner in which they apply.'

One of the problems in relation to these purposes of sentencing is that some of them may be in conflict in particular cases. For example, the sentence which is most suitable for reforming an offender may not be the same sentence which would be imposed if the judge merely considered the purpose of punishment. In most cases the judge is performing a balancing act but always keeping in mind the need to reduce crime. Also, although there are five purposes of sentencing set out here, academics have always considered that there are six aims of sentencing. The additional one not covered in s 142 is denunciation. Each of these aims of sentencing will be examined in turn.

12.2.1 Punishment

This is aim is also referred to as retribution. It is based on the idea that punishment should be imposed because the offender deserves punishment for his or her acts. It does not seek to reduce crime or alter the offender's future behaviour. This idea was expressed in the nineteenth century by Kant in *The Metaphysical Elements of Justice* when he wrote:

'Judicial punishment can never be used merely as a means to promote
some other good for the criminal himself or for civil society, but instead
it must in all cases be imposed on him only on the ground that he has
committed a crime.'

Retribution is therefore concerned only with the fact that the offence was committed and making
sure that the punishment inflicted is in proportion to that offence. The crudest form of retribution
is seen in the old saying 'An eye for an eye and a tooth for a tooth and a life for a life'. This was
one of the factors used to justify the death penalty for the offence of murder. The offender had
taken a life and so had to forfeit his own life. In other crimes it is not so easy to see how this
principle can operate to produce an exact match between crime and punishment. For this reason
sentencing guidelines are produced to help judges in deciding an appropriate punishment.

Sentencing guidelines

Under the Criminal Justice Act 2003, the Sentencing Guidelines Council has the responsibility for
producing such guidelines. They receive advice from the Sentencing Advisory Panel and this Panel
consults widely before tendering its advice. In addition the Secretary of State, under s 170(2) of the
Criminal Justice Act 2003, may at any time propose to the Council that sentencing guidelines be
framed or revised. All documents produced by both the Sentencing Guidelines Council and the
Sentencing Advisory panel can be found at www.sentencing-guidelines.gov.uk.

Prior to the creation of the Sentencing Guidelines Council, the Court of Appeal (Criminal
Division) had responsibility for setting guidelines. These were only a specific type of offence. For
example in *R v McInerney; R v Keating* [2002] All ER (D) 300 the Court of Appeal gave guidelines
on sentencing for burglary. This caused some controversy as the Sentencing Advisory Panel had
recommended that for non-violent domestic burglary the appropriate sentence for a first offence
should be nine months, with 18 months for a second offence and the three-year minimum
sentence for a third offence. The Court of Appeal guidelines were that the initial approach should
be:

> **J** 'to impose a community sentence subject to conditions that ensured that the
> sentence was an effective punishment and one which offered action on the part of
> the Probation Service to tackle the offender's criminal behaviour and, when
> appropriate, would tackle the offender's underlying problems such as drug addiction
>
> The Court of Appeal thought that if, and only if, the court was satisfied that the
> offender had demonstrated by his or her behaviour that punishment in the community
> was not practicable, should the court resort to a custodial sentence.'

In *R v Billam* [1986] 1 WLR 349 the Court of Appeal had set out tariffs for rape, with the guideline being that rape offenders should be given a custodial sentence. Five years was considered as the normal starting point where there were no aggravating features. However, where there were aggravating features, such as a very young victim or excessive use of violence, there should be starting points of eight or 15 years. These guidelines were revisited in *R v Milberry* [2002] All ER (D) 99. The idea of the starting point of five years' imprisonment remained where there was a single rape on an adult by a single offender. Similarly the starting point of eight years was applicable where there were aggravating features. Fifteen years was the starting point recommended for a campaign of rape. The Court of Appeal also added that a life sentence might be appropriate if there was a likelihood of the offender remaining a danger for an indefinite time. This has now been reinforced by ss 225 and 226 of the Criminal Justice Act 2003 which create a mandatory life sentence for dangerous offenders.

The new system of the Sentencing Guidelines Council creating guidelines allows wider principles to be developed. It is hoped that this will lead to greater consistency in sentencing.

Tariff sentences

Some states in America operate a very rigid system in which each crime has a set tariff with the judge being allowed only to impose a penalty within the tariff range. This removes almost all the element of discretion in sentencing from the judges and ensures that sentences for offences are uniform. The objections to this are that it does not allow sufficient consideration of mitigating factors, and may produce a sentence which is unjust in the particular circumstances. The concept of retribution and giving the offender his 'just deserts' should not be so rigid as to ignore special needs of the offender.

12.2.2 Deterrence

This can be individual deterrence or general deterrence. Individual deterrence is intended to make sure that the offender does not re-offend through fear of future punishment. General deterrence is aimed at preventing other potential offenders from committing crimes. Both are aimed at reducing the future levels of crime.

Individual deterrence

There are several penalties that can be imposed with the aim of deterring the individual offender from committing similar crimes in the future. These include a prison sentence or a suspended sentence, electronic tagging or a heavy fine. It is noticeable, however, that prison does not appear to deter, as about 60 per cent of adult prisoners re-offend within two years of release. With young offenders custodial sentences have even less of a deterrent effect as the re-offending rate is even higher.

Critics of the theory of deterrence point out that it makes an assumption about criminal behaviour that is not borne out in practice. It assumes that an offender will stop to consider what the

consequences of his action will be. In fact, most crimes are committed on the spur of the moment and many are committed by offenders who are under the influence of drugs or alcohol. These offenders are unlikely to stop and consider the possible consequences of their actions.

It is also pointed out that fear of being caught is more of a deterrent and that while crime detection rates are low, the threat of an unpleasant penalty, if caught, seems too remote. Fear of detection has been shown to be a powerful deterrent by the success rate of closed-circuit televisions used for surveying areas. In one scheme on London's District Line of the Underground system there was an 83 per cent reduction in crime in the first full year that surveillance cameras were used.

General deterrence

The value of this is even more doubtful as potential offenders are rarely deterred by severe sentences passed on others. However, the courts do occasionally resort to making an example of an offender in order to warn other potential offenders of the type of punishment they face. This will usually be where there is a large increase in a particular type of crime. General deterrence also relies on publicity so that potential offenders are aware of the level. It is in direct conflict with the principle of retribution, since it involves sentencing an offender to a longer term than is deserved for the specific offence. It is probably the least effective and least fair principle of sentencing. The Sentencing Guidelines Council in the draft guidelines, *Overarching Principles: Seriousness and New Sentences: Criminal Justice Act 2003,* published in 2004, recognise this and point out:

Q	'1.36 The seriousness of an individual case should be judged on it own dimensions of harm and culpability rather than as part of a collective social harm. It is legitimate for the overall approach to sentencing levels for particular offences to be directed by their cumulative effect. However, it would be wrong to further penalise individual offenders by increasing sentence length for committing an individual offence of that type.'

12.2.3 Reform and rehabilitation

Under this the main aim of the penalty is to reform the offender and rehabilitate him into society. It is a forward looking aim. The hope is that the offender's behaviour will be altered by the penalty imposed so that he will not offend in the future. It also aims to reduce crime in this way. This principle of sentence came to the fore in the second half of the twentieth century with the development of sentences such as probation and community service orders. The Criminal Justice Act 2003 has extended the range of orders that can be made within a community sentence. The details of this are examined at section 12.4.

Reformation is a very important element in the sentencing philosophy for young offenders, but it is also used for some adult offenders. The court will be given information about the defendant's background, usually through a pre-sentence report prepared by the probation service. Where relevant the court will consider other factors, such as school reports, or job prospects, or medical problems.

Individualised sentences

Where the court considers rehabilitation, the sentence used is an individualised one aimed at the needs of the offender. This is in direct contrast to the concept of tariff sentences seen in the aim of retribution. One of the criticisms of this approach is, therefore, that it leads to inconsistency in sentencing. Offenders who have committed exactly the same type of offence may be given different sentences because the emphasis is on the individual offender. Another criticism is that this aim tends to discriminate against the under privileged. Offenders from poor home backgrounds are less likely to be seen as possible candidates for reform.

Persistent offenders are usually thought less likely to respond to a reformative sentence.

12.2.4 Protection of the public

Protection usually involves incapacitating the offender in some way. That is, the offender is made incapable of re-offending. Of course, the ultimate method of incapacitation is the death penalty. In some countries the hands of thieves are cut off to prevent them from re-offending. Another controversial method of incapacitation is the use in some American states of medical means to incapacitate sex offenders and thus ensure that they cannot re-offend.

Incapacitation is also thought of as protecting society from the criminal activities of the offender, so today in Britain this is achieved by removing dangerous offenders from society through the use of long prison sentences. This is shown by the Criminal Justice Act 2003 where dangerous offenders must be given a life sentence in certain circumstances. Also, the use of minimum sentences for persistent offenders is aimed at protecting the public from their repeated criminal activities.

There are other penalties that can be viewed as incapacitating the offender. For example, in driving offences, the offender can be banned from driving. There is also a move to using community-based sentences that will incapacitate the offender in the short term and protect the public. These include exclusion orders under which an offender is banned from going to the place where he offends, usually a pub or a football ground, and curfew orders which order an offender to remain at a given address for certain times of the day or night. There is also the provision of electronic tagging to help supervise curfew orders.

12.2.5 Reparation

This is where the offender has to make reparation to the victim or community who have suffered as a result of the offence. At the lowest level this may be done by compensating the victim of the crime. This is usually by ordering the offender to pay a sum of money to the victim or to make restitution, for example by returning stolen property to its rightful owner. The idea that criminals should pay compensation to the victims of their crimes is one that goes back to before the Norman Conquest to the Anglo–Saxon courts. In England today, the courts are required to consider ordering compensation to the victim of a crime in addition to any other penalty they may think appropriate. Under s 130(2) of the Powers of Criminal Courts (Sentencing) Act 2000, courts are under a duty to give reasons if they do not make a compensation order.

The concept of restitution also includes making reparation to society as a whole. This can be seen mainly in the use of unpaid work requirements in a community sentence when offenders are required to do so many hours' work on a community project under the supervision of the probation service.

Reparation is now often viewed in the wider concept of restorative justice. This has two aims. The first is to prevent the offender from re-offending through an understanding of the trauma the crime has caused to the victim. At the same time the offender will be expected to make reparation. A widely accepted definition of 'restorative justice' is:

> 'A process whereby all the parties with a stake in a particular offence come together to resolve collectively how to deal with the aftermath of an offence and the implications for the future.'

> (T Marshall, *Restorative Justice: An Overview* (Home Office, 1999))

The trend today is towards more focused reparation in which the offender is brought face to face with the victim and there have been pilot schemes bringing offenders and victims together, so that the offender may make direct reparation. A Home Office study *Implementing Restorative Justice Schemes (Crime Reduction Programme): A Report on the First Year* by Shapland *et al* was published as Home Office Online Report 32/04. This looked at three schemes operating in different areas of England and Wales in their first year. All had found that setting up schemes had taken more time and funding than expected and that it was really to early to judge whether the schemes were being successful in preventing re-offending.

Reparative justice is used in youth justice. Youth Offender Panels often use it as part of the package in the contract for a young offender's future behaviour.

12.2.6 Denunciation

This is society expressing its disapproval of criminal activity. A sentence should indicate both to the offender and to other people that society condemns certain types of behaviour. It shows people that justice is being done. Denunciation also reinforces the moral boundaries of acceptable conduct and can mould society's views on the criminality of particular conduct. For example, drink-driving is now viewed by the majority of people as unacceptable behaviour. This is largely because of the changes in the law and the increasingly severe sentences that are imposed. By sending offenders to prison, banning them from driving and imposing heavy fines, society's opinion of drink-driving has been changed.

The ideas of retribution and denunciation were foremost in the concepts behind the Criminal Justice Act of 1991, as shown by the Government White Paper on Crime and Punishment (1990) which preceded the Act. However, in the 2003 Criminal Justice Act denunciation was not included as one of the purposes of sentencing in s 142.

■ Key facts chart on purposes of sentencing

KEY FACTS

Purpose	Explanation	Suitable punishment
Punishment	Punishment imposed only on ground that an offence has been committed also known as retribution	Tariff sentences Sentence must be proportionate to the crime
Protection of the public	Society is protected from crime by making the offender incapable of committing further crime	Death penalty for murder Long prison sentences Tagging
Deterrence	Individual – the offender is deterred through fear of further punishment General – potential offenders warned as to likely punishment	Prison sentence Heavy fine Long sentence as an example to others
Reform and rehabilitation	Reform offender's behaviour	Individualised sentence Supervision requirement Unpaid work requirement
Restitution	Repayment/reparation to victim or to community Restorative justice	Compensation order Unpaid work requirement Reparation order
Denunciation	Society expressing its disapproval Reinforces moral boundaries	Reflects blameworthiness of the offence

12.3 Custodial sentences

This book does not seek to give a detailed examination of all the sentences available, but merely to examine briefly the different categories of custodial sentences, community-based sentences, fines and discharges. A custodial sentence is the most serious punishment that a court can impose. Custodial sentences range from 'weekend' prison to life imprisonment. They include:

• mandatory and discretionary life sentences

- fixed-term sentences
- Custody Plus (short-term sentence)
- intermittent custody
- suspended sentences.

12.3.1 Life sentences

The only penalty available where an offender aged 21 or over pleads guilty or is found guilty of murder is life imprisonment. This is, therefore, a mandatory sentence where the judge has no discretion in sentencing. However, the judge does state the minimum term that should be served before the offender is eligible for release on licence. This minimum period used to be set by the Home Secretary but this procedure was held to be a breach of the European Convention on Human Rights, since it gave the Executive power over sentencing. There was also a challenge as to whether having a mandatory life sentence for murder was a breach of human rights, but it was ruled in *R v Lichniak; R v Pyrah, The Times*, 26th November 2002 that it was not incompatible with Arts 3 and 5 of the Convention.

The minimum term to be served in a life sentence is now governed by s 269 and Sch 21 to the Criminal Justice Act 2003. This gives judges clear starting points for the minimum period to be ordered. The starting points range from a full life term down to 12 years. A whole life term should be set where the offence falls into one of the following categories:

- the murder of two or more persons, where each murder involves a substantial degree of premeditation or planning or the abduction of the victim or sexual or sadistic conduct
- the murder of a child if involving the abduction of the child or sexual or sadistic motivation
- a murder done for the purpose of advancing a political, religious or ideological cause or
- a murder by an offender previously convicted of murder.

Cases which have a starting point of 30 years include where the murder is of a police or prison officer in the course of his duty, or a murder using a firearm or explosive or the sexual or sadistic murder of an adult or a murder that is racially or religiously aggravated. Any offence of murder which is not specifically given a starting point of a whole life term or 30 years has a starting point of 15 years, although where the offender was under the age of 18 at the time of the offence this period is 12 years.

Aggravating and mitigating factors

Once the judge has decide on the starting point, any aggravating or mitigating factors must then be considered. Aggravating factors which can increase the minimum term ordered by the judge include the fact that the victim was particularly vulnerable because of age or disability or any mental or physical suffering inflicted on the victim before death. Mitigating factors include the fact that the offender had an intention to cause grievous bodily harm rather than an intention to kill, a lack of premeditation or the fact that the offender acted to some extent in self-defence (though not sufficient to give him a defence). Where there are mitigating factors the judge can set a minimum term of less than any of the starting points. In addition, Lord Woolf, the Lord Chief Justice, has issued a Practice Direction *(Crime: Mandatory Life Sentences (No 2)*, 29th July 2004) giving practical guidance to judges as to the procedure for passing a mandatory life sentence.

Where the offence carries a discretionary life sentence and the judge decides that a life sentence should be imposed, then again the judge must set a minimum term to be served before the offender can be released on licence. However, there are no statutory guidelines for such cases and the judge may select the term he thinks appropriate.

12.3.2 Fixed-term sentence

A fixed-term sentence is one for a definite period, for example six years' imprisonment. Under the Criminal Justice Act 2003, all offenders serving fixed-term sentences of 12 months of more will be released on licence after they have served half their sentence. They will remain on licence until the full term of the sentence and if, at any time during the licence period, they breach their licence condition, they can be recalled to prison. It is also possible for offenders to be released up 135 days before the half-way stage of their sentence under a curfew condition.

12.3.3 Custody Plus

For short-term sentences, s 181 of the Criminal Justice Act 2003 has introduced a new concept: that of Custody Plus. This is a short prison sentence of up to three months followed by a period on licence in the community during which the offender must meet requirements set by the court. The overall length of the sentence cannot exceed a maximum of 12 months. This sentence was brought in following the Halliday Review of the Sentencing Framework for England and Wales, *Making Punishments Work*. The Report pointed out that prison sentences of less than 12 months had little meaningful impact on criminal behaviour.

During the licence period, the court can add on one or more of the following requirements:

* as unpaid work requirement
* an activity requirement
* a programme requirement
* a prohibited activity requirement
* a curfew requirement
* an exclusion requirement
* a supervision requirement and
* in the case where the offender is aged under 25, an attendance centre requirement.

These requirements are also available as part of a community order and are explained more fully in the section on community sentences (section 12.4).

12.3.4 Intermittent Custody

Intermittent Custody is a new approach in which a prison sentence and community sentence are served alternately. For example, a prison sentence at weekends (or at night) with a community programme during the week (or during the day). The aim of the sentence is to allow offenders to keep their jobs, family ties or education. It cannot be used for those convicted of sex offences. Pilots began in January 2004 and by September 2004 103 orders had been given and only three had been breached. An offender who fails to return to prison at the required time risks being sent back into full-time custody for the remaining period of his sentence. In September 2004 the Home Secretary called for an expansion of the use of intermittent custody, so that an additional 1,300 spaces are to be created during 2005.

The period to be served in prison must be between 14 and 90 days and the time that the sentences lasts must be between 28 weeks and 51 weeks. Any days when the offender is not in prison are regarded as periods when he is on licence and the court can make one or more of the following four requirements:

- as unpaid work requirement
- an activity requirement
- a programme requirement
- a prohibited activity requirement.

12.3.5 Suspended sentences

A suspended sentence of imprisonment is one where the offender will only serve the custodial period if he breaches the terms of the suspension. The prison sentence can only be between 28 and 51 weeks. The period of suspension can be between six months and two years. The idea is that the threat of prison during this period of suspension will deter the offender from committing further offences. If the offender complies with the requirements of the suspended sentence he will not serve the term of imprisonment. The suspended sentence can be combined with any of the requirements used in a community order (see section 12.4). If the offender fails to meet the requirements the suspended sentence may be 'activated'. That is, the offender will be made to serve the term of imprisonment. Prior to the Criminal Justice Act 2003, a suspended sentence could only be combined with a fine or a compensation order, leaving the offender unsupervised. As a result, a suspended sentence was seen as a 'soft option' and rarely used by the courts.

12.4 Community sentences

Prior to the Criminal Justice Act 2003, the courts had individual community sentences which they could impose on an offender. They could combine some of these sentences, in particular, unpaid work with a supervision order. Also, they could add requirements about treatment and residence to a supervision order, but they could not use a whole range of orders. The Halliday Report recommended that:

> **Q**
>
> '6.1 To ensure that a non-custodial sentence reduces the likelihood of re-offending, courts should have the power to impose a single, non-custodial penalty made up of specific elements – which would replace all existing community sentences. These elements would include:
>
> - treatment for substance abuse or mental illness;
> - curfew and exclusion orders;
> - electronic monitoring;
> - reparation to victims and communities;
> - compulsory work;
> - attendance at offending behaviour programmes.'

This was brought into effect by the Criminal Justice Act 2003 and there is now a community order available to the courts which is a customised community sentence combining any requirements which the court thinks necessary. These requirements include all the previous existing community sentences which became available as 'requirements' and can be attached to the sentence. There are also new 'requirements' available. The sentencers can 'mix and match' requirements allowing them to fit the restrictions and rehabilitation to the offender's needs. The sentence is available for offenders age 16 and over. The full list of requirements available to the courts is set out in s 177 of the Criminal Justice Act 2003.

'177(1) Where a person aged 16 or over is convicted of an offence, the court by or before which he is convicted may make an order imposing on him any one or more of the following requirements:

(a) as unpaid work requirement

(b) an activity requirement

(c) a programme requirement

(d) a prohibited activity requirement

(e) a curfew requirement

(f) an exclusion requirement

(g) a residence requirement

(h) a mental health treatment requirement

(i) a drug rehabilitation requirement

(j) an alcohol treatment requirement

(k) a supervision requirement, and

(l) in the case where the offender is aged under 25, an attendance centre requirement.'

Each of these is defined within the Criminal Justice Act 2003. Most are self-explanatory from their name, such as drug rehabilitation and alcohol treatment. Much crime is linked to drug and alcohol abuse and the idea behind these two requirements is to tackle the causes of crime, hopefully preventing further offences. Mental health treatment is also aimed at the cause of the offender's behaviour. The main other requirements are explained briefly below.

12.4.1 Unpaid work requirement

This requires the offender to work for between 40 and 300 hours on a suitable project organised by the probation service. The exact number of hours will be fixed by the court and those hours are then usually worked in eight-hour sessions, often at weekends. The type of work involved will vary, depending on what schemes the local probation service have running. The offender may be required to paint school buildings, help build a play centre or work on conservation projects. When Eric Cantona, the French footballer, was found guilty of assaulting a football fan, the court ordered that he help at coaching sessions for young footballers. More recently, Leeds footballers Lee Bowyer and Jonathan Woodgate were order to do unpaid work after they were convicted of assault.

12.4.2 Activity requirement

The offender has to take part in set activities on certain days for up to a maximum of 60 separate days. The activities can include activities for the purpose of reparation, including contact between the offender and the victim.

12.4.3 Curfew requirement

Under a curfew requirement an offender can be ordered to remain at a fixed address for between two and 12 hours in any 24-hour period. This order can last for up to six months and may be enforced by electronic tagging under which the offender has to wear a tag which sends signals of his whereabouts to a central monitoring system. This is usually via a radio receiving unit connected to a telephone line. However, in September 2004, the Home Secretary announced that the use of satellite tracking to monitor the whereabouts of offenders would be piloted. He also indicated that he would like to see more use of tagging as a requirement, with the number of offenders being tagged increasing from 9,000 a year to 18,000 a year.

12.4.4 Exclusion order

Under s 205 of the Criminal Justice Act 2003 courts may order that an offender be banned from entering a specified place or places. It can be just for certain days or it can be a complete ban. Such an order can be for up to two years. An exclusion requirement may be used for a variety of offences: for example banning football hooligans from attending at certain football clubs or persistent shop-lifters from entering certain shops. Tagging and satellite technology is also being piloted as a way of monitoring whether an offender is keeping out of the excluded area.

12.4.5 Supervision requirement

This places the offender under the supervision of a probation officer for a period of between six months and three years. During this time the offender must attend appointments with the probation officer or another person determined by the probation officer. A supervision requirement will be made for the purpose of promoting the offender's rehabilitation.

12.5 Young offenders

12.5.1 Custodial sentences

Custodial sentences are viewed as a last resort for young offenders. When a custodial sentence is imposed young offenders are kept separate from adult offenders and there is a considerable emphasis on education and training. Despite this, statistics show that custodial sentences are not effective in preventing young offenders from re-offending. A report, *The Lost Generation* (2004), by Community Care magazine and the Prison Reform Trust showed that 71 per cent of young offenders given a custodial sentence re-offended within two years. In the Queen's Speech in November 2004, the Government stated that it intended to bring in a Youth Justice Bill aimed at moving punishment of young offenders away from custody and towards community sentences with greater use of electronic tagging. However, there may not be enough parliamentary time for this Bill in the 2004–05 session as there is the possibility that the session will finish early because of a General Election being called.

Detention at Her Majesty's Pleasure

Any offender aged 10–17 who is convicted of murder must be ordered to be detained during Her Majesty's Pleasure. This is an indeterminate sentence which allows the offender to be released when suitable. The judge in the case can recommend a minimum number of years that should be served before release is considered. This must be in accordance with the guidelines set out in the Criminal Justice Act 2003 (see section 12.3.1). The sentence will be initially be served in a special unit for young offenders. When an offender reaches 21 he will be transferred to an adult prison.

Detention for serious crimes

For very serious offences the courts have additional power under s 53 of the Children and Young Persons Act 1933 to order that the offender be detained for longer periods. For 10–13 years olds this power is only available where the crime committed carries a maximum sentence of at least 14 years' imprisonment for adults or for is an offence of indecent assault on a woman under s 14 of the Sexual Offences Act 1956. For 14 to 17 year olds it is also available for causing death by dangerous driving or for causing death by careless driving while under the influence of drink or

drugs. The length of detention imposed on the young offender cannot be more than the maximum sentence available for an adult.

Young offenders' institutions

Under s 91 of the Powers of Criminal Courts (Sentencing) Act 2000 offenders aged 18–20 can be sent to a young offenders' institution as a custodial sentence. The minimum sentence is 21 days and the maximum is the maximum allowed for the particular offence. If the offender becomes 21 years old while serving the sentence, he will be transferred to an adult prison.

Detention and training orders

Under s 100 of the Powers of Criminal Courts (Sentencing) Act 2000 the courts can make a detention and training order in relation to an offender aged 10–21. The sentence is for a specified period with a minimum of four months and a maximum of 24 months. In between these, the order can be for six, eight, 10, 12 or 18 months. For a summary offence the maximum is six months. For offenders under the age of 15 an order can only be made if they are persistent offenders. For those under 12 there is an additional requirement that the court must be of the opinion that only a custodial sentence is adequate to protect the public from further offending by that offender.

12.5.2 Other sentences

There are number of community orders which can be used for young offenders. The main ones are referral orders, action plan orders, reparation orders and are available for offenders under the age of 18. There are also attendance centre orders which are available for those up to the age of 25. The orders are largely aimed at the cause of the offending and preventing a repetition of the offending behaviour.

Referral orders

Where an offender under the age of 18 pleads guilty to an offence which carries a sentence of imprisonment for adult offenders, and the offender has no previous convictions, the Youth Court must refer the offender to a Youth Offending Panel. The court can also decide to make a referral order where the offence is non-imprisonable, but do not have to make one.

Once a referral order is made the Youth Offending Panel will arrange a meeting involving the offender, his parent(s) or guardian(s), two volunteer members of the community and a member of the local Youth Offending Team (YOT). The victim can be invited to attend, but the 2004 Annual Report: *Joint Inspection of Youth Offending Teams: The First Phase* found that the number of victims attending panel meeting was disappointingly low. The aim of the Panel is to 'reach an agreement with the offender on a programme of behaviour the aim (or principal aim) of which is the prevention of re-offending by the offender' (s 23(1) Powers of Criminal Courts (Sentencing) Act 2000).

The agreement should include an element of reparation: this may be financial of otherwise. If the victim agrees, the Panel may require the offender to attend mediation sessions with the victim. The agreement is also likely to require the offender to take part in sessions and activities, such as anger management or alcohol or drug awareness schemes if these played a part in causing him to commit the offence.

Action plan orders

This type of order is a short intensive programme of community intervention which is intended to combine punishment, rehabilitation and reparation and to change offending behaviour and prevent further crime. The order places the offender under supervision and also sets out requirements which the offender has to comply with for a period of three months. The requirements can be for the offender to do any or all of the following:

- participate in set activities
- present himself to a specified person at set times and places
- attend at an attendance centre
- stay away from certain places
- comply with arrangements for his education
- make reparation.

Reparation orders

This is an order for the offender to do a maximum of 24 hours work to make reparation either to the community or, where the victim consents, to the victim direct. The work has to be carried out under supervision within three months of the making of the order.

Attendance centre orders

This involves attendance at a special centre for two or three hours each week, usually on a Saturday. The minimum number of hours is usually 12, although for offenders under the age of 14 it can be less. The maximum hours are 24 for those aged under 16 and 36 hours for older offenders. The sessions are managed by the probation service and will usually include organised leisure activities and training.

12.6 Fines and discharges

As seen at the beginning of this chapter a fine is the most common way of disposing of a case in the Magistrates' Court. In the Crown Court only a small percentage of offenders are dealt with by way of a fine. One of the problems is the number of unpaid fines. This has two bad effects: it makes the punishment ineffective; and it leads to defendants being imprisoned for non-payment. In order to overcome these, the Courts Act 2003 introduced the concept of discharge of fines by unpaid work. Pilots on this were being run from September 2004 to March 2005 in various area of the country. The fine which is owed is remitted at a rate of £6 per hour of unpaid work.

In deciding on an appropriate sentence, it is necessary to consider both aggravating and mitigating factors. The two charts that follow are taken from the Magistrates' Court Sentencing Guidelines. These guidelines are accurate until April 2005. These guidelines are issued to each magistrate. They give a guideline starting point for a first-time offender pleading guilty and on each chart are examples of aggravating and mitigating factors. It can be seen that these will vary according to the type of offence committed.

The overall approach is given by the Sentencing Guidelines Council in its draft guidelines, *Overarching Principles: Seriousness and New Sentences: Criminal Justice Act 2003* (2004) which point out that:

Q	'1.3 The sentencer must start by considering the seriousness of the offence, the assessment of which will: • determine which of the sentencing thresholds has been crossed; • indicate whether a custodial, community or other sentence is the most appropriate; • be the key factor in deciding the length of a custodial sentence, the onerousness of requirements to be incorporated in a community sentence and the amount of any fine imposed.'

12.7.2 Reduction for a guilty plea

On the other hand, the 2003 Act allows for a reduction in sentence for a guilty plea, particularly where made early in the proceedings (s 144). This provision was previously included in s 152 of the Powers of Criminal Courts (Sentencing) Act 2000. The Sentencing Guidelines Council has suggested that the reduction for a guilty plea at the first reasonable opportunity should attract a reduction of up to one-third, whereas a plea of guilty after the trial has started would be given only a one-tenth reduction. The amount of reduction is on a sliding scale, as shown in Figure 12.2.

Assault-actual bodily harm	Offences Against the Persons Act 1861 s.47 Triable either way -see Mode of Trial Guidelines Penalty: Level 5 and/or 6 months

CONSIDER THE SERIOUSNESS OF THE OFFENCE
(INCLUDING THE IMPACT ON THE VICTIM)

IS DISCHARGE OR FINE APPROPRIATE?
IS IT SERIOUS ENOUGH FOR A COMMUNITY PENALTY?
GUIDELINE: → IS IT SO SERIOUS THAT ONLY CUSTODY IS APPROPRIATE?
ARE YOUR SENTENCING POWERS SUFFICIENT?

THIS IS A GUIDELINE FOR A FIRST-TIME OFFENDER PLEADING NOT GUILTY

 CONSIDER AGGRAVATING AND MITIGATING FACTORS AND THE WEIGHT TO ATTACH TO EACH

for example	for example
Abuse of trust (domestic setting) Deliberate kicking or biting Extensive injuries (may be psychological) Headbutting Group action Offender in position of authority On hospital/medical or school premises Premeditated Victim particularly vulnerable Victim serving the public Weapon *This list is not exhaustive*	Minor injury Provocation Single blow *This list is not exhaustive*

If offender is on bail, this offence is more serious
If offender has previous convictions, their relevance and any failure to respond to previous
sentences should be considered—they may increase the seriousness. The court should make
it clear, when passing sentence, that this was the approach adopted.

TAKE A PRELIMINARY VIEW OF SERIOUSNESS, THEN CONSIDER OFFENDER MITIGATION

for example
　　Age, health (physical or mental)
　　Co-operation with police
　　Evidence of genuine remorse
　　Voluntary compensation

CONSIDER YOUR SENTENCE

Compare it with the suggested guideline level of sentence and reconsider
your reasons carefully if you have chosen a sentence at a different level.
Consider a reduction for a timely guilty plea.

DECIDE YOUR SENTENCE
NB. COMPENSATION-Give reasons if not awarding compensation

As a result the Home Office is running a three year programme which aims to increase opportunities to tackle women's offending in the community and to ensure that prison is reserved for the most serious offences or for public protection. One of the aims of the programme is to improve community-based mental health services since 40 per cent of women prisoners reported receiving help for mental or emotional problems in the year before imprisonment. Another priority is to increase the number of women receiving treatment for drug abuse, as 43 per cent reported using crack cocaine and 44 per cent heroin in the year before entering prison. Better service in the community could provide sentencers with options other than prison for women offenders who have drug abuse problems.

Further reading

Davies, M, Croall, H and Tyrer, J, *Criminal Justice* (2nd edn, Longman, 1998) Chapter 9.

Lewis, P, 'Can prison prevent reoffending?' [2003] NLJ 168.

appendix 1 ACTIVITIES ON JUDICIAL PRECEDENT AND STATUTORY INTERPRETATION ■

1. Activity on judicial precedent

Read the extract of the judgment below and answer the following questions:

(a) Briefly summarise the most important (ie the material) facts of the case.

(b) Summarise the company's defence.

(c) What is the *ratio decidendi* of *Carlill v Carbolic Smoke Ball Co* [1892] All ER Rep 127?

(d) Give an example of *obiter dicta*.

CASE EXAMPLE

Carlill v Carbolic Smoke Ball Co [1892] All ER Rep 127

On 13th November 1891 the following advertisement was published by the defendants in the *Pall Mall Gazette*:

'£100 reward will be paid by the Carbolic Smoke Ball Co. to any person who contracts the increasing epidemic influenza, colds, or any diseases caused by taking cold, after having used the ball three times daily for two weeks according to the printed directions supplied with each ball. £1,000 is deposited with the Alliance Bank, Regent Street, showing our sincerity in the matter . . .'

The plaintiff [this term is now claimant] bought a smoke ball and used it three times every day, according to the instructions, for several weeks, but then had an attack of influenza. She wrote to the defendants, telling them what had occurred, and asking for the £100 promised by them in the advertisement. The defendants refused to pay and she sued for the money. At the trial, the defendants denied that there was any contract between them and the plaintiff; and, alternatively, that, if there were any, it was void. Judgment was nevertheless given for the plaintiff and the defendants appealed.

CONTINUED ▶

J

'We were asked by counsel for the defendants to say that this document was a contract too vague to be enforced. The first observation that arises is that the document is not a contract at all. It is an offer made to the public. The terms of the offer, counsel says, are too vague to be treated as a definite offer, the acceptance of which would constitute a binding contract. He relies on his construction of the document, in accordance with which he says there is no limit of time fixed for catching influenza, and that it cannot seriously be meant to promise to pay money to a person who catches influenza at any time after the inhaling of the smoke ball. He says also that, if you look at this document you will find great vagueness in the limitation of the persons with whom the contract was intended to be made – that it does not follow that they do not include persons who may have used the smoke ball before the advertisement was issued, and that at all events, it is a contract with the world in general. He further says, that it is an unreasonable thing to suppose it to be a contract, because nobody in their senses would contract themselves out of the opportunity of checking the experiment which was going to be made at their own expense, and there is no such provision here made for the checking. He says that all that shows that this is rather in the nature of a puff or a proclamation than a promise or an offer intended to mature into a contract when accepted.

Counsel says that the terms are incapable of being consolidated into a contract. But he seems to think that the strength of the position he desires to adopt is rather that the vagueness of the document shows that no contract at all was intended. It seems to me that in order to arrive at this contract we must read it in its plain meaning as the public would understand it. It was intended to be issued to the public and to be read by the public. How would an ordinary person reading this document construe it upon the points which the defendant's counsel has brought to our attention? It was intended unquestionably to have some effect, and I think the effect which it was intended to have was, that by means of the use of the carbolic smoke ball, the sale of the carbolic smoke ball should be increased. It was designed to make people buy the ball. But it was also designed to make them use it, because the suggestions and allegations which it contains are directed immediately to the use of the smoke ball as distinct from the purchase of it. It did not follow that the smoke ball was to be purchased from the defendants directly or even from agents of theirs directly. The intention was that the circulation of the smoke ball should be promoted, and that the usage of it should be increased . . .

CONTINUED ▸

J

I think that the expression is equivalent to this, that £100 will be paid to any person who shall contract influenza after having used the carbolic smoke ball three times daily for two weeks. It seems to me that that would be the way in which the public would read it. A plain person who read this advertisement would read it in this plain way, that if anybody after the advertisement was published used three times daily for two weeks the carbolic smoke ball and then caught cold he would be entitled to the reward.

Counsel says: "Within what time is this protection to endure? Is it to go on for ever or what is to be the limit of time?" . . . I think it means during the use. It seems to me that the language of the advertisement lends itself to that construction.

Was the £100 reward intended to be paid? It not only says the reward will be paid, but it says: "We have lodged £1,000 to meet it." Therefore, it cannot be said that it was intended to be a mere puff. I think it was intended to be understood by the public as an offer which was to be acted upon . . . The answer to that seems to me to be that, if a person chooses to make these extravagant promises, he probably does so because it pays him to make them, and if he has made them the extravagance of the promises is no reason in law why he should not be bound by them.

It is said it is made to all the world, i.e., to anybody. It is not a contract made with all the world. There is the fallacy of that argument. It is an offer made to all the world, and why should not an offer be made to all the world which is to ripen into a contract with anybody who comes forward and performs the conditions? It is an offer to become liable to anyone, who before it is retracted performs the conditions. Although the offer is made to all the world the contract is made with that limited portion of the public who come forward and perform the conditions on the faith of the advertisement . . .

Then it was said that there was no notification of the acceptance of the offer. One cannot doubt that as an ordinary rule of law an acceptance of an offer made ought to be notified to the person who makes the offer, in order that the two minds may come together. Unless you do that, the two minds may be apart, and there is not that consensus which is necessary according to the English law to constitute a contract. But the mode of notifying acceptance is for the benefit of the person who makes the offer as well as for the opposite party, and so the person who makes the offer may dispense with notice to himself if he thinks it desirable to do so . . . And if

CONTINUED ▸

J the person making the offer expressly or impliedly intimates in his offer that it will be sufficient to act on the proposal without communicating acceptance of it to himself, and the offer is one which in its character dispenses with notification of the acceptance, then according to the intimation of the very person proposing the contract, performance of the condition is a sufficient acceptance without notification . . . in the advertisement cases it seems to me to follow as an inference to be drawn from the transaction itself that a person is not to notify his acceptance of the offer before he performs the conditions, but that, if he performs the conditions at once, notification is dispensed with. It seems to me, also, that no other view could be taken from the point of view of common sense. If I advertise to the world that my dog is lost and that anybody who brings him to a particular place will be paid some money, are all the police or other persons whose business is to find lost dogs to be expected to sit down and write me a note saying that they have accepted my proposal? Of course they look for the dog, and as soon as they find the dog, they have performed the condition. The very essence of the transaction is that the dog should be found. It is not necessary under such circumstances, it seems to me, that in order to make the contract binding, there should be any notification of acceptance. It follows from the nature of the thing that the performance of the condition is sufficient acceptance without the notification of it. A person who makes an offer in an advertisement of that kind makes an offer which must be read by the light of that common sense reflection. In his offer he impliedly indicates that he does not require notification of the acceptance of the offer . . .

In the present case the promise was put forward, I think, with the intention that it should be acted upon, and it was acted upon. It seems to me that there was ample consideration for the promise, and that, therefore, the plaintiff is entitled to recover the reward.'

Bowen LJ

2. Activity on statutory interpretation

Read the extract from the judgment below and answer the following questions. References to the relevant paragraphs of the judgment are given for some of the questions.

(a) What was the purpose of the Human Fertilisation and Embryology Act 1990? Whereabouts in an Act is the purpose normally expressed?

(b) Explain in your own words what Lord Bingham says about parliamentary draftsmen (para 7).

(c) When, according to Lord Bingham, it is likely that cases on statutory interpretation will reach the appellate courts?

(d) Why does Lord Bingham reject the use of a purely literal interpretation (para 8)?

(e) Explain what Lord Bingham means when he says there is a rule that a statute is always speaking (para 9).

(f) In your own words, briefly explain the background to the Act.

(g) Why did the court need to consider the words 'where fertilisation is complete'?

(h) What view did Lord Bingham take of the words 'where fertilisation is complete' (para 14)?

CASE EXAMPLE

R v Secretary of State for Health (Respondent), ex parte Quintavalle (on behalf of Pro-Life Alliance) (Appellant) [2003] UKHL 13

J

'1.   The issues in this appeal are whether live human embryos created by cell nuclear replacement (CNR) fall outside the regulatory scope of the Human Fertilisation and Embryology Act 1990 and whether licensing of such embryos is prohibited by section 3(3)(d) of that Act. Crane J at first instance held such creation fell outside the scope of the Act and was not prohibited by section 3(3)(d): [2001] 4 All ER 1013: [2001] EWHC Admin 918. The Court of Appeal (Lord Phillips of Worth Matravers MR, Thorpe and Buxton LJJ) agreed with the judge on the second point but reversed his ruling on the first [2002] QB 628; [2002] EWCA Civ 29. Both points were argued before the House.

2.   This case is not concerned with embryos created in the ordinary way as a result of sexual intercourse. Nor is it directly concerned with the creation of live human embryos *in vitro* where the female egg is fertilised by the introduction of male sperm outside the body. CNR, a very recent scientific technique, involves neither of these things. In the Court of Appeal and in the House the parties were content to adopt the clear and succinct explanation given by the judge [Crane J] of what CNR means:

CONTINUED ▶

J

Q

"In the ovary the egg is a diploid germ (or reproductive) cell. It is described as 'diploid' because its nucleus contains a full set of 46 chromosomes. By the process of meiotic division the nucleus divides into two parts. Only one of these, a pronucleus containing only 23 chromosomes (described as the 'haploid'), plays any further part in the process. Fertilisation begins when the male germ cell, the sperm, whose pronucleus contains 23 chromosomes, meets the haploid female germ cell and is a continuous process taking up to 24 hours. As part of the process the male and female pronuclei fuse to from one nucleus with a full complement of 46 chromosomes, a process know as syngamy. The one-cell structure that exists following sygamy is the zygote. After several hours the cell divides to create a two-cell zygote. At this stage it is generally referred to as an embryo. At about 15 days after fertilisation a heaping up of cells occurs which is described as the 'primitive streak'. Fertilisation may of course take place in the normal way or *in vitro*.

CNR is a process by which the nucleus, which is diploid, from one cell is transplanted into an unfertilised egg, from which . . . the nucleus has been removed. the [replacement] nucleus is derived from either an embryonic or a foetal or an adult cell. The cell is then treated to encourage it to grow and divide, forming first a two-sell structure and then developing in a similar way to an ordinary embryo.

CNR is a form of cloning. Clones are organisms that are genetically identical to each other. When CNR is used, if the embryo develops into a live individual, that individual is genetically identical to the nucleus transplanted into the egg. There are other methods of cloning ... CNR of the kind under consideration does not . . . involve fertilisation."

CONTINUED ▶

The Act

3. The 1990 Act was passed "to make provision in connection with human embryos and any subsequent development of such embryos; to prohibit certain practices in connection with embryos and gametes; to establish Human Fertilisation and Embryology Authority", and for other purposes. The sections at the heart of this appeal are sections 1 and 3, which I should quote in full:

"1(1) In this Act, except where otherwise stated –

(a)   embryo means a live human embryo where fertilisation is complete, and

(b)   references to an embryo include an egg in the process of fertilisation,

and, for this purpose, fertilisation is not complete until the appearance of a two cell zygote.

(2) The Act, so far as it governs bringing about the creation of an embryo, applies only to bringing about the creation of an embryo outside the human body; an in this Act –

(a) references to embryos the creation of which was brought about *in vitro* (in their application to those where fertilisation is complete) are to those where fertilisation began outside the human body whether or not it was completed there, and

(b) references to embryos taken from a woman do not include embryos whose creation was brought about *in vitro*.

(3) This Act so far as it governs the keeping of use of an embryo, applies only to keeping or use of an embryo outside the human body.

(4) References in this Act to gametes, eggs or sperm, except where otherwise stated, are to live human gametes, eggs of sperm but references below in this Act to gametes or eggs do not include eggs in the process of fertilisation.

. . .

3(1) No person shall –

(a) bring about the creation of an embryo, or

(b) keep or use an embryo,

except in pursuance of a licence.

CONTINUED ▸

J

(2) No person shall place in a woman –

   (a) a live embryo other than a human embryo, or

   (b) any live gametes other than human gametes.

(3) A licence cannot authorise –

   (a) keeping or using an embryo after the appearance of the primitive streak,

   (b) placing an embryo in any animal,

   (c) keeping or using an embryo in any circumstances in which regulation prohibit is keeping or its use, or

   (d) replacing a nucleus of a cell of an embryo with a nucleus taken from a cell of any person, embryo or subsequent development of an embryo.

(4) For the purpose of subsection (3)(a) above, the primitive streak is to be taken to have appeared in an embryo not later than the end of the period of 14 days beginning with the day when the gametes are mixed, not counting any time during which the embryo is stored."

7. . . . Such is the skill of parliamentary draftsmen that most statutory enactments are expressed in language which is clear and unambiguous and gives rise to no serious controversy. But these are not the provisions which reach the courts, or at any rate the appellate courts. Where parties expend substantial resources arguing about the effects of a statutory provision it is usually because the provision is, or is said to be, capable of bearing more two or more different meanings, or to be of doubtful application to the particular case which has now arisen, perhaps because the statutory language is said to be inapt to apply to it, sometimes because the situation which had arisen is one which the draftsman could not have foreseen and for which he has accordingly made no express provision.

8. The basic task of the court is to ascertain and give effect to the true meaning of what Parliament has said in the enactment to be construed. But that is not to say that attention should be confined and a literal interpretation given to the particular provisions which give rise to difficulty. Such an approach not only encourages immense prolixity [long-windedness] in drafting, since the draftsman will feel obliged to provide expressly for every contingency which may possibly arise. It may also (under the banner of loyalty to the will of Parliament) lead to the frustration of that will, because undue concentration on

CONTINUED ▶

J

the minutiae of the enactment may lead the court to neglect the purpose which Parliament intended to achieve when it enacted the statute. Every statute other than a purely consolidating statute is, after all, enacted to make some change, or address some problem, or remove some blemish, or effect some improvement in the national life. The court's task, within the permissible bounds of interpretation, is to give effect to Parliament's purpose. So the controversial provisions should be read in the context of the statute as a whole, and the statute as a whole should be read in the historical context of the situation which led to its enactment.

9. There is, I think, no inconsistency between the rule that statutory language retains the meaning it had when Parliament used it and the rule that a statute is always speaking. If Parliament had, however long ago, passed an Act applicable to dogs, it could not properly be interpreted to apply to cats; but it could properly be held to apply to animals which were not regarded as dogs when the Act was passed but are so regarded now. The meaning of "cruel and unusual punishments" has not changed over the years since 1689, but many punishments which were not then thought to fall within that category would now be held to do so. The courts have frequently had to grapple with the question of whether a modern invention or activity falls within old statutory language . . . A revealing example is found in *Grant v Southwestern and County Properties Ltd* [1975] Ch 185, where Walton J had to decide whether a tape recording fell within the expression "document" in the Rules of the Supreme Court. Pointing out that the furnishing of information had been treated as one of the main functions of a document, the judge concluded that the tape recording was a document . . .

The background to the Act

11. The birth of the first child resulting from *in vitro* fertilisation in July 1978 prompted much ethical and scientific debate which in turn led to the appointment in July 1982 of a Committee of Inquiry under the chairmanship of Dame Mary Warnock DBE to

Q

"consider recent and potential developments in medicine and science related to human fertilisation and embryology; to consider what policies and safeguards should be applied, including consideration of the social, ethical and legal implications of these developments; and to make recommendations."

CONTINUED ▸

J attempt themselves to supply the answer, if the answer is not to be found in the terms of the Act itself.'

Lord Wilberforce

Lord Bingham then went on to apply the guidance given in Lord Wilberforce's judgment. Lord Bingham considered three points:

1. Does the genus of live human embryos by CNR fall within the same genus of facts as those to which the expressed policy of Parliament has been formulated?

2. Is the operation of the Human Fertilisation and Embryology Act 1990 to be regarded as liberal and permissive in its operation or is it restrictive and circumscribed?

3. Is an embryo created by CNR different in kind or dimension from that for which the Act was passed?

Look back at the facts in *R v Secretary of State for Health (Respondent), ex parte Quintavalle* (2003), apply the guidance of Lord Wilberforce yourself and answer the three points above.

Having done this, compare your answers with those of Lord Bingham which can be found in the online report for the case at para 15.

House of Lords decisions can be found at www.publications.parliament.uk . Click on House of Lords', then 'Judicial Work' and then 'judgments'.

appendix 2 ANSWERING QUESTIONS ■

Essay title 1

Baz has been charged with an either way offence. He has many previous convictions for minor offences. Explain and comment on the procedure for determining the trial venue.

Advice

Where you have to answer a question about the courts and the question is based on a mini-scenario, the first and most fundamental point is to identify whether the matter involves civil or criminal procedure. This should be quite clear from the information given in the question. In this particular question there should be no problem. You are told that Baz is charged with an either way offence. This immediately identifies it as a criminal case.

Then check on the exact focus of the question. Here, the final sentence of the question gives a very definite area which must be discussed: the procedure for determining the trial venue. But do not forget that you are only dealing with a triable either way offence, so you would not receive any credit if you discussed summary or indictable offences. Also note that as well as explaining the procedure, you are required to comment on it.

Having identified the points it may then be helpful to draw a rough flow chart reminding yourself of the different directions such a matter can take. Here, the most important point is whether Baz is going to plead guilty or not guilty. You are not told this so you must cover both possibilities:

Originally, the grounds for allowing an appeal against conviction following trial on indictment under the Criminal Appeal Act 1968 were that the conviction was either 'unsafe' or 'unsatisfactory'. The Criminal Appeal Act 1995 amended the 1968 Act, using the term 'unsafe' only. Professor J C Smith argued (see [1995] Crim LR 920) that this should not necessarily entail a narrowing of the grounds of appeal. Initially, however, the Court of Appeal in *Chalkley* [1998] 2 All ER 155, despite disapproving the trial judge's decision to allow the relevant evidence to be admitted (ie this was unsatisfactory), held that it did not have the power to quash the conviction unless that conviction was unsafe. It appeared that a conviction was viewed as unsafe only where the person convicted was actually not guilty. Subsequently, the Court of Appeal in *Mullen* [1999] 2 Cr App R 143 held that abuse of pre-trial process can cause a conviction to be unsafe, a safe conviction is a lawful conviction and the word 'unsafe' bears a broad meaning. Accordingly, no trial should have taken place because of the prosecution's abuse of process of the court prior to trial. In *Togher* [2001] 3 All ER 463, the Court of Appeal pointed out that both approaches (the narrower approach in *Chalkley* (1998) and the wider approach in *Mullen* (1999)) had subsequently been followed, but in that case, the wider approach was endorsed and the dust appears to have settled regarding the meaning of the word 'unsafe'.

Article 6(1) European Convention on Human Rights provides that:

> (A) 'Art 6(1) In the determination of his civil rights and obligations or of any criminal charge against him, everyone is entitled to a fair and public hearing within reasonable time by an independent and impartial tribunal established by law.'

Do proceedings that fall foul of Art 6 automatically render a conviction unsafe? In *Togher* (2001), the Court of Appeal stated that if a defendant had been denied a fair trial, it was almost inevitable that his conviction would be regarded as unsafe. This was the first consideration of this question after the ECHR became part of UK domestic law under the Human Rights Act 1998. However, in *R v Davies, Rowe and Johnson* [2001] 1 Cr App R 115, and later in *R v Williams, The Times*, 30th March 2001, the Court of Appeal asserted that Art 6 required an examination of the fairness of the trial, and that would not necessarily lead to a finding that the conviction was unsafe.

Sections 8–12 of the Criminal Appeal Act 1995 replaced the role of the Home Secretary to refer suspected miscarriages of justice to the Court of Appeal with the Criminal Cases Review Commission, a body independent of the Executive. It was found that the Home Secretary had exercised his power to refer four or five times a year on average. In the first six years of the CCRC, 196 cases had been referred to the appeal courts, providing clear evidence that the CCRC has an invaluable role in prompting the appeal courts to meet the purposes set out by Lord Woolf above. For the 77 unsafe convictions that have been quashed, justice is done in individual cases. This increases public confidence in the administration of justice and will confirm the view of the quote above; the Court of Appeal will quash unsafe and, under *Togher* (2001), unfair convictions.

It could be said that the fairness of a trial is not solely the concern of the defendant, but the whole trial must be fair to all parties. Accordingly, as as a result of the Auld Report the prosecution now may appeal against a judicial ruling which effectively terminates the prosecution's case (and therefore the case as a whole collapses) before the jury delivers its verdict. The rationale of this new power under s 58 Criminal Justice Act 2003 is to balance the defendant's rights to appeal in similar circumstances.

The common law doctrine of *autrefois acquit* is another way to ensure a fair trial for a defendant, but it has been perceived as preventing justice for victims where the accused has been wrongly acquitted. First inroads were made into the doctrine by allowing a referral in a case of jury tampering if a person has been convicted of the tampering. More recently, under the Criminal Justice Act 2003, the prosecution's rights of appeal from the Crown Court have been broadened effectively to end the rule against double jeopardy and are retrospective in effect. Sections 75 and 76 of the Criminal Justice Act 2003 enact these changes. They make it possible in certain cases for a re-trial to take place despite an earlier acquittal. This may occur if there is:

- new (not adduced in the proceedings in which the person was acquitted) **and**
- compelling (reliable, substantial and highly probative) evidence of the acquitted person's guilt **and**
- it is in the public interest (including the defendant's fair trial rights) (s 78).

This latter factor is vital to ensure that defendants are tried fairly or not at all.

INDEX ■

Note: Page numbers in italics refer to diagrams; the suffix (prop) refers to proposed legislation or administration.

UNLOCKING
THE ENGLISH
LEGAL SYSTEM